FROM GEORGE WASHINGTON TO
COL. ELIAS DAYTON,
26.7.1777

"The necessity of procuring good Intelligence is apparent & need not be further urged—All that remains for me to add is, that you keep the whole matter as Secret as possible. For upon Secrecy, Success depends in Most Enterprizes of the Kind, and for want of it, they are generally defeated, however well planned and promising a favorable issue.

> I am Sir
> Yr. Most Obed. Sev."

THE BALLANTINE ESPIONAGE/INTELLIGENCE LIBRARY

is the first cohesive collection of true chronicles of the greatest, most important, and most intriguing events in the history of international espionage and intelligence gathering. The series offers astonishing new information for the professional and an exciting introduction for the uninitiated. The books delve deeply into the people, events, and techniques of modern espionage—the puzzles, wiles, ruthlessness, romance, and secrets of this endlessly fascinating world.

Written by eyewitnesses or experts, they read "like fiction." But they are undeniably more powerful, because they are *true . . .*

⊞ ESPIONAGE/INTELLIGENCE LIBRARY ⊞

THE PHILBY CONSPIRACY

Bruce Page

David Leitch

Phillip Knightley

updated

BALLANTINE BOOKS • NEW YORK

Copyright © 1981 by Page, Leitch, and Knightley

All rights reserved. Published in the United States by Ballantine Books, a division of Random House, Inc., New York,
and simultaneously in Canada by Random House of Canada,
Limited, Toronto, Canada.

Library of Congress Catalog Card Number: 68-20487

ISBN 0-345-29726-1

Printed in Canada

First Ballantine Books Edition: September 1981

Author's Preface

We do not say this is the whole story of Kim Philby's career. That story may never be told, for its authors would need simultaneous access to the files of the British secret departments concerned, the American CIA and the Soviet KGB. Philby himself, while he might be willing to reveal details about Western intelligence operations with which he was concerned, will never be so frank about his work for the KGB, as witness his coyness on this topic in his own book, *My Silent War*.

Our account is based on several hundred interviews with diplomats, politicians, scientists, intelligence officers and ordinary citizens in the West. All these people, however, were acting in a private capacity. So far from receiving official help, our investigation has been conducted in the face of consistent official reluctance to see the full truth emerge. Our inquiry did not rely on aid from Mr. Philby himself, or from any other Communist or Eastern source with the exception of Philby's first wife, who now lives in East Berlin and furnished us with some personal biographical details of her marriage.

When we originally wrote a series of articles in *The Sunday Times* on the Philby case, Mr. Philby commented on these articles to Western visitors—including colleagues of ours. We have made strictly limited use of some of his remarks, which have been passed on to us. Our rule has been to make use of such remarks only when they correspond with other, and objectively verifiable evidence. Although Mr. Philby says that the articles we published represent "more or less a true bill," he has not chosen to volunteer any information of substance to us. We have no way of knowing whether he will regard this book, and its new material, as a "true bill" or not.

Stories of espionage are bedevilled by difficulties with sources. In some chapters—such as those dealing with Philby's affair in Spain—we have been able to identify our sources plainly. In other chapters, chiefly because of the intimidatory effects of the Official Secrets Act, we have been forced to be far more circumspect.

These circumstances make it difficult for us to thank people without it at once appearing that they have told us things that they should not have told us, or have in some way been indiscreet about official matters.

We should, however, like to thank several colleagues of ours on *The Sunday Times*—in particular Mr. Hugo Young, Mr. Murray Sayle, Mr. Adam Hopkins, Mr. Stephen Fay, Mr. John Barry and, especially, Mr. Ritchie McEwan who worked with us on the original inquiries. We must also thank the former editor of *The Sunday Times*, Mr. Harold Evans, for his consistent encouragement.

Most of all, however, we must thank our two research assistants, Mr. Nelson Mews and Mr. Alexander Mitchell, who together with Mrs. Jenni Davies made the writing of this book possible.

Some people object to any such enterprise as ours in this book, on the grounds that it "glorifies treachery." We can only say that we have not tried to glorify what Philby and his associates did, but merely to describe it, without moralising over it. Bacon said that we are much indebted to those who write what men do, and not what they ought to do: this book attempts to record what certain men did. It seems to us that the story is of some interest to those who are concerned for the security of democracy.

BRUCE PAGE
DAVID LEITCH
PHILLIP KNIGHTLEY

Contents

Something I owe to the soil that grew—
More to the life that fed—
But most to Allah, Who gave me two,
Separate sides to my head.

RUDYARD KIPLING, *Kim*

Introduction

The avenger stole upon the citadel and destroyed it from within. Yet both the avenger and the citadel were largely creations of the same historical condition. The avenger was the son of a British Raj; the citadel was dedicated to the preservation of British power; both had been displaced by the evanescence of the Empire. The avenger was an embittered solitary with the arrogance of a man familiar with the terrain of personal philosophies: the Arabian desert. He would root out the old fort with the indifference of the timeless wind, the cunning of the Levantine and the amoral loyalty of Kipling's chosen boy: yet he was still one of them, at war with his own shadow. The avenger would destroy the past; the citadel would preserve it. Yet it was a past they had in common. In the unequal duel between Kim Philby and the British Secret Service, a new dimension is added to the relationship between the privileged Englishman and the institution which he collectively comprises. Let anyone who derides the notion of the Establishment read this book.

I sit back now, the manuscript put away, and reach for the apt phrases of outrage. But none of us is yet equal to the dimensions of this scandal. Like a great novel, and an unfinished one at that, the story of Kim Philby lives on in us: it conveys not merely a sense of participation but of authorship. Still, listening to our own judgements we can discern in ourselves the social attitudes and opinions which account as much for Philby's survival as for his determination to destroy us. Hardly a tear was shed for George Blake: Blake was half a foreigner and half a Jew; only the length of his prison sentence seriously excited the public conscience. Vassall was an upstart; Burgess and Maclean were psychiatric misfits. But Philby, an aggressive, upper-class enemy, was of our blood and hunted with our pack; to the very end, he expected and received the indulgence owing to his moderation, good

Introduction © by LE CARRÉ PRODUCTIONS Ltd 1981

1

breeding and boyish, flirtatious charm. In our very notion of the "Thirties Spies" there is an implicit confession of weakness. "The Thirties" we say, "The Thirties" were the last lot to care; as if we were so far past the peak of our national and emotional energy that neither the grouse-moor complacency of Macmillan nor the Pygmy grandeur of Wilson could stir us into becoming enemies of our own political incompetence. I am uncomfortably conscious, in-cidentally, of the "we": Philby's is one of those cases which force us to define our own place in society. I suppose by "we" I mean the world to which I my-self vaguely belong: middle-class, graduate, intellectual. Philby's world, but indoors.

This book is massively incomplete, as the authors are the first to admit. We should never forget the gaps. In this most Marxian of novels, where thesis and antithesis are endemic to protagonist, institution and reader alike, it is arguable that even the principal character is still missing. In the lives of Burgess, Maclean and Philby we discern his hand, his influence, his shadow: never once do we see his face or consciously hear his name. He is the Soviet re-cruiter. For these men were recruited. By whom? Between the ages of nineteen and twenty-one, it seems, these chil-dren of Cambridge were recognised, courted and con-sciously seduced into a lifetime of deceit. By whom? As they grew to manhood, and the youthful dream of an ad-venturous crusade gave way to the tedium and fears of criminal betrayal, who sustained them in their faith? Who serviced them, paid them? Who trained, welfared, con-soled and commanded them? Who kept them in play and taught them the clandestine arts? Whom did Philby meet and when? What were the methods of communication? Was Philby a photographer, a radio operator; did he rely on the pelmanism of his namesake? Did Philby in turn recruit others? Did he run them? This was his secret life; it is a secret still. The street corner, the hurried handover in the cab, the timed dialogue from kiosk to kiosk; those were the moments when the hunter was hunted, and we know nothing of them at all.

When a boy of twenty gives himself body and mind to a country he has never visited, to an ideology he has not deeply studied, to a regime which even abroad, during those long and awful purges, was a peril to serve; when he remains actively faithful to that decision for over thirty years, cheating, betraying and occasionally killing, surely we must speculate on the nature of his master; no novitiate can last indefinitely without a confessing father. He understood us better than we understood ourselves: was he our countryman? He recruited only gentlemen: was he himself a gentleman? He recruited only from Cambridge: was he a Cambridge man? All three recruits would travel far on the reputations of their families alone: was he too a man of social influence? Today, if he exists, he may be walking the streets of London; very probably he did nothing which at that time was against the law of the land.

And did he only pick winners, whoever he was? Or are there, among the surviving contemporaries of Burgess, Maclean and Philby, men whom he unsuccessfully approached? This is but one of numberless questions provoked by this brilliant but necessarily incomplete account of the Philby story. Philby may wish to enlighten us but probably never will: the Russian apparatus of bureaucratic sanction is even more lugubrious than our own: and though he is avid for praise, he is not yet ready for re-defection.

I do not much believe in the political motive of Kim Philby; but I am sure that the British secret service kept it alive as no other environment could have done. The British intelligence world described here is apolitical. Once entered, it provides no further opportunity for spiritual development. The door that clanged behind the new entrant protected him as much from himself as from reality. Philby, once employed, met spies, conundrums, technique; he had said goodbye to controversy. Such political opinions as sustained him were the opinions of his childhood. The cleaner air of the outside world would have blown them away in a year. Instead, he took into the soundless shrine of the secret world the half-formed jargon of his intellectual betters, the brutal memories of his father, Vienna and Spain; and from there on, simply ceased to develop. He was left with a handful of clichés whose application had ceased in 1931. Similarly, the posturing chauvinism of his superiors would long have passed for idiotic in the outside world; in the secret world it passed for real. Thus in the same secret place, under the same secret sun, the anachronisms of his quarry were sheltered from the changing frosts of reality. Citadel and avenger, both unnaturally protected, were fighting out the battles of the thirties. For this reason, the early life of Kim Philby is doubly important: all Kim's life was early.

Duplicity for Kim Philby was something of a family tradition. However Philby reacted to his eminently distasteful father, whether he wished to destroy or outshine him, or merely to follow in his footsteps, he could hardly fail, in the outposts where they lived, to inherit many of his characteristics. A little king in his desert palaces, St. John Philby did not hide from Kim his contempt for his superiors in London; the loyalties he preached were at best dynastic; at worst they constituted a doctrine of militant arrogance. St. John himself was a man of unreconciled and wilful paradox; he was an empire man, a decider, a builder, a collector of intelligence in the best Kipling tradition; an Arabist, a Lawrence mystic, a solitary adventurer capable of violence and rapacity. He was also a salesman, dealing in consumer goods: cars, refrigerators and the rest. Metaphorically, St. John was the man who brought Cadillacs to the Sheiks. Now and then, operating the reverse market, he sold off oil concessions to the Americans. Later in his life, with that perverse puritanism which survived in Kim, he repented his shiftier commercial enterprises.

From his father, Kim acquired the neo-Fascist instincts of a slightly berserk English gentleman; from his father, the Establishment's easy trick of rationalising selfish decisions and dressing them in the clothes of a higher cause; from his father the cartographer's memory; for he no more forgot a word or a gesture than another man forgot the way home; from his father the scholar's perception which enabled him to keep track of his own complicated treachery. And he could hardly fail, when his father delivered him over to the Establishment for his education, to feel already that he was being trained in the enemy camp. Like Kipling's boy, one feels, he was already waiting for the call: *"It was intrigue, of course—he knew that much, he had known all evil since he could speak—but what he loved was the game for its own sake—the stealthy prowl through the dark gullies and lanes. . . ."*

I dream in mad moments—but anything is possible between those two—that St. John recruited his own son for service against the *"missionaries and white men of serious aspect,"* against the soft town-dwellers of Whitehall ignorant of real men's ways. He did not, of course; but if he had laboured all his life to create in Kim the irresistible chemistry of the boy's later betrayal, he could not have done much more. Kim prowled the edges of the Establishment as his namesake stalked the back-streets of Lahore: *"in headlong flight from housetop to housetop under cover of the hot dark."* For the Philbys strode from peak to peak, and fools lived in the valley.

Through his father, moreover, Kim Philby acquired his richest asset as a spy: an effortless familiarity with the quarry. Through his father, and the education which his father gave him, he experienced both as a victim and as a practitioner the capacity of the British ruling class for reluctant betrayal and polite self-preservation. Effortlessly he played the parts which the Establishment could recognise—for was he not born and trained into the Establishment? Effortlessly he copied its attitudes, caught its diffident stammer, its hesitant arrogance; effortlessly he took his place in its nameless hegemony. So well indeed did he perceive its nature that years later, when the security services and the press came to suspect him for what he was, Philby was able to rally the Establishment to his side and manoeuvre it into protecting him as its own.

It is, I am sure, part of the ambivalence of Philby's position that he never altogether took leave of the world he foreswore. He enjoyed the Establishment; he enjoyed its comaraderie, its inside track, its institutional warmth, its comforting distaste for intellectual pyrotechnics; to the very end he remained dependent on the people he deceived. Hence, perhaps, his extraordinary reluctance to defect to Russia; hence his confession abroad; hence his long and perilous hesitation in Beirut. Kim was homesick. Even now in Moscow, his obsession is not with Russia, but with England.

Kim loved the absent parent best; and even though he had marked down the parent authority of England as his lifelong enemy, Kim Philby never quite absolved it from its parental duty to protect. And I think there was even a moment—it is part of cracking up—when Philby wanted to be discovered and punished for what he had done; and that moment also came in the last days in Beirut.

There is little to be learnt of Philby's mother. We may assume that a man of his father's temperament would not tolerate a woman of any force. Certainly in the Arab world where they "were at home," there was not much doubt where women stood. Later Philby's own attitude to women recalls the ambivalence of those days: the mother-goddess of Kipling mingled unhappily with the mindless, curtained amenity of Arab life. "I must have women," said John Gay. "Nothing unbends the mind like them."

Women were also his secret audience. He used them as he used society; he performed, danced, phantasised with them, begged their approbation, used them as a response for his histrionic talents, as a consolation for a manhood haunted by his father's ghost. When they came too close, he punished them or sent them away, either as unsatisfactory mother-figures or the spent instruments of his expression. Sometimes they were the actual currency in which he paid old scores or satisfied his treacherous impulse. But whatever they were, they were second to that one elected mother who held his heart: Russia.

As the authors repeatedly demonstrate, Philby was not a political animal. We do not find him plunged into an agony of doubt during the Stalin purges, the Doctors' Plot, the Hungarian revolution. I cannot relate the crises in his personal life to crises within the Communist world: this was not the nature of his commitment. Mother Russia was the boy's absolute.

We can only speculate about his motive, and we can only guess at the scope of his deceit. Did Philby initiate the operations he betrayed? Did he *propose* the Albanian infiltrations in which he sent agents to their deaths? We know barely the tiniest part of the havoc he caused; the codes, the men, the strategies, the techniques, the policies he betrayed. We shall get little help from either side in working out *that* bill. Some intelligence secrets, as I said elsewhere, are known in any capital of Europe, but they are still too hot for the taxpayer.

For those who enjoy tortuous speculation, there is one intriguing coincidence. Sikorski, whose assassination Rolf Hochhuth notoriously attributes to Winston Churchill, took off from Gibraltar on July 4, 1943. At that time Kim Philby was in charge of SIS[1] counter-intelligence opera-

---

[1] Secret Intelligence Service (MI 6). Its relationship to MI 5 is set out in Ch. 9.

tions in the Iberian peninsula. If Sikorski *was* assassinated, is it conceivable that Philby planned the operation on behalf of his Russian masters, and that the assassin whom he hired believed he was working for the British?

Deceit was Philby's life's work; deceit, as I understand it, his nature. "I have come home," he said in Moscow. Philby has no home, no woman, no faith. Behind the political label, behind the inbred upper-class arrogance, the taste for adventure, lies the self-hate of a vain misfit for whom nothing will ever be worthy of his loyalty. In the last instance, Philby is driven by the incurable drug of deceit itself. Philby, a policeman would say, is bent. It comes as no surprise that, safely arrived in the land of his dreams, the old deceiver stretches out his fingers once more and steals the only thing left to steal: the wife of Donald Maclean. That is the law of the desert; and the desert is all he has.

Such was the avenger. What of the citadel? If Philby's relationship to the Establishment was ambivalent and paradoxical, the relationship of the Establishment to Philby affords an even richer study in English attitudes. It is a considerable and original virtue of this book that treats the British secret services for what they surely are: microcosms of the British condition, of our social attitudes and vanities. In this sense, the book is a milestone in the Englishman's education of himself. We can never again suppose that Intelligence is a world populated by people we have not met or known. The spy world revealed here is not a *Nibelungenland* shrouded in the covering mist of Gothic conspiracy and high national affairs; it is peopled by men and women as susceptible as the rest of us to self-delusion. Its borders spill over into almost every area of our public life; its viability depends upon our tolerance, upon our money and to a sizeable extent upon our complicity.

Every government department, like every business, parliament, school or profession, carries its fair share of the world's idiots. There has never been any reason to suppose that the Secret Service should be absolved from this responsibility. Indeed, it is probably the one point on which ex-Intelligence officers, of whatever nationality, are agreed: we had our clowns. But the presence of such people in SIS should not blind us into believing that Philby survived by making fools of people who were fools already.

Nevertheless, there are plenty of external reasons why SIS and the Security Service were, in the immediate postwar years when Philby did his greatest damage, in a pretty poor way. The five years between 1944 and 1949 saw the greatest historical failure and the greatest historical reversal of all time. Soldiers who had fought at Bastogne were now required to fight in Korea. Airmen who had defended London were now required to defend Berlin. In Germany itself there were those who were taking away and those who were handing back, there were those who spoke of the allies and no longer meant the Russians, those who spoke of the enemy and no longer meant the Germans.

Simultaneously, the patriotism which had kept us afloat for six years was suffering a healthy recession. The dons, artists and intellectuals who had swollen the ranks of SIS and engineered its greatest triumphs, returned with the rest of us to cultivate their old professions and enjoy the fruits of the peace they had won. As a society, we had resolutely lived without ideological doubt for six years; we were constipated with slogans, archaisms and compromise. Our national intellect had too long been mobilised for war. Our painters had decorated the walls of the Imperial War Museum, and even our arch satirist Noël Coward had spoken like a boy scout from the bridge of a studio destroyer. The intellectual tradition we had abandoned in order to fight fascism was leftist; everything pointed to a gentle, pragmatic form of international socialism. Instead, we were called upon to march in a new crusade, and to demonstrate if anything a greater confidence in our identity than even Hitler had called forth.

Inevitably, SIS was to recruit against the trend. If the prevailing political sentiment of the nation was vaguely leftist, the posture and tradition of SIS—as well as its present role—were frankly anti-Bolshevist. It was in the world of capital that SIS had its traditional heart, in the preservation of trade routes, in the defence of foreign investment and Colonial wealth; in the protection of "ordered society." In re-discovering this tradition, and bringing to it the new techniques and brutalities it had learned in the war, SIS was hardly likely to win the hearts of the intellectuals whose wit had once saved it from disbandment. The Attlee administration was content to leave the leadership as it stood. The social democrat, far more than the capitalist, is the sworn enemy of Communism. There is no sign, in the account given here, that Attlee tried to put a Socialist spin on our Intelligence effort. Let SIS expand, he seems to have said; in the fight against Communism, Left and Right are united.

The irony goes further. The more apparent it became that we were neither emotionally nor economically capable of taking sides in the Cold War and retaining our former world position, so we placed ever greater trust in the magic formulae and hocus-pocus of the spy world. When the King is dying, the charlatans cash in. It is to this daft underworld of fast-talking charm-sellers that Guy Burgess, incidentally, belonged. I do not think that SIS can be blamed for employing Philby in the first place; it is nothing short of incredible that they kept him on after 1944. By 1945 at the latest the recruitment policy of SIS had put loyalty above intelligence; and pedigree above originality. The shaming fact of Philby's continued employment after this date is that SIS quite clearly identified class with loyalty. Yet this too illustrates another point that must be made about the collective mentality of professional intelligence men: they think they know the score. Wholly taken up with the modalities of national self-advancement, they are professionally incapable of comprehending ideology, however it was born, as a serious motivating force in people of their own kind. This absence of ideological fuss is called common sense, or level-headedness, and is the first qualification of recruitment. Moreover, since they clearly select only from their own class, they are, or at least in Philby's day *were,* frankly undemocratic: in the upper reaches of the British administrative tradition, they argued, our secrets are most safely cradled.

The belief went further: SIS would not merely *defend* the traditional decencies of our society; it would embody them. Within its own walls, its clubs and country houses, in whispered luncheons with its secular contacts, it would enshrine the mystical entity of a vanishing England. Here at least, whatever went on in the big world outside, England's flower would be cherished. *"The Empire may be crumbling; but within our secret élite, the clean-limbed tradition of English power would survive. We believe in nothing but ourselves."* It was the kind of music Kim Philby had heard from his cradle.

Small wonder that they became both protective and competitive. Theirs was a society united by one thing only: collectively and individually its members had abdicated the responsibility to develop. Behind the sealed doors, puzzled men could take refuge from the swiftly changing world, here defend the absolutism of British policy. Here loyalty and patriotism found silent and, as they thought, secure expression. An inescapable concomitant of this mental condition was the identification of the fortunes of the Service with the fortunes of the nation. They themselves replaced the ideologies they dismissed. *Their* image, *their* repute, were the nation's prestige; *their* infallibility the nation's bond; *their* survival evidence of the inarticulate supremacy of the English gentleman.

This was the citadel which took in Philby and made him passionately its own.

There seem to be four distinct stages in the Establishment's attitude to Kim Philby. The first stage accounts for his recruitment:

A decent, diffident boy, son of old St. John; Westminster and Cambridge; goodish reports; plenty of guts and knows how to get on with intellectuals without being tarred with their brush. And his left-wing associations? *Wild oats. Open the door and let him in.*

The second stage, post 1944, sees the Establishment rejoicing in its judgement:

Kim is not only a good operator—fit to teach those rash Americans wisdom—but when he wants to be, presentable. He rides hard, likes his drink and is a bit of a bastard with the girls; but he knows when to accept the bit. Capable of rising very high. We were wise to choose Kim. And his left-wing associations? *All got up by MI 5.*

The third stage follows the defection of Burgess and Maclean, and is by far the most interesting, covering both the Mock Trial, and Macmillan's official clearance of Philby in the House of Commons:

Kim has been monstrously misused. He has been playing a damned difficult game flushing out Russians and his actions have been misinterpreted by a lot of outsiders, including those lower class buffoons in Five. He may have been a bit naughty but no more. We must get him back on the rails. And, aside, the voice pleaded:

Kim, persuade us you are not one of them.

For how else are we to interpret that scandalous Mock Trial? A good interrogator never specifies the charges, never reveals the extent of his knowledge, does not give to his suspect the comfort and security of being accompanied by his colleagues, nor the fillip of an examination before an appreciative audience. Least of all does he guarantee to abide by the sporting procedures of the English courts. By staging a trial at all, the Establishment reaffirmed certain guarantees. They demonstrated that they feared for the *image* of the Secret Service and would go to great lengths to avoid publicity. (Our Secret Service has no face, but it does have an image.) They told him, if he did not know already, that they were uncertain of their ground; and they assured him, by providing him with a trial before his peers, that he was still one of them.

One is reminded irresistibly of the secret nocturnal trial of John Profumo conducted by the Conservative Party a few years later. Both Philby and Profumo, significantly, enjoyed Macmillan's professional confidence on the floor of the House of Commons. Each, of his own sphere, was so much a part of the Establishment he betrayed that it was impossible for his colleagues to judge him. Each was incompetently tried in private and incompetently exonerated in public. Each held out, with astonishing gall, against what seemed to be a foregone conclusion. Each ultimately knew the great weakness of the Establishment: *"This Club does not elect liars, therefore Profumo is not a liar; this Club does not elect traitors, therefore Kim is not a traitor."* This Establishment is a self-proving proposition.

To this third stage also belongs the mystery of Philby's reinstatement, and his employment by the *Observer: "We have given Astor assurances that Kim will not be working for SIS. We have given similar assurances at one time or another to Ambassadors, Ministers and firms, and nobody seriously believes. . . ."*

We know from Mr. Astor's very strenuous denials that he at least did seriously believe SIS, and that he was grossly misled. Nevertheless there seems to have been

room for genuine misunderstanding. SIS is used to keeping people in a state of semi-awareness, not least those
who have to speak for them in public. Possibly SIS felt
that it had left Mr. Astor in a similar frame of mind: and
possibly it took comfort in the modest salary which Mr.
Astor paid to Philby; and possibly it felt, quite errone-
ously as it turned out, that Mr. Astor had obligingly left
the way clear for SIS to pay him—and employ him—for
the greater part of his time.

The fourth stage follows the revelation that Philby was
a Soviet spy. Once again we are simply without knowledge. From the account given here, we can only assume
that the old SIS instincts reasserted themselves. No other
explanation, on this evidence, is possible. It is the pleasant assumption of the authors of this book that the contemporary regime of SIS is professional, self-critical and
efficient. It can only be said that on the evidence given
here these virtues were not apparent in the management
of Philby's case once SIS knew that he was a Soviet spy.
Did they want him to go to Russia? The argument
seems to be that they could not prevent him. Why not? A
common swindler could have been arrested and extra-
dited: Why not Philby? He was a criminal: an accessory
before the fact of murder; he had misappropriated government funds. If the British Government had wanted
Kim Philby back in England, I am persuaded that SIS
could have got him. Even if the law could not be
stretched, the task of SIS is to do by underhand means
what cannot be achieved by overt means. If they had
wanted him, they would have got him.
So what happened? Did they, in a sporting way, allow
Kim to run for it? Did the Service want him back and
Macmillan forbid it? By now Philby had confessed. He
was cracking up. His old defences were slipping, he was
by turns cruel and sentimental. Both dream and reality
were closing in on him: Russia, for so long an illusion,
was threatening to become a reality; the citadel, roused
at last, was apparently preparing to strike the avenger.
Philby wavered; but so, disgracefully, did the Establishment. It was not a question of justice: a *full* confession
from Philby would have been one of the most valuable intelligence prizes on the market. It would have demanded
prolonged "debriefing" and might have taken a year or

more. But they wavered, and once again, as at the time of the trial, the simplest rules of interrogation were thrown aside. A man who has confessed is an altered man; excited, alarmed, proud and off balance; still very far from telling the truth. There will be a cover story, a story within a story, perhaps a story within that. Confession by a man of Philby's expertise is like the peeling of an onion; even the most gifted interrogator may never reach the heart. But one rule rings out like a bell: cling to him. Do not for an instant lose him from your sight; bear on him, attack him before he can regroup. No one doubted—the Mock Trial had demonstrated—that Philby could think on his feet. Yet what happened? What voice did the Establishment use?

I will leave a loaded pistol in the library. . . . It's got up by the press. . . . Let sleeping dogs lie. . . . The nation's prestige is already sufficiently damaged. . . . We can't absorb another George Blake scandal . . . by exposing Philby, we're playing the Russians' game. So the scandal never happened. No Minister resigned. Everyone and no one was to blame.

If we can only guess at the scope of Philby's betrayal, let us at least make an assessment of the damage he caused.

From the mid-forties, when SIS first took up arms in earnest against Communism, clean through the coldest years of the Cold War, operations were forfeit, officers compromised, agents shot, imprisoned or forced to become channels of misleading information. A major atomic spy (Maclean) was protected and a vast quanity of intelligence about Russia withheld from us. This was Philby's work and it is not an academic loss. A secret service, in designating its intelligence targets, declares its own ignorance and thereby points to the areas in which it is most easily deceived. A penetrated secret service is not just a bad one: it is an appalling liability. In place of an all-seeing eye, it becomes a credulous ear and a misleading voice, innocently deceiving its own customers in every sphere of the national security: diplomatic, strategic and economic. This was the condition in which SIS functioned, at a charitable estimate, for ten years. Worst of all, because it had taken leave of reality, it continued to believe in its own impregnability. But what of the rest of White-hall?

What of the *customers?* Had they also taken leave of reality? What of our vigilant Secretaries of State, our Foreign Office, Treasury, Joint Intelligence Committees, our economists, Armed Services and all of those who were themselves, each in his separate world, the recipients of these trumped-up wares? God knows what the Secret Service spent in those years: the Berlin tunnel alone must have cost as much as an extra branch of the London Underground. Throw in the Secret Vote and a few hidden subsidies and put it at two hundred million pounds over ten years. Did the Treasury ever draw a profit and loss account of that little bill? How could any public service spend so much on so little and get away with it for so long? The answer, I believe, lies with the prevailing nature of our society, and our predicament as a fading world power. In speaking of the world Philby deceived, I have described it without compunction either as the Establishment or as SIS. At the operative time, the two were indistinguishable.

But let us be fair in this respect at least: no secret service can be more clear-headed than its government. Everything rests upon a clearcut statement of requirements by those who formulate the nation's policy. If the Secret Service is properly used, it is a fighting arm, an extension of Government policy. But in times of dismay and national corruption it sinks swiftly into intrigue, slovenly security and inter-departmental rivalry. I believe that SIS in its worst years, far from being a putrescent arm upon a healthy body, was infected by a general sickness which grew out of the sloth and disorientation of afterwar. It is arguable that Kim Philby, spiteful, vain and murderous as he was, was the spy and catalyst whom the Establishment deserved. Philby is a creature of the post-war depression, of the swift snuffing out of the Socialist flame, of the thousand-year sleep of Eden and Macmillan.

If the secret services were negligent in controlling Philby, so Parliament and we ourselves, society at large, were equally negligent in controlling the secret services. It was *our* politicians who fronted for them, *our* editors who suppressed for them, *our* dons who informed for them, recruited for them; *our* Prime Ministers who protected them.

Thus, no doubt, the life and loves of Kim Philby have demonstrated his original thesis. The Establishment *is* shown to have behaved with grotesque ineptitude; it has produced most of the moods and attitudes that Kim Philby secretly sneered at. And of course he has proved to us what a superior chap he is. Better than all of *us*, or all of *them*, which ever way you care to take it. Constitutional scrutiny of Intelligence Services is largely an illusory concept. If they're good, they fool the outsiders—and if they're bad they fool themselves.

A Marxian novel; a novel without humanity; a novel rich in scenes of social decay. They will call him a vanguard man; they will give him medals, publish his arid, post-office prose, extol his ideological virtue. On either side of the Iron Curtain they will lift their glasses to Kim, wherever he is, the Felix Krull of the intelligence war. *"He crossed his hands on his lap and smiled, as a man may who has won salvation for himself and his beloved."* Thus ended Kipling's boy.

I have no such affection for Philby and no admiration. We shall never, I hope, create a society that is proof against his kind: the little man who found a big name for cheating. Philby is the price we pay for being moderately free; for being able to read this book; and there is a side to Philby's head which knows it, and will know it till he dies. Stupid, credulous, smug and torpid as the Establishment may have been, it erred on the side of trust.

How will he spend the rest of his days? Drinking? Reading the cricket scores in the London newspapers? Waiting for the English holocaust? Now he is exclusive. In ten years' time he may be stopping British tourists in the Moscow streets. Imagine that leaky eye and whisky voice, that hesitant, soft-footed charm: "Britain is Fascist, you know," he will say. "That's why I had to do it."

JOHN LE CARRÉ

BEGINNINGS

1. The Man in Dzerzinsky Square

Chance does nothing that has not been prepared beforehand.
            —ALEXIS DE TOCQUEVILLE, *Recollections*

Western visitors to Moscow, exploring the city in the first mild warmth of a Russian summer, can expect sometimes to come across a stocky, middle-aged man who does not look his age, though in fact he will be seventy on his next birthday, walking briskly across Dzerzinsky Square. They will know, as tourists, that this is the square named after Feliks Dzerzinsky, Lenin's dreaded secret-police boss of the twenties. Today the square is the place where the KGB, the Committee for State Security, has its offices. And if the visitors know anything of the reputation of the KGB, they will probably feel a certain chilly unease.

What to make of the man? At first sight, he appears to be a Russian. He swells slightly over his waistband in the comfortable style of prosperous Muscovites. He wears a Russian-looking suit of somewhat baggy cut, with a woollen sports-shirt without a tie. If spoken to, he will answer in Russian.

And yet there could be a hint of something Western about him: a pair of suede boots that look English, a whiff of French tobacco (he likes to smoke Gauloises sometimes). If anyone should follow him, which is probably not a wise procedure, he would be seen to enter the KGB building as an obvious habitué. But sometimes, very oddly, he carries an airmail edition of *The Times,* and if it happens to be the cricket season, he may pause to turn to the sports pages and check up on the county or Test cricket results. An Englishman who looks like a Russian? A Russian who behaves like an Englishman? In either case, he is a man who can walk into the headquarters of the Soviet Union's secret police and espionage organisation. And when this man meets a Western visitor by appointment he carries a pistol in his briefcase and is "covered" by watchful Russian bodyguards.

The Anglo-Russian is Harold Adrian Russell Philby,

known more usually as Kim Philby, born sixty-nine years ago in British India, and now a citizen of the Soviet Union. The nature of his career can be spelt out swiftly in a list of his titles and decorations: Order of the Red Banner and the Order of Lenin (U.S.S.R.), Red Cross of Military Merit (Franco Spain), Order of the British Empire, civil division (withdrawn), member of the Athenaeum (struck off), former Director of the counter-Soviet section of the British Secret Intelligence Service (MI 6), formerly liaison officer between that service and the American Central Intelligence Agency (with an "astronomical" security clearance), and now a Major-General in the KGB espionage service. He worked for thirty years under cover in the West, and for five of those years was one of the most destructively successful agents in the shadowy history of espionage.

As a reward for his services, the Soviets have continued to heap on him both honours and extravagant praise. As recently as July 1980, seventeen and a half years after his defection, the Moscow evening paper *Izvestia* announced that he had been awarded the People's Friendship Order, a special decoration reserved for foreigners (by birth at any rate) who had rendered signal services to the U.S.S.R. The paper described him as "a wonderful man who remains at his combat post" and ran a prominent serialisation of his book, *My Silent War*. Not surprisingly, given this publicity fanfare, *My Silent War* led to what the manager of Moscow's leading military bookshop called "a mad scramble" on publication day, and every last copy was sold out.

Like Kipling's hero Philby was a man with "two separate sides to his head." On one side was an unmistakable son of the British establishment: a slightly taciturn, obviously charming product of a good public school and a smart Cambridge college; industrious, clear-headed, and believed to be trustworthy to a remarkable degree. This was the man who entered the Secret Intelligence Service in 1940, who set up in 1944 the special new section to deal with the Soviet Union, who was sent in 1949 to represent the British in Washington.

Unfortunately, the "other side of the head" was the real Philby. And the real Philby was a lifelong Communist, who was recruited by the Soviet intelligence organisation when he was only twenty-two. The real Philby was a man who never felt any loyalty to the British causes he pretended to serve: it merely happened that he had been equipped by birth and upbringing with all the outward qualifications of a loyal Englishman, and was prepared to use them in the service of another power. It is now known that during the whole period when he worked at the centre of the Western intelligence community, he made no move without first referring it to his Soviet masters.

At the height of Philby's career, every Western intelligence initiative was doomed before it began. For the agents he sent into ambushes, the results are known and measurable: usually death, sometimes imprisonment. For the nations and governments who were betrayed, the results are harder to assess. The secret intelligence battles of the Cold War, in which Philby was able to strike so many powerful blows for the Russians, were part of a confrontation between East and West which still continues, if in a modified form. It is too early to strike a profit-and-loss account. The accounting, also, depends to some extent on the degree to which secret operations influence the movements of international affairs—and we cannot yet be sure that we have enough information to judge this question.

This book sets out to tell a particular story of espionage, not to assess the entire significance of the role that espionage played in the Cold War. It is a description of a battle, and an attempt to discover why the battle was won and lost. At an immediate glance, the presence of the Englishman Philby in Dzerzinsky square seems astounding, as well as dangerous. But investigated in retrospect, it becomes easy enough to understand. Indeed, there seems to be a certain inevitability about the progression of events that took Philby to Moscow.

Our work began as an inquiry into the career of Philby alone. But we soon found that his career was inextricably linked with those of Guy Burgess and Donald Maclean, also Soviet espionage agents, and his contemporaries at Cambridge in the early thirties. We have therefore tried to investigate and explain the three careers together, while concentrating on Philby, as the most dangerous and effective agent of the three.

2. Boyhood of Three Spies

Why shouldn't the Indians win? After all, it's their country.

—DONALD MACLEAN, aged seventeen.

The child was born of British parents in the dusty cantonment of Ambala in the Punjab on New Year's Day, 1912. He used to pass hours waiting for his civil servant father on the court-house steps, playing with the Indian children. Burnt brown by the sun, he could himself have passed as an Indian; he spoke Hindi before English. The boy had been sonorously named Harold Adrian Russell Philby but he was nicknamed "Kim," after the hero of Kipling's novel—with whom he shared certain characteristics. The Philby family took their names seriously. The father, who when Kim was born had been five years in the Indian Civil Service, was himself christened Harry St. John Bridger. Later he deserted India, his first passion, for Arabia and began a lifelong love affair with the country and its peoples. Then he started to call himself Abdullah, "slave of God," to which he added Al Hajji, the honorific title to which Muslims who have made the pilgrimage to Mecca are entitled. The son settled for plain "Kim" and the name stuck with him through the rest of his life.

The circumstances of Kim's birth are rich in ironies and allusions which resonate throughout his later life. The British Raj, amongst whose proud administrators he spent his first years, displayed in an exceptionally rarefied form those British middle-class, imperialist virtues which the adult Philby was to despise so passionately in secret. Even more important was the fact that India had been for many years a vital area for British intelligence endeavour. This was aimed at charting the political currents moving through the complex masses of the Indian population, and at guarding against the "threat from the North"—from Tsarist Russia. The novel *Kim*, one of Rudyard Kipling's most potent pieces of myth-making, is concerned with the intelligence exploits of a cunning Irish boy who grows up among Indians. It seems an almost unbearable coinci-

21

dence that young Philby should have acquired, irremovably, the same nickname and started his life in the self-same milieu. This life was very nearly abruptly foreshortened by an incident which might easily have been one of his fictional namesake's adventures. One day his Punjabi *ayah* ran screaming through the house; she had found a cobra in Kim's bath. St. John despatched the monster with his shotgun and the son survived to go to England and school.

The father was one of those Englishmen who, like his contemporary T. E. Lawrence, felt a mystical and even fanatical attachment to the Arab world. St. John often found himself at odds with the British ruling classes, of which he himself was a characteristic but maverick representative.

He was *of* the Establishment, but never in it, and his son was to experience a similar kind of ambivalence. Early on Kim developed a stammer; he was a silent, self-contained and introverted boy. People thought his cantankerous father bullied him when he was at home in the family's London house at 18 Acol Road, Hampstead, in intervals between wandering round the more barren areas of the Arabian desert. There is no evidence that St. John ill-treated his son, though he always insisted that children should be kept strictly in their places. To the day he died the old man preserved the birch twigs he had been allowed to use on small boys during his period as head boy of Westminster School in the early 1900s; which suggests, at the least, a certain nostalgia for those good old authoritarian days.

In any case St. John only made spasmodic visits to London; he was far too busy with his travels. Kim's dominant influence was his mother Dora, a pleasant, very domesticated woman whose personality tended to be overshadowed by her husband, but who blossomed in his absence. There were three other children, Helena, Patricia and Diana. The boy was brought up in a house full of women and he found it agreeable; he was to re-create this situation constantly in his adult life.

When it came to choosing a school St. John's latent conservatism emerged—Kim must follow his father to Westminster. Kim was a King's Scholar in this ancient school tucked behind the Abbey; but the slightly scruffy boy, wearing a scholar's gown with the regulation top hat and tails, did not equal his father's brilliant record. He is remembered as an average pupil kicking a football about Dean's Yard (though he was not an outstanding athlete) and lining up with his friends at "Suts," the school tuck shop. His overriding passion was music—he collected enormous quantities of classical records—but despite sterling efforts to master the French horn he never achieved any particular expertise. The year he was sixteen he visited Spain on a summer holiday and came back full of enthusiasm for King Alfonso XII and the Royal family; at this period he evidently shared his father's enthusiasm for hereditary rulers. About this time he also had a conversation with a friend on the subject of marriage, which, he said, was a lunatic institution. "Can you imagine any *boy* you could stand to spend your whole life with? Do you think it would be any different with a woman? I don't understand why anybody ever gets married."

Academically, he was not thought by his friends to be outstanding, though on one occasion a don from Christ Church, Oxford, Professor E. F. Jacob, set the History Sixth an essay and irritated the rest of the class by announcing afterwards that Kim's effort was "head and shoulders" above the rest. Apart from his Kim was conscientious, meticulous even, but never brilliant. On the other hand it seemed that the quiet boy with the stammer was ideal Indian Civil Service material: the family were keen that he should follow this career and Kim in his taciturn way seemed happy to the prospect. The boy lacked his father's eccentric independence and compelling personality but, it was thought, these very deficiencies might be no bad thing as far as the ICS was concerned. One St. John was enough for the family. In October 1929 Kim went up to Trinity College, Cambridge to read history preparatory to taking the Civil Service examination. The thick-set, untidy lad was nearly eighteen but he looked more like a schoolboy than an undergraduate.

By contrast, a fellow Trinity historian, Guy Francis de Moncy Burgess, gave an impression of having been born a sophisticate. At seventeen his passions were Proust, Firbank and the glittering Michael Arlen. He also admired Cézanne and had a talent, which he never really developed, for dashing off satirical and sometimes obscene drawings, rather in the style of Daumier. Burgess was a precocious adolescent out of the pages of early Huxley.

The Burgesses, who claimed descent from Huguenot settlers originally called de Bourgeois, were far richer than the Philbys. Guy's father, Naval Commander Malcolm Kingsford de Moncy Burgess, died when he was eleven; subsequently his mother re-married a Colonel John Retallack Basset and lived the life of a society lady, taking up apartments in Arlington House, Piccadilly. Mrs. Basset was much closer to Guy than to Nigel, the younger child. In January 1924, at the age of thirteen, Guy went to Eton, and a year later to Dartmouth; like his father he was destined for a naval career. But after spending more than two years there he developed a slight defect in vision which meant the Navy was closed to him. By a special dispensation he was allowed to return to Eton, which was probably just as well, despite family tradition the Navy and Guy Burgess were quite evidently not made for each other. In Eton's hot-house atmosphere, relieved from the austerities of life at Dartmouth, Guy became affected and rather pretentious, even though he was a good enough athlete to get into the soccer team, and also a fine swimmer. He developed into a kind of Oscar Wilde of the sixth form, but he was something more than an adolescent *poseur*. In his last year he won the prestigious Gladstone Memorial Scholarship and in October 1930 went up to Trinity with a scholarship gained more by well-polished epigrams than any profound learning.

For the rest of his life brilliance, particularly in conversation, was to serve him as a substitute for application. He was also quite exceptionally handsome, and adroit at exploiting his looks. A woman who met him at this period recalls feeling that he was trying to dominate her with his personality and charm. She found it odd and unpleasant; she had not realised that Guy was really playing a game with her, and that he was homosexual. "I'd never even heard the word."

Sir Donald Maclean, who died in that summer of 1932 when his son, also called Donald, was first espousing Marxism at Cambridge, was one of the finest flowers of the British nonconformist, Liberal tradition. He was born in 1864 and his family came from Tiree, an island off the Argyll coast; he himself was a figure of almost claustrophobic rectitude, whose lifetime preoccupations were Presbyterian Christianity, the Liberal Party, and high principle.

Sir Donald's background was almost identical to that of Harold Macmillan. Macmillan's grandfather, like Sir Donald Maclean's father, was a crofter who spent his life in the Highlands without ever having seen "either a train or a tree." The two families were in fact related by marriage, though they were never close to each other. But Sir Donald spent comparatively little time in Tiree or Scotland. He was brought up in middle-class Cardiff where, in due course, he founded a firm of solicitors, which flourished because of his industry, parsimony and impressive public *persona*. He became an energetic lay-preacher and moraliser, a co-founder of the National Society for the Prevention of Cruelty to Children, and a passionate partisan of the Liberal Party, in whose interest he stood (unsuccessfully) as Parliamentary candidate in 1900. Six years later he won Cardiff and thereafter became a prominent man in the Party, which he led in 1918 for three years while Asquith was forced into the political wilderness. In 1907 he had married a quiet girl from Surrey called Gwendolen Devitt and bought a house in London. Their second son, Donald, was born on May 25, 1913.

Life in the dark, three-storey house in Southwick Street, Paddington, was reinforced with family prayers and punctuated with regular visits to the Marylebone Presbyterian Church in George Street. The head of the family's overwhelming probity and industry seems to have produced formidable inhibition in the son, who found his mother easier than his father. Members of the family believe that he was a convinced Christian only for a short period as an adolescent, but he did not openly rebel against religion for many years. Instead he said nothing. In September 1927 he was sent to Gresham's School, a mile away from the village of Holt in Norfolk.

Gresham's in 1927 was a fairly small minor public school with less than 250 pupils and a reputation for progressive, slightly cranky views. It was precisely the kind of establishment calculated to appeal to the Macleans—its headmaster, an unconventional liberal called J. R. Eccles, was an opponent of corporal punishment who operated the so-called "honour" system. In effect this meant that the boys were responsible for their own discipline, a scheme intended to promote a sense of responsibility.

Donald was a slight, fair-haired boy, clever, but rather supercilious and reserved. He was neither popular nor good at games; the general view was that he was effeminate, and when the Old School House put on a play in his first term he was given a female part. Later, when they tried their hand at a Noël Coward play, *I'll Leave It To You,* young Donald again played the female lead. He did, on the other hand, enjoy a good deal of reflected glory from his distinguished parents. Eccles admired Sir Donald and the feeling was reciprocated—the celebrated Liberal was frequently invited to address the boys; Lady Gwendolen graced prize days, where the *grande dame* manner she had acquired made her one of the centres of attraction.

The young Donald Maclean was shy, awkward, obsessed by sex and overwhelmed with guilt—it took him another thirty years to accept fully the homosexual element in his make-up that was so obvious to his friends, who sometimes unkindly called him "Lady Maclean." But he worked hard at school and had a vehement sense of rectitude, even if it was more confused than that of his father, who went through life finding it easy to see issues, and personalities, in black and white. He also displayed unusual social concern, and considerable independence of mind. When he was twelve, he wrote an essay against capital punishment. And Maclean's younger brother Alan recalls a week in 1929 when both of them were suffering from influenza and sharing a bedroom. Donald was always kind and he spent long hours playing soldiers with the smaller boy. Donald, however, played the game eccentrically. Young Alan always arranged the lead soldiers so that the splendid, kilted Highlanders outmanoeuvred the ragged Indians and finally decimated them. In Donald's variation the natives won. When Alan complained Donald said it was only right that the Highlanders should be beaten. "Why shouldn't the Indians win? After all, it's their country."

What conclusions can be drawn from these twentieth-century biographies, all of which fit with minor variations into traditional patterns of British middle-class life of the period? Both Kim Philby and Donald Maclean were potential ideologues; Maclean had been a Christian as a young boy and though his beliefs appear to have lasted only a very short time his temperament always remained fundamentally a religious one. He was also highly suggestible. Maclean was the kind of man who might possibly have become a Roman Catholic, or even a Moral Re-Armer.

Kim Philby was also temperamentally an extremist and there was a strong element of the adventurer in him. He might have had a successful career in the Army, or as a journalist, which of course he was at one period, or even, as originally intended, in some remote outpost of the British Raj. Burgess was apparently the most gifted, the best-connected, and by far the most polished. If Etonians had been unsophisticated enough to elect their classmate most likely to succeed, he would have been a formidable contender.

Decades later, after the three boys had grown up and acquired the ambiguous celebrity accorded to traitors, various analysts fastened on their father-relationships, or lack of them, as a key to their subsequent behaviour. Burgess, of course, barely knew his father, though the posthumous influence was evidently powerful enough for him to have tried an obviously unsuitable naval career. Certainly neither the opinionated, autocratic St. John nor Sir Donald, with his exaggerated façade of a Victorian paterfamilias, could have been the easiest of parents to live with or follow. Such psychological speculation should not, of course, be allowed to overshadow the importance of the social and political forces which acted on Philby, Burgess and Maclean. But Kim Philby's father St. John was so extraordinary a character in himself that it is impossible to consider the son's career without relating it to the father's. If father-relationships count for anything, St. John's character must have moulded the character of the future master-spy.

3. The Slave of God

God, I'm bored.
—ST. JOHN PHILBY, on his deathbed

One of the constant side effects of having an Empire on which the sun never set was the emotional adjustment required during a lifetime of administering the Raj. The less sensitive officers of the Indian Civil Service survived being born in India, educated in Britain, serving in India, taking leave in Britain, promoted in India and finally retiring in Britain, without feeling any great degree of alienation. Others, beginning probably with Clive and ending with John Masters, found the demands of two Motherlands impossible. It is all very well to live in the colonies and speak for years of England as home—but what happens to those who cannot stand home when they finally get there? What happens to those who find the call of the sunburnt plains of empire just as appealing as the ordered woods and gardens of Cheltenham—and can deny neither?

St. John Philby fell into this schizoid group. He spent a lifetime renouncing his native land, railing against her perfidy, deceit and moral decline. He abandoned Christianity to become a Muslim. He took a Saudi slave-girl as a second wife. He lived in Mecca, dressed as an Arab, ate camel meat and had a "bodyguard" of four huge Abyssinian baboons. (The baboons, on chains, guarded the entrance to his house in Mecca: no one could enter until he told them to lie down.) But he kept up his membership of the Athenaeum, enjoyed dining the Establishment, contributed to *The Times* and tried never to miss a Test Match. He wanted to be an MP, and stood twice for Parliament. But even when he was expelled from his beloved Saudi Arabia he preferred to live in exile in the Middle East rather than face life in Britain again.

He frequently said that the only England he ever admired was England under Cromwell, "which laid the firm moral foundations of subsequent intellectual and spiritual development," yet his own moral behaviour was, by Western standards, inexcusable. He was an authoritarian, difficult to like, more difficult to love, and shatteringly wrong on many of the major events of his time (he was convinced Hitler had "no earthly intention" of attacking Britain and thought that the Italians were the "New Romans" who were going to sweep through a decadent Europe). Yet he was a tough, brilliant explorer and even his enemies respected his integrity. "Get your facts right," he would say, "then always go through to the end with whatever you think right, no matter what it is"—a *simpliste* piece of advice which appears to have affected his son deeply.

St. John Philby's early life was completely conventional, the background of an upper-middle-class Englishman heading for distinction in the service of his King and Country. He was born in 1885 in Ceylon, the son of Henry Montague Philby, an unremarkable tea planter. He was sent home to go to Westminster (where he was captain), then to Trinity, Cambridge, where he took a degree in Oriental Languages (he mastered Urdu, Persian, Arabic, Baluchi, Pushtu and Punjabi). There was nothing in his behaviour at university to indicate the eccentric years that lay ahead. The political climate was conservative; students spent anguished, soul-searching days deciding whether to become Fabians. St. John at this point never wavered. He remained a moderately liberal Conservative. When he graduated he returned to India in the Indian Civil Service—for the most unromantic motives. He did not believe in Indian nationalism or in self-determination for colonial peoples. He looked on the job as a duty—sharing the white man's burden.

After his marriage in 1910 to Dora Johnson (the daughter of an officer of the Indian Public Works Department) he moved from the Punjab to Calcutta. He had already been marked for promotion and despite one superior's rather damning report—"he mixes a bit too much with the native element"—he was made secretary to the Board of Examiners of Bengal. At the outbreak of war he was appointed to the British forces in Mesopotamia in charge of the financial side of the intelligence department. Here he had his first taste of the intrigue which went on in the bazaars of Bagdad. Years later when his treks across Saudi Arabia and the many reports of his disappearances had made his name familiar to most British newspaper readers, the novelist William J. Makin wrote a brief account of Philby's secret activities in the First World War. It is worth quoting here because it shows the aura which built up around the man, and made him seem so much larger than life, even to his family. "Twice St. John Philby disappeared from base, each time wandering the by-ways of Bagdad disguised as an Arab beggar. Two clever Germans were causing concern to the British forces at this time. One was the famous Wassmuss, who ranged with a band of guerilla fighters throughout Persia, swooping down on oilfields and generally upsetting the British lines of communication between India and

Mesopotamia. The other German was Preusser, who claimed to be the master of the Persian Gulf. St. John Philby had to pit his brains against these two clever men. The sequel was inevitable. Preusser was knifed by an Arab one night and died. Wassmuss found a cordon closing around him in Persia and only escaped by a sensational ride through the night towards the rooftop of the world, where he took refuge in a Central Asian state. When this work was finished St. John Philby again disappeared."[1]

Philby did not stay long in Bagdad. He was caught up in Britain's policy of promoting revolution against Germany's Turkish allies—and found he disagreed over the means of doing it. He fell out with the deputy chief political officer, Arnold Wilson, a fiery-tempered Army officer (well remembered in later years in the House of Commons for threatening to horsewhip journalists who wrote ill of him), and was happy to accept charge of a political mission to Ibn Saud, then a courageous if intolerant tribal leader in a bitterly divided Arabia.

The British approach to the Arabian situation was equivocal. The Arab Bureau (for which T. E. Lawrence worked) felt reasonably certain that Hussein of Mecca and his son, Feisal, had ensured that the Hashemites would be the ruling power. But the Government of India, which had a large degree of autonomy, was worried about the effects that this policy was having on its relations with the Muslim community in India and thought it wiser to court Ibn Saud. St. John Philby seemed the ideal man for the job, and there was no indication at that time that his success would become the embarrassment it did later.

Philby fell in love with Arabia and conceived a durable hero worship for Saud, the man who in his heyday could outrun, outride and outshoot anyone in the desert. The feeling was reciprocated. Saud was fascinated by the stocky argumentative Englishman who was more Bedouin than the Bedouin (an Arab agent in Taif was to report: "It was possible to distinguish Philby from the thirty-five Bedouin in his group only by the fact his feet were

---

[1] If Philby did help the pursuit of Wassmuss he played a part in one of the greatest British intelligence coups of the century (see Ch. 11).

not quite dirty enough") and came to trust him more than any of his own advisers.

What had happened was that Philby had succumbed to a still unexplained force which affects so many Englishmen who dabble in Arab affairs, a force which tends to loosen the most traditional men from their loyalties to their Governments. Lawrence could not bring himself to carry out British policy in Arabia; Wilfred Blunt carried on a vast campaign against Cromer in Egypt; Gertrude Bell and Percy Sykes substituted themselves for government in Iraq; Arnold Wilson, after a brilliant career in Mesopotamia, joined Mosley's blackshirts. Philby, too, went against Britain; and as Saudi Arabia changed from a biblical desert kingdom into a twentieth-century oil state he was there at Saud's side, pleading his cause to the West, interpreting the West to the King. He adopted the Arab way of life completely and with little effort. The austerity, the strict moral code, the social system based on a benevolent if autocratic monarchy, appealed to the puritanical side of his personality. He willingly gave up material comforts, boasted frequently that he needed neither bed, nor table nor chair, and when at Test Matches during his rare visits to England insisted—to the astonishment of other spectators—on sitting cross-legged on the grass throughout the match. He wore Arab clothes most of the time in Arabia, and was soon reduced to one outfit of Western attire—a grey suit two sizes too small and a pair of battered brown canvas shoes. He never touched alcohol in his Arab life. But in the West, he lived well, drank freely, travelled first-class, and smoked big cigars.

It is significant that the man he so much admired, Ibn Saud, was the exemplar of one of the most strict, devout and narrowminded of Muslim sects: the Wahhabis. When they captured Mecca they made bonfires of 100,-000 hookahs. This was the sect St. John joined. He made a pilgrimage to the Holy City, performed the customary circumambulation of the Kaaba and took as his new Islamic name, Abdullah, the prefix of the King's own name.

Like many other British Arabists, St. John held that his country had behaved with unforgivable duplicity towards the Arabs in the First World War. The British promised Arab self-determination in Arabia in exchange for Arab help against the German-Turkish alliance. But these public promises were cynically ignored in the secret Sykes-

Picot agreement, by which Britain and France agreed to divide the Middle East to their own advantage after the war. This duplicity was then compounded by the Balfour Declaration, promising Palestine to the Jews. St. John's reaction seems to have been that the rulers of Britain simply could not be trusted.

It did not take Whitehall long to realise that Philby's zeal was greater than that required of an ICS officer devoted to his job. Philby had "gone Arab" and his prospects of advancement began to wane. The final break came in 1925 when Philby took it upon himself to act as mediator between Saud and Shariff Ali while Saud was laying siege to Jeddah. The British Government was attempting to maintain strict neutrality in this struggle between two Arabian leaders and took a poor view of St. John's interference. It was suggested to him that he might like to retire, and Philby agreed.

To earn a living he set up in business in Jeddah, importing cheap cars, prams, cough mixture and radios. Almost as an afterthought he developed a second career, begun on his first visit to Saud, that of Arabian explorer. When all his eccentricities have been forgotten it is for this that he will be remembered. He crossed parts of Arabia unknown to Burton or Doughty, mapping them with such precision that oil prospectors still use his maps today. He received the Founder's Medal of the Royal Geographical Society and was awarded the first Burton Memorial Medal of the Royal Asiatic Society. He made large additions to British collections of geological and zoological specimens from Arabia. The British Museum owes to him five new species of birds, including a partridge named after him and a woodpecker named after his wife. He took up the collection and study of early Semitic inscriptions in Arabia and he increased from some two thousand to over thirteen thousand the number of known Thamuddic inscriptions.

His personal finances prospered. Ibn Saud gave him a house worth ten thousand pounds and he acted as Saud's go-between in most business negotiations—with appropriate commissions. He wrote regularly for *The Times* and other British newspapers and published many books. No Westerner was better informed of events in the Middle East, but on the world political stage he remained a novice. In 1939 he offered himself as Labour candidate for Epping but was rejected. Instead he joined the People's Party ("Peace with Germany by agreement") and stood at Hythe. When the south coast was already having its first practice blackout and a large scale civil defence exercise made movement in the area difficult, Philby was addressing election meetings begging voters to "resist the blandishments of Mr. Churchill." When the first Territorials were arriving at Shorncliffe Camp he was saying "I am perfectly convinced that Mr. Hitler does not want war and anyone who tells you that he does is a liar." Philby polled 576 votes and lost his £150 deposit.

St. John returned to the Middle East, but as the war gained momentum in 1940, he felt "unwilling to go on enjoying the complete security of Arabia in wartime," and set out to go to America. In Karachi—on the only route he could travel at the time—he was arrested and repatriated to Britain, where he was imprisoned under Regulation 18b, the famous mechanism which was used for dealing with potential Nazi sympathisers.

The reason for St. John's detention was the fact that he had advised Saud that Britain was unlikely to do well in the war against Germany and that the King would be wise to withdraw his sterling investments to a safer place. Word of this reached Herbert Morrison, who was furious. St. John's friends deny that his anti-British sentiments were very serious, and certainly he was released after four months. It was said at the time that he would have been released earlier if only someone could have remembered what he had been imprisoned for. Philby obviously felt strongly about his detention and took pains to record in *Arabian Days* (1948) that the tribunal which examined him not only set him free but revoked unconditionally the order of detention. At the end of the war St. John joined the short-lived Commonwealth Party, then, disillusioned with British politics, he returned to the Middle East for good. He found Arabia greatly changed. Income from concessions to exploit the country's vast oil deposits had brought undreamed-of riches to Saud and his people. Philby did not like it. In his last published work, *Forty Years in the Wilderness* (1957), he lamented the decadence which prosperity had brought to his adopted country: "I belonged to the generation of his father [Ibn Saud I] and he to a generation that learned its manners from the old Wahhabi dispensation. Alas that his sons and their contemporaries should have had their lessons in the gutters of the West!"

His disgust for the younger generation's lust for Western consumer durables drew rebukes from him which carried a strong flavour of anti-Semitism. He was fond of saying that the Arabs and the Jews were both Semites and therefore traders, and that the only difference lay in the fact that the Jews were honest traders and the Arabs were not. The more Arabia became westernised the more outspoken he became.

At a Privy Council meeting in 1953 in the Royal Palace at Riyadh, while old King Saud lay dying in an adjacent room, Philby, moved by grief, made his bitterest attack on the corrupting influence of the West. Using the flowery Arabic rhetoric he had grown to like, he began by saying that although he had no official position in the court the King had often been pleased to take his advice. Having established his position, Philby came to the point: "Unless you abandon your present corrupt practices you are doomed. You lost Palestine because you bought worthless arms and pocketed the profits . . ." There was more in the same vein. The young Saud was furious and their relationship steadily deteriorated until, in 1955, he expelled St. John. The ostensible reason was a dispute which arose over the construction of a new palace for one of the Saudi princesses. St. John had obtained the contract for a British firm he represented, but the royal family demanded so many changes to the original plan that St. John had to tell them that the palace could not be built at the price first quoted. The real reason was Saud's resentment at Philby's continuing criticism of his rule.

St. John took up residence in Damascus and then the Lebanon, where he had a house in the mountains outside Beirut. He had separated from his English wife Dora by this time and was living with the former slave girl, Umferhat—a gift from King Saud I—and their two children. His last years with Dora had been stormy. Strangely, she expressed no jealousy over Umferhat and would probably have remained a quiet if slightly dull wife, had not a sadistic streak in St. John compelled him to tell Dora—in some detail—of his affair with another Englishwoman. (One of the monumental rows between St. John and Kim occurred when each accused the other of treating his wife abominably—St. John with Dora, Kim with Aileen.) Dora began to drink heavily and died, possibly by her own hand, in 1956.

After two years Saud II relented and invited St. John to return from exile. He accepted with alacrity. Although he was now seventy he was as active as ever. He spent his time collating and indexing all the material he had gathered during forty years in Arabia, preparing papers for the Royal Geographical Society and writing more books (described by one disgruntled reader as "one damned wadi after another").

In 1960 he visited Russia as a guest of the Royal Geographical Society and returned via London, where he made a great show of displaying a medal Khrushchev had given him. He took his grandchildren on a fortnight's holiday to Falmouth, where he spent some time calling on Doughty's sisters. Then he stopped off at Beirut on his way back to Riyadh and stayed with Kim. The reunion was gay and hectic. On September 29, after a particularly heavy party, St. John had a heart attack and was taken to hospital unconscious. Kim sat with him throughout the night. In the morning St. John regained consciousness briefly, looked vaguely around the ward and then focused on his son. His last words, worthy of any deathbed anthology, were: "God, I'm bored."

He was buried with simple Muslim rites the following day. Kim, who had a tombstone placed on his father's grave with the inscription THE GREATEST EXPLORER OF THEM ALL, was strongly affected by his father's death. Their relationship had been a complicated one. In the early years St. John had alternated a smothering affection with public humiliation until Kim lost an important factor in a child's development—the certainty of parental love. After St. John had repeatedly belittled his son in front of others, Kim reached a stage where he could not speak to his father without having difficulty in getting the words out. It seems highly probable that Kim's stammer stems from this period and that St. John was to blame. On the other hand St. John was every boy's dream of the romantic parent. While other fathers went to the City or toiled in banks, St. John strode ten feet tall across the Empty Quarter, glory and honour by his side. There is no doubt that Kim hungered to follow in his father's footsteps. So was Kim's final rejection of Britain an extension of his father's rejection? The similarity of their lives certainly suggests it. Yet in his later years St. John seemed to mellow towards his country. He even became perversely proud of Kim's appointment as First Secretary in Washington and told his friends that he was certain Kim would one day become Ambassador.

What then would he have felt about Kim's defection? One reverts to an impression which outweighs all others: St. John Philby was a man who listened to a different drum and the sense of individual purpose that this gave him was his son's strongest inheritance. If St. John had known the nature of the game which Kim had chosen, with its years on lonely and dangerous paths, one feels he might not have approved but he would most certainly have understood.

Such was Kim Philby's father. But there were, of course, other influences on him—and whether or not he, Burgess and Maclean shared defective parental relationships, they certainly had one powerful formative influence in common. All of them were affected by the growth of Marxist passion at their University, Cambridge.

4. The Cambridge Marxists

> . . . . *beneath the surface of an ever more sophisticated society what dark passions and inflammable credulities de we find, sometimes accidentally released, sometimes deliberately mobilised.*
>
> —HUGH TREVOR-ROPER, *The European Witch Craze of the Sixteenth and Seventeenth Centuries.*

In December 1933 Julian Bell wrote to the *New Statesman* that "in the Cambridge that I first knew, in 1929 and 1930, the central subject of ordinary intelligent conversation was poetry. . . . By the end of 1933 we have arrived at a situation in which almost the only subject of discussion is contemporary politics, and in which a very large majority of the more intelligent undergraduates are Communists, or almost Communists. . . ."

It was in October 1929 that Kim Philby went up to

Cambridge, dressed in flannel bags and tweed jacket. If St. John had gone up with his son for the day (which he did not) he might well have observed that the old place was much as he had left it in the Edwardian, pre-Great War era nearly two decades earlier. In fact the surface similarity was misleading and the university was on the brink of one of the most radical, and sudden, changes in its history. But 1932 was to be the crucial year. In 1930 and 1931, which marked the successive arrivals of Burgess and Maclean, the atmosphere was still Cambridge, old style. The clock was still standing, as it were, at ten to three, but only just.

For middle-class boys, fresh out of public school, Cambridge's beauty and freedom were intoxicating. Cushioned by their backgrounds, cossetted by the college servants and tradesmen, flattered by the attention of the popular press, who regarded them, with their counterparts at Oxford, as an extension of smart London society as well as the heirs to Westminster and Whitehall, they comported themselves with the assurance of the nation's future rulers. The university formed a self-regarding and escapist society, which fitted in well with the Baldwin Government's brand of complacent Conservatism. Neither industrialism nor traffic jams had yet shattered the college calm; few scholarship boys had managed to penetrate the citadel of privilege; the town existed for the benefit of the university, and servants were dirt cheap. Public schoolboys only needed a little private money to cultivate their leisure elegantly and enjoy the Cambridge of punts and patties, late night conversations and strawberry teas. It was a bewitching atmosphere, and even more so when recalled in later years. Nostalgia—with Rupert Brooke's Grantchester poem as its most fulsome expression—was this Cambridge generation's occupational vice.

Trinity, which sheltered both Philby and Burgess, was the biggest and, enjoying massive endowments, the richest college. King's, its finances still in the process of being rehabilitated by Maynard Keynes, the resident financial wizard, was poorer but perhaps intellectually even more prestigious. Its tentacles spread to the Bloomsbury of the Woolfs and E. M. Forster, the Eton of Lytton Strachey and so many other aesthetic Kingsmen. King's was the spiritual home of the Apostles, an exclusive and bizarre mixture of dining club and secret society divided in its membership between King's and Trinity. It had been founded in the early nineteenth century, and its most distinguished early members were Tennyson and Arthur Hallam. Its members were regarded, certainly by themselves, as a kind of intellectual super-élite. They met regularly to enjoy two activities typifying a certain stratum of Cambridge society—conversation, and the cultivation of personal friendship. In 1932 the Apostles elected Guy Burgess a member, thereby playing a strange, ambiguous role in the story of class and national betrayal that was to emerge over the years.

Burgess gained this social and intellectual accolade thanks to his close friendship with another Trinity man, Anthony Frederick Blunt, who had just become a Fellow of the college. This art historian, who was to become Keeper of the Queen's Pictures in his middle-age, was one of the most overtly brilliant—and homosexual—lights of Cambridge society. The son of the Rev. Arthur Blunt, a Church of England clergyman, he had been educated at Marlborough, a notably religious public school that provided subsidised places for sons of the clergy. Burgess's sponsor, however, had long replaced his schoolboy Christianity with agnosticism and was flirting with Leftist politics. Apart from his academic gifts, Blunt also enjoyed distinguished family connections, which were to become even more glittering with the passage of time. His second cousin was Lady Elizabeth Bowes-Lyon, daughter of the fourteenth Earl of Strathmore. She became the Duchess of York when she married George, the Prince of Wales's younger brother. And after he in due course became Edward VIII, and then abdicated to marry his American lover, Wallis Simpson, the Duke of York became King of England, as George VI. The dandified art connoisseur thus found himself related to Elizabeth, the future Queen of England.

The Apostles were an exclusively male society; the university itself very much a male enclave. In a period when a proposal to permit mixed bathing in the Serpentine could provoke irate and extended controversy it is not surprising to find the sexes firmly, almost crudely, segregated. Girls had been permitted to titular degree-taking status in 1922, but they were still plainly second-class citizens. They were widely regarded by their male contemporaries as frowsty blue-stockings—Julian Bell, one of the more celebrated undergraduates of the period, unkindly called them "bottled snakes"—and most of the gayer university members preferred to find their girl-friends at deb-parties in London. Conditions for friendship, let alone seduction, were clearly more favourable outside the university limits. Girton and Newnham girls were even forbidden to go to a man's rooms for tea unchaperoned; if they themselves received male visitors alone they were required to wheel their iron bedsteads out into the corridors. Girton had been deliberately sited three miles out of town on the Huntingdon Road in the hope that the distance would inhibit assaults on their inmates' virtue. A special blue bus ferried the Girtonians in to lectures, and when they were over, out again. Not surprisingly Rosamund Lehmann makes the heroine of her classic novel of the period, *Dusty Answer,* comment on the prevailing atmosphere of sexual separation. She feels a growing awareness "of fundamental masculine apartness; of the other sex mysteriously calling to and avoiding it across an impassable gulf."

This then was the Cambridge world the three boys found when they came up between 1929 and 1931. At one extreme it was frivolous, dilettante, aesthetic; at the other, typified by the blue-blood and thunder Pitt Club which Burgess joined, philistine and snobbish. Scarcely anywhere did Cambridge make contact with the world outside, living in the shadow of the steadily worsening depression. (When the Hunger Marchers passed through the town in 1933 undergraduates stared in wonder at these shabby creatures from a world they had never seen.) But despite the economic climate the university, if largely apathetic, was still politically more Tory than otherwise. Union debates stirred no passion; on the contrary they were thought of as a kind of whimsical game.

Yet there was a much more serious side to the university, which indicates its subterranean strength and vitality. Rutherford, with his pupils Chadwick, Drummond and John Cockroft, had made the Cavendish Laboratory the most important centre of experimental physics in the world. Peter Kapitza, a young Russian who was to leave Cambridge in dramatic circumstances, was only one of the young physicists who came to the Cavendish to sit at the feet of the mighty. Another, at Trinity Hall with Donald Maclean, was Alan Nunn May. Cambridge was enjoying an extraordinary renaissance in scientific research, which extended to some of the humanities. Wittgenstein was probably the most important philosopher of the decade; literary criticism was being revolutionised by I. A. Richards and re-written by F. R. Leavis.

Neither Philby nor Maclean had much wide-ranging academic interest beyond their own subjects—History with Economics for Kim, French and German for Donald. But Burgess, basically a historian, was a voracious reader who worked through books with the same animal passion he brought to all his activities (surprisingly, he was a devotee of Jane Austen and George Eliot, as well as writers with a higher erotic content). Burgess was made for Cambridge and it for him. He was one of those men who reach the height of their distinction as a university student, without ever progressing. He was so ideally cast in the role of a brilliant undergraduate at Cambridge in the early 1930s that he continued to play it, with diminishing spontaneity and success, for the next three decades.

At twenty Burgess was remarkably handsome in an epicene way which attracted both women (whom he had little to do with) and men, who appealed to him more. Cambridge had enjoyed a tradition of sentimental friendships between men from the days of Hallam and Tennyson onwards, which not infrequently developed sexually. (The luminaries of Bloomsbury, Strachey, Keynes, Duncan Grant, had devoted a great deal of time to falling in and out of love with each other, and their impact was still strong.) A lot of young men, of course, played at it because they were used to an exclusively male society and were awkward with girls, who were in any case in short supply.

With Burgess there was never any question about whether he was in earnest. He was not remotely effeminate but brought to homosexual conquest the kind of energy usually associated with heterosexual seducers. In his rooms on I staircase in the timid Gothic of Trinity New Court, he started a collection of whips (Philby, who lived only a matter of yards away, may well have been invited to admire them; this was the time that their lifelong friendship was beginning). Though Philby was fairly clearly *not* among them, Burgess's conquests were soon legendary. On occasions he claimed to have seduced Donald Maclean but years later he contemptuously denied this: "That great white body, never. It would have been like sleeping with Dame Nellie Melba." Cutting a swathe from Trinity to King's, bellowing with laughter in Hall, parading a pair of sixteen-year-old "nephews" along the banks by the Cam, he became one of the best-known figures in the University. There was always a new Burgess anecdote and when one went down particularly well he would repeat it again and again. "I could never travel by train," he used to announce at parties in his gruff, blurred voice. "Why? Because I would feel obliged to seduce the engine-driver."

In June 1932 his intellectual facility was rewarded with a First in Part One of the History Tripos—a series of three examinations. At the beginning of his next Michaelmas term, in November 1932, he was elected to the Apostles and on November 12 he attended his first meeting in King's. He seemed ideally suited to play the fool cleverly and fit in to the Apostles' ingrown world of mutual admiration. But times were changing.

In April 1931 a frail, untidy young man called David Haden Guest walked into evening "Hall" at Trinity and attracted a good deal of attention, much of it ribald. Guest, an undergraduate mathematician whose father had been a Labour MP, was wearing a hammer and sickle badge on his lapel.

A month earlier Guest had been in Braunschweig prison, detained after a demonstration the local Nazi-controlled police had decided was Communist inspired, which it probably was. Guest himself, however, had not at this stage been a Party member. He was simply a student at Gottingen University on sabbatical leave from Cambridge. He had gone to Gottingen without political motivation simply because he wished to study under the great mathematician Hilbert.

In Cambridge the signs of impending chaos in Europe seemed a long way off, but in Nazi-dominated Gottingen they were as real as the armed police in the streets and the drunken Nazi meetings which went on to the small hours of the morning in the beer cellar next to Guest's *pension*. In Gottingen anti-Semitism had already reached an advanced point and Guest, who had been brought up in an atmosphere of delicate liberal consciences, was deeply shocked to find that the works of Heine had been removed from the university library. But it was the two weeks in prison and the fact that his release was engineered thanks to the assistance of some friendly comrades that made up his mind. As soon as he returned to England he joined the Communist Party and in April 1932 he started a cell in Cambridge University. There had been occasional university Communists before this date but they had all worked on routine canvassing chores through the town Party organisation.

The new university cell was very different. Its members worked openly through the Cambridge Socialist Club, a numerically weak, basically Labour Party organisation which they tried to strengthen, imbue with thorough-going Marxist principle, and tap for recruits to the Party itself. There were also private cell meetings attended by two Marxist dons in the university—Maurice Dobb an economist then at Pembroke College, and J. D. Bernal, a crystallographer who was considered the finest young scientist the university had seen for ten years. Guest had managed to recruit four undergraduate members, one of whom was a fellow Trinity undergraduate, Maurice Cornforth. The names of the others have always been kept secret but it seems certain that Guy Burgess was either a founder member or came in very shortly after. Certainly at his first Apostles' meeting in November 1932 he made it clear that he was a Communist. In the course of the next two years he contrived on a number of occasions to inject a passionate, left-wing political content into the artistic, literary and philosophical debates of the Apostles. In these endeavours, he was usually supported by Hugh Sykes Davies, a surrealist writer who became a fellow of St. John's, and naturally also by Anthony Blunt. Three years earlier it had been very different; then members had agreed without dissent that such a sordid subject as "practical politics," as opposed to more elevated preoccupations like philosophy or aesthetics, was not worthy of Apostolic consideration. Things were changing.

The disastrous defeat of Labour in the autumn of 1931 and Ramsey MacDonald's inglorious decision to continue as Prime Minister at the head of a National Government without policy or conviction aroused deep disillusion. So, cumulatively, did the third year of Depression and, in September, two events which occurred within forty-eight hours of each other—the Japanese invasion of Manchuria and the sailors' strike at Invergordon. Capitalism appeared to be in precipitate decline; a doctrine whose orthodox exponents denied that overproduction was possible began to look shaky—even in insulated Cambridge. The crisis of faith in capitalism had begun. It had taken a long time to reach Cambridge but once there the political climate changed with quite remarkable speed; politics became fashionable and virtually everyone with intellectual pretentions was either on the left or, more likely, the extreme left. David Guest's Cambridge cell was only ahead of events for a matter of months as far as the student world was concerned. A Communist fellow-travelling "anti-war" group came into being at the London School of Economics in October 1931; a Communist cell was founded at University College, London, at almost exactly the same time. The three, previously unaware of each other's existence, met over Easter, 1932, in a flat overlooking Hampstead Heath.

Here for the first time a plan to coordinate student Communist activities throughout British universities was formulated and agreed. After this there were certain outstanding landmarks in the progress of university movements of the extreme left, among them the foundation of the October Club—a Marxist splinter group from the Oxford Union Debate where "this House" decided on February 9, 1933, that it would "in no circumstances fight for King and Country"; and the whole complex of demonstrations and counter-demonstrations that occurred in Cambridge in November 1933. The university leftists demonstrated at the Tivoli Cinema which was showing a jingoist film—*Our Fighting Navy*—but were broken up by university Tories determined to teach "the cads" a lesson. This provoked a reaction in favour of the pacifist socialists, who by now were Communist led and organised. Because of this they were able to use the annual "Poppy Day" Rag, traditionally an apolitical bacchanal designed to produce money for ex-servicemen's funds, as an anti-war demonstration. John Cornford, a young Trinity historian and Communist, succeeded in persuading the Christian representatives on the march to the War Memorial to agree that the protest should be more than just against the Great War. The wreath the demonstrators carried announced they were there "to prevent similar crimes of Imperialism." The following February, Hunger Marchers from Tyneside marched through Cambridge and received an impressive welcome. An eye-witness described the undergraduates lining the streets "staring a little frightened at the broken boots and old mackintoshes."

It would be a mistake to assume that these incidents—the most newsworthy of the time which the Press fastened on—meant that the whole university had turned into a Red enclave overnight. The majority of undergraduates carried on as before without feeling involved one way or the other—on the day that the Hunger Marchers arrived, for instance, the *Varsity Weekly,* the undergraduate newspaper, decided they only rated a two-column photograph on an inside page while the main story of the week was a preview of a wrestling match scheduled to take place in the City Baths. But the fact remained that the "thinking people," those undergraduates who thought of themselves as the intellectual leaders of the university, were almost all on the left. It was a development which deeply grieved John Maynard Keynes, the veteran Apostle, who found many of the young men he would like to have elected to the Apostolic ranks had made a prior commitment to Marxism. Keynes's biographer, Roy Harrod, wrote: "He could not but observe the tendency towards Communism among the young at Cambridge, and most markedly among the choice spirits, those whom thirty years before he would have wished to consider for membership in 'The Society.' He attributed it to a recrudescence of the strain of Puritanism in our blood, the zest to adopt a painful solution because of its painfulness."

Whether or not the cause was innate Puritanism, the immediate effect was a suspension in the proceedings of "The Society" after a series of meetings, which Keynes must have found deeply wounding, where members considered whether the Apostles could sensibly—or honestly —continue in the light of the social situation.

Burgess pitched in to Cambridge left-wing politics with the same zest he had previously reserved for seduction and drinking. He began in Trinity itself where he organised a strike of waiters—there was so much cheap labour around that the College paid meagrely and discharged many of the staff at the end of each term, knowing there would be no shortage of manpower when the next term started. Burgess was also involved, with the tireless David Guest, in a protest by Cambridge council-house tenants against high rents, and he made a characteristically ebullient contribution to the ani-war demonstration of November 1933. He and Julian Bell, the Bloomsbury Apostle and poet who for so long hovered on the edge of the Communist Party, joined the march in Bell's 1925 Morris Cowley, which they used as a battering ram against the "hearties," mainly from the Jesus College Boat Club, who pelted the marchers with eggs and rotten fruit. It was only a month after this, in a flurry of enthusiastic political consciousness, that Bell sent a letter to the *New Statesman*, ". . . we are all Marxists now," it continued, after referring to the sudden revival of political consciousness. In retrospect it is clear that Marxists were indeed thick on the ground at Cambridge but that they divided into two distinct categories.

The first were the commonest—young men disillusioned with the smug prophecies of the traditional economists and appalled by the social situation they saw around them. They found a means of expressing their indignation by joining the Party or flirting with it. As time went by, and economic conditions improved, they either changed their minds about left-wing solutions or simply grew out of them. The *Trinity Review* for the years 1931 onwards is riddled with references to the Leftist sympathies of men who are now diplomats, millionaires, bulwarks of the Church, the Establishment and the established. They include people like Victor (now Lord) Rothschild and Anthony Blunt (later Sir Anthony). F. E. Cumming-Bruce, now a distinguished diplomat, was said to sing the "Red Flag" in his bath. Apart from Blunt, none of these people were Communists even then: and it might be fair to guess that most of them have moved a good deal to the Right since those days. Thirty years later, when the matter became one of crucial importance for the security of the Western world, it proved damnably difficult to separate the serious, committed, life-long (and, by definition, underground) Communists from the jejune undergraduates who had simply "gone through a Leftish phase" or enjoyed a modish, soon to be forgotten infatuation for a fashionable ideology most of them only superficially understood. The middle-aged tended to laugh off the middle-class communism, or Communist sympathy, as a kind of minor adolescent affliction, analogous to acne: almost everyone went through it at a certain stage, there was no point in worrying and no cure, except to wait for puberty to end.

But something more than post-adolescent rebelliousness underlay this discontent. An Apostle of the period wrote to us of the "real sense of moral shock—above all, to those brought up more or less 'in the Establishment' as it became clear that nothing effective was to be done either about unemployment in this country, or the rapid breakdown of peace. . . .

"It was very difficult to get jobs for anyone who went down in the early thirties, and the fate of those who had gone down a year before, simply to join the unemployed, pressed very realistically on those who were still up. We were all, moreover, of obviously military age, and the war which we saw coming was clearly not going to be one that we wanted to fight. It was already clear to anyone with any sense that the main aim of British policy was to send a re-armed Germany eastwards. We didn't think that it would work, or that it ought to work, and we were damned well right. And it gave us, our consciousness of what was going on, a special kind of disgust for our elders, the politicians and so forth. It left me, for example, permanently an anarchist, at any rate in the sense that I never expect to find much decency or honesty in any government. And I can very easily imagine that for men like Philby, Burgess and Maclean, the same disgust could lead on to more active 'treachery,' as you evidently want to call it.

"It may deserve the name, but a good part of the blame lies with 'the Establishment' of which they were so much a part that their disgust with it was intensely personal . . . so much under their own skins . . . any government or state of society which fails to win for itself some measure of the generosity and loyalty natural to youth is in for grave trouble."

It was this "special kind of disgust" in specially strong concentration which sustained the smaller numbers of "hard-liners" at Cambridge. This group, in turn, fell into two sub-groups. These were the overt Communists like David Guest, John Cornford and James Klugman, a brilliant Trinity historian, later a member of the British Communist executive. These were men whose allegiance to the Party never wavered. Only a handful of them survived to serve the Communist Party beyond the thirties, but not through any weakness on their part; Cornford, Guest and a number of other Cambridge graduates like Julian Bell who never quite became a Communist, volunteered to go to Spain and were killed.

And then there were the Communists who went underground, the covert Communists, who had worked out—or been told—that they would be most useful to the party working under a "cover"—whether they fully realised that this meant they were to be used as spies is open to question. Kim Philby was the archetype of this group. For him the turning point was the 1931 General Election, Labour's crushing humiliation, and Ramsay MacDonald's betrayal of socialism when he stayed on as head of the National Government.

In the election Kim had campaigned for Labour with John Midgley, a Trinity contemporary. This was still before the upsurge of left-wing thought: Philby must have been one of the very few undergraduates who felt deeply enough to go and work for socialism. "My friends," Kim's set speech began, "the heart of England does not beat in stately homes and castles. It beats in the factories and on the farms." Oddly enough, these stirring sentiments are the only surviving record of Philby's political thought at the period. Unlike virtually all his contemporaries on the left he never committed his undergraduate opinions to print (neither, in fact, did Burgess, but all his life he found writing difficult and boring: conversation was his forté). Because of this early discretion Philby's political progress can only be charted via the memories of his friends. A school-friend from Westminster visiting Cambridge in 1932 was alarmed at the vehement extremism of Philby's Marxism defined in the course of a Trinity lunch party. "Almost everyone was to some degree left. But Kim, I would have said, was a fellow-traveller at least." A Cambridge contemporary said of the same period: "Kim was almost certainly in the Party—I expect he had been approached by the Soviets about undercover work. Everybody was." The second part of this statement is questionable but there are plenty of surviving witnesses ready to confirm the first—now that Philby's defection is part of history. Whether they would have been equally open with MI 5 investigators when his guilt was in the balance is another matter. Kim wrote no articles, signed no speeches. The only people who could have betrayed him were his close friends, themselves all Leftists or former Leftists, all the more ready to condone such youthful ideological peccadilloes in others. Before he was twenty-two Philby had learnt how to dissemble and how to cover his tracks. His natural talent for the business of espionage was formidable, even as an undergraduate. The stammer, which could always be produced to avoid answering a question or provide time to think, was another built-in advantage.

Donald Maclean's situation was slightly different. He was a public Communist and he told his mother, Lady Maclean, that as soon as he had finished with Cambridge he would be off to Russia to help in the Revolution, probably as a teacher. This was in 1933, the same year that he wrote an article in *Cambridge Left*, a socialist review, talking about the capitalist society, "which is doomed to disappear" and referring triumphantly to "the rising tide of opinion which is going to sweep away the whole crack-brained criminal mess." This sentence expresses admirably the disgust that Maclean and people like him felt at the picture of decay and confusion which Western society presented in the early thirties. It also catches the slightly credulous faith in a swift, violent and absolute cure which many of them shared. It was this faith which it was the business of the Soviet recruiters to seek out and to encourage.

Soon after the appearance of this piece which could hardly have made his position clearer, Maclean suddenly went into reverse gear. Lady Maclean heard with relief that her son had changed his mind about the Russian Revolution and had settled instead for a career in the Foreign Office. Even allowing for the violently conflicting impulses of a very young man the *volte-face* was so extreme that those close to Maclean might have found another explanation had they thought to search for it. Burgess, as usual, was the most idiosyncratic. He visited Russia at the end of his fourth year in Cambridge, in the 1934 long vacation, accompanied by an Oxford Communist, Derek Blaikie. Mr. David Astor, son of Nancy Astor, succeeded in arranging some letters of introduction to Communist leaders, but when Burgess returned he was noticeably less enthusiastic about Revolutionary life than most British devotees of the period who brought their testaments back. When he described life in the Soviet Union to the Cambridge Communists he surprised many of the comrades by his lukewarm tone. Shortly afterwards, having prepared his ground, he resigned from the Party and abandoned his political activities. As he was to explain in a statement made to Donald Maclean over twenty years later in Moscow, this implied no disagreement with the Marxist analysis of the situation.

They had both decided that they could promote Marxism more effectively by penetrating the Establishment, not launching outside attacks on it. The fact that both of them were members of the Establishment by birth and upbringing made the task that much easier. Philby was thinking along similar lines but, as usual, kept his thoughts to himself.

At this point the three temporarily severed their links and their careers diverged. Burgess and Maclean started to look for jobs, significantly in the public service. As an undergraduate Philby had made a series of trips abroad on his terrifying old motor-bike, often accompanied by a friend from Westminster days. Philby had been particularly interested by Austria. Already a theoretically convinced—if not deeply learned—Marxist he set out for Vienna, to pursue some post-graduate studies in practical Communism.

5. Commitment in Vienna

We're in for fifty years of undeclared wars, and I've signed up for the duration. I don't exactly remember when it was, but I signed up all right.
—ERNEST HEMINGWAY, *The Fifth Column*

Kim Philby came down from Cambridge in the autumn of 1933 and left almost immediately for Vienna. It was his second visit to a city still famous for beautiful women, leisurely elegance, polished manners, and the *Gemütlichkeit* of an ancient and decadent capital. He could have been any slim young Englishman just down from University with a year in romantic Vienna ahead of him— Schlagobers on the terrace of the Café Heinrichshof, long afternoons in the Hotel Sacher, new wine at Grinzing and intermittent study of German. But it was not like that for him.

He found lodgings in the ninth district in the house of Israel Kohlman, Latschkagasse 9. Kohlman, a Pole who had arrived in Austria before the First World War, was a minor civil servant who spent most of his spare time in Jewish welfare work. He had a self-effacing wife called Gisella, who was always busy in the kitchen, and a dark vivacious daughter, christened Alice, but usually called by the diminutive Litzi, then twenty-three.

Litzi had been married at eighteen to Karl Friedman, but they were divorced after fourteen months. She was short, tending to plumpness, had a snub nose and dressed like a gypsy. But she had that effervescent zest for life—with its hint of great sexuality—common in Middle-European Jewish girls, and had never wanted for admirers. She had been a member of the Blau Weiss, a Zionist organisation founded by Friedman, generally apolitical and interested mainly in providing healthy activity for Jewish youth—mountain-climbing, sailing, hiking, and vigorous gymnastics, all under conditions of giddying abstinence. Litzi did not really fit because she drank in moderation, and, in conformity with her views on female emancipation, saw no reason why a healthy young woman should not be as entitled as any man to sexual pleasure.

She found Philby handsome and charming and since they were thrown together with the casual intimacy of paying guest and landlady's daughter, it was probably inevitable that they should become lovers. The actual moment seems to have occurred when they were out for a walk in the snow. (Philby later told this to a close friend in Spain, adding "I know it sounds impossible but it was actually, quite warm once you got used to it.") This affair was a highlight in Philby's life. Several of his men friends in Vienna at that time insist that it was his first sexual experience and that his emotional involvement was, as a consequence, much deeper than Litzi's.

If this was so it would help to explain the speed with which Litzi was able to sweep Kim into the deadly underground of European politics. From the isolated and idealistic politics of Cambridge he was brought into personal contact with the bloody clash of ideologies which was to shake Austria until the Anschluss. At an impressionable twenty-two Philby saw for himself the effects in human terms of the theories he had debated in the abstract in Britain. This was the real stuff of general strike, police violence, sabre-charges, street battles and broken heads, when life or death could literally depend on which political party you were known to support. It is clear that Kim's *emotional* commitment to the left, and probably to Communism hardened at this moment.

It was a time of turmoil, and to a Marxist it would have seemed that many of the events he watched were the master's texts springing to life before his eyes. Austria was still suffering from the effects of losing her empire after the First World War. The Hapsburgs had ruled a country which stretched from the Carpathians to the Adriatic. With the Allies' victory this had been reduced to Vienna and its scenic but unproductive hinterland. The population, cut to six millions, was divided into the Socialist anti-clerical dwellers and the poor and backward Roman Catholic peasants.

The country, ruled by a succession of Conservative coalition governments, rapidly became crippled by inflation. Eric Gédye, *Times* correspondent in Vienna at this period, writes in his book *Fallen Bastions:* "In the decayed salons of inflation-battered Vienna one walked across Oriental rugs to dine off costly plate on a little cold sausage and black bread beneath the eyes of Old Masters." Such privations might have endured indefinitely. The Czechs, Slovaks, Rumanians, Yugoslavs and Hungarians, intent on maintaining their recently celebrated freedom, had no intention of offering aid to the Austrian economy only to see a return of the hated Hapsburgs. As far as the rest of Europe was concerned, Austria could go on adding zeros to its notes and dining off dry bread and acorn coffee.

But a great churchman and subtle political intriguer, Monsignor Seipel, Chancellor of Austria, knew the cards to play. "Leave us the political Cinderella and we throw ourselves into the arms of Berlin. . . . Let the masses continue to starve and they will bring Moscow to Central Europe." This was a brilliant line, playing as it did on the Allies' fear that Germany would rise from the rubble of defeat and revive its *Drang nach dem Osten*—down through the Balkans via the granaries of Rumania, across Bulgaria, cutting the British artery at Suez, on to the oil-fields of Mesopotamia, spreading on the way to encompass the colonial empire of France. This, with the new

nagging worry that a starving Austria would be ripe for
Bolshevism, finally forced a grudging relief programme
from the Allies, and Austria's reconstruction through the
League Loans began.

Unfortunately, Seipel, a bitter anti-Bolshevist, was unable to stop. Once foreign investment was flowing freely
into Austria, he set about sowing the belief that this
money would never be really safe until the Austrian left
was crushed. So while the Socialists laboured to turn Vienna into an early model welfare state with huge blocks
of well-designed workers' flats and free clinics, baths,
schools, kindergartens and gymnasiums, the Conservatives
and Monarchists fomented subversion, hoping to "drive
the Reds out of Austria," and bring the Hapsburgs, who
were unhappily drifting from capital to capital, back to
the Schönbrunn Palace.

The Socialists viewed these manoeuvres with alarm. To
defend themselves they formed a private army, the
Schutzbund, or Republican Defence Corps. In turn, the
Conservatives raised their own private army, the Heimwehr, led by Prince Starhemberg, a dissolute aristocrat
who had taken part in Hitler's abortive beerhall putsch in
Munich in 1923, and Major Emil Fey, a tough professional soldier.

The first clash between the armies occurred on July 15,
1927. Two weeks previously the Heimwehr had opened
fire on a Socialist procession, killing a child and a cripple.
Several men had been arrested and put on trial but had
been promptly acquitted. A massive Socialist demonstration had been called, both as a gesture of solidarity and
as a protest at the court's decision. When the Socialist
marchers reached Parliament House, a police officer and
a detachment of armed police barred their way. There
were struggles. The police drew their sabres and charged.
The fight spread quickly throughout the city and by night-
fall eighty-five civilians and four policemen had been
killed and the Palace of Justice destroyed by fire.

This was a crucial moment for the Socialists. They had
to decide whether to fight (they had hidden arsenals) or
whether to rely on the more traditional weapon of a general strike. Their choice of a strike turned out to be disastrously wrong. In three days the Government had
broken it by using blackleg labour. The Heimwehr, exul-
tant, now knew that, faced with violence and terrorism,

the Socialists would collapse. The pattern for future clashes was set.

These early signs that Democratic Austria was in serious trouble were watched with alarm by the socialist movement in the rest of Europe, and the early thirties saw an influx of concerned disciples of the left, including Hugh Gaitskell, future leader of the British Labour Party —and Kim Philby.

Kim and Litzi were in the thick of it; Litzi sparkling, argumentative, opinionated; Kim already displaying the discretion about his own part in events that was later to become an integral part of his professional façade. An Austrian writer who settled in Britain met Kim at one of the intellectual socialist gatherings that were the centre of Vienna's international social life at the time. He described him: "He was a shaggy bumbling Englishman overwhelmed by the passions swirling around him. To what extent he shared them I don't know. Certainly he talked. But more often he listened."

Litzi for her part had already flung herself into work for the Communist Party. When Friedman met her she had been, he said, "an hysterical *petite bourgeoise*." He had converted her to the left, made her a member of the Zionist Socialist Movement, only to see her rapidly embrace Communism. After their divorce she met three Hungarians, refugees from Admiral Horthy's dictatorship. All three were Communist Party members and one, Gabor Péter, was of high rank. Friedman, who has settled in Israel, remembers him as "a real Stalinist, a tough, ruthless and professional operator." Physically he was most unattractive. He limped, had a slight hunchback and a thin, ugly face. But his powerful personality overrode all this and he had easy success with women. Péter recruited Litzi and she has remained a devoted member ever since. (At the time of writing, recently divorced from her fourth husband, turning slightly grey but still an attractive woman, she lives in Wildensteinstrasse in East Berlin. She has a daily maid, her own car and a good salary from dubbing English and German films. Péter had a less happy fate. In 1945 he became head of the secret police in Hungary with a notorious reputation for his treatment of Monarchists and dissident Communists— "the Beria of Hungary." He was purged in 1953, imprisoned until 1959, and is now working as a tailor again.)

By early 1934 the political situation was deteriorating steadily towards civil war. Dr. Engelbert Dolfuss had assumed power, all 4 feet 11 inches of him. (He was, the irreverent Austrians said, the only leader ever to issue postage stamps bearing his portrait—life size.) Dolfuss ran a repressive clerical dictatorship but, worried by the growing strength of the Austrian Nazis, made a nervous attempt at negotiation with Hitler then turned for help to Mussolini. Mussolini advised Dolfuss to crush one of his antagonists, preferably the Socialist, immediately, so as to be free to deal with the other.

On February 12 the Heimwehr and police provoked an incident that was to lead to open civil war. A group of Heimwehr guardsmen stormed one of the huge blocks of workers' flats to search for hidden arms and met with determined opposition. As the echoes of rifle fire rattled over the city a Socialist plan for a general strike went into action. Unfortunately the city's electrical workers had struck at the sound of the first shots and the power supply failed just as the Socialist presses printing the strike manifesto had started to run. The manifesto was never printed and the strike never really got started.

The Government rapidly arrested the Socialist leaders and the rank-and-file blundered around in confusion. The militants waited for orders to take up arms and fight but no orders came. The custodian of one of the arms caches refused to hand rifles to the workers without orders from his superior. The superior was already in gaol. By the time the Socialists had found new leaders and had armed themselves it was too late. The one-sided battle lasted four days and a thousand people were killed. Two of the biggest blocks of workers' flats, the Karl Marx Hof and the Goethe Hof, were destroyed by Heimwehr artillery fire. In the courtyard of the Supreme Court nine Socialist leaders were clumsily hanged, strung up and allowed to strangle to death. One of them, Münichreither, had been wounded in the fighting and was carried to the gallows on a stretcher. A wave of arrests began.

In the underground there was a hasty and uneasy alliance of communists and socialists in an organisation called Revolutionary Socialists. Philby and Litzi were closely involved in this movement, working with a group to smuggle wanted socialists and communists out of the country.

Philby was invaluable because, as an Englishman, he could move anywhere without restraints—"the authorities considered it unthinkable," one of Kim's friends said, "that an English gentleman like Kim could have any contact with Communists, Jews, Liberals or people of that sort."

So Philby was there when the Karl Marx Hof and the Goethe Hof were shelled. He helped a group of workers who had escaped from the flats to hide in a nearby sewer. The men, probably Communists, were in blood-stained rags. To appear in the streets like this would have been dangerous, so Philby called at Eric Gédye's office and asked him if he had clothing for six men. Gédye gave him three old suits. Philby borrowed the rest from other friends and moved his small band to a safer hiding place and finally onto the underground line out of Austria and into Czechoslovakia.

Everywhere the left was on the run and it did not take long for Philby to decide that he had seen the lesson: ordinary democratic Socialism was apparently incapable of resisting Fascism. The collapse of the Austrian socialist movement, the sordid end of its leaders, the rise of the Nazis, their revival of beheading for political offences, the general repression of any form of political dissent, convinced him that only the Communist Party could offer any hope for Europe growing increasingly dark.

There was another factor in his involvement, a more personal, human one. This was Philby's first taste of intrigue, his first experience of the Great Game. At twenty-two it would be difficult to resist the temptation to romanticise his part in events, to see himself as one of Kipling's few: "From time to time God causes men to be born who have a lust to go abroad at the risk of their lives and discover news . . . today it may be of far-off things, tomorrow of some hidden mountain, and the next day of some nearby men who have done a foolishness against the State. These souls are very few and of these few not more than ten are of the best."

It is clear from what occurred next that Philby was motivated at least in part, by this romantic, quixotic view of his role. He contacted Lilly Jerusalem, the daughter of a former Austrian Government official. "Kim telephoned me and asked me to meet him urgently. I suggested that he come to our house but he said it wasn't safe, so finally we met in some little café.

"Then he told me in a whisper that he wanted me to hide in our house his girlfriend Litzi Friedman, who was underground since the Dolfuss revolt. I knew Litzi was an extreme left-winger but I couldn't help because of my father's position. I never saw Kim again."

The police were obviously closing in on Litzi, and Philby's worried attempts to find her a sanctuary were not very successful. He took, as he saw it, the only way out. On February 24, 1934, in the Vienna Town Hall, Harold Adrian Russell Philby, student, "without religious faith," born January 1, 1912, in Ambala, British India, married Alice Friedman, née Kohlman, born May 2, 1910, in Vienna. It was a quiet, hurried ceremony. Litzi, looking back over the years and over two subsequent marriages, remembers it: "The police were hunting down active Communists and I found out that they were after me. One way I could avoid arrest was to marry Kim, get a British passport and leave the country. This is what I did. I wouldn't exactly call it a marriage of convenience. I suppose it was partly that and partly love. We left Austria and went to stay in England."

The sudden marriage caused quite a stir. Ilse Barea, an energetic Austrian lady who divided her time between London and Vienna lecturing to seminars of young Socialists, remembers Hugh Gaitskell telling her how horrified he was to hear of Philby's marriage to "that young communist girl, Alice Friedman." Apparently both Mrs. Barea and Gaitskell saw Philby as "a rather altruistic left-winger, mixed-up and Byronic in outlook, eager to assist the left-wing cause without leaning quite as far as Communism."

Others saw him differently. Lilly Jerusalem's mother, who now lives in Israel, sent Lilly a cutting of the *Sunday Times* series on Philby with a note in the margin. "In Vienna everyone knew that Kim Philby was a Communist but apparently no one knew that in England." And the writer Naomi Mitchison recorded in her diary for March 2, 1934, that Philby, "a nice young Cambridge Communist" came to see her "all het up about some of the Reichstag prisoners and wanting to know if I or anyone I knew could fly at once to Berlin and see about it."

Lady Mitchison can still recall the meeting and says she knew that Philby was a Communist because "he told me so."

So Philby considered himself a Communist in March 1934 (and was prepared to say so under the right circumstances) even though he might not have been a card-carrying member of the Party. He says in his own book that he was never a member of any Communist organisation but that he left university in the summer of 1933 "with the conviction that my life must be devoted to Communism." Had he already received his life-long assignment—to penetrate British intelligence? The best witness here would obviously be Litzi, but she is very careful on this subject. "As far as I know, apart from marrying me, a Communist, Kim took no part in Communist underground activities while he was in Vienna. He knew some Communists, of course, through me, and was very progressive with strong leftish leanings."

If Litzi did know of Kim's recruitment she is not likely to admit it. Litzi is an old Party member, well-regarded, with a congenial job and status—things not easily come by in a Communist state—and has no intention of saying anything to imperil them. But every piece of evidence we have been able to gather points to Philby's assignment being given him in Vienna in this period. The evidence is, admittedly, all circumstantial but it is also all objective. And it coincides with accounts Philby has given to his children visiting him in Moscow since the defection and in his book. He told his children, "I was recruited in 1933, given the job of penetrating British intelligence, and told it did not matter how long I took to do the job." In *My Silent War* he says, "I was invited, *at so early an age*, to play my infinitesimal part . . . How and when I became a member of the Soviet intelligence service is a matter for myself and my comrades" [emphasis ours]. The formidable Gabor Péter would have possessed all the necessary qualifications to be the initial recruiter.

Again the circumstantial evidence is strong, because the moment he returned to London in May 1934, Philby buried the image of the young left-wing activist and in its place began to construct the careful, apparently apolitical disguise that was to protect him during his next thirty dangerous years. He began his penetration of the Establishment power-structure by getting himself a minor job in journalism, on the highly respectable magazine *Review of Reviews*. Guy Burgess and Donald Maclean set about their tasks of penetration in slightly more glamorous circumstances.

6. Joining the Establishment

> *I am a Comintern agent.*
>   —GUY BURGESS in 1938

Like many young men who have been outstandingly successful undergraduates, Guy Burgess found the process of accommodating himself to the world outside irritating and frustrating. The very qualities which had made him a Trinity "character"—the bohemianism, and patrician disdain for reliability or discipline—were disadvantages when it came to getting a job. Although he muddled through in the end (Burgess invariably did) the problem of beginning a career was not eased by the fact that though he was sublimely unfitted to be an organisation man, he was nevertheless irresistibly attracted throughout his life by institutions of all kinds.

He came down from Cambridge, jobless, in the spring of 1935. He felt considerable regret at parting from this comfortable matrix after four and a half agreeable years on the inside, all the more so because he discovered it left him over the age limit to take the Civil Service examinations. This was the result of his schoolboy failure to be accepted by his first institutional target the Royal Navy, on which he had wasted nearly two and a half years as a boy. Because of this he had gone up to Cambridge at nineteen and a half, rather old by the standards of the early thirties, and then, after taking his degree, had remained in Trinity, working on an abortive thesis and casting round wistfully for a Fellowship, which eluded him. All this meant he was debarred from the Foreign Office, which appealed to him, and was obliged to find a substitute. True to type, his eye settled in turn on three other prestigious Establishment hulks against which, limpetlike, he hoped to clamp himelf. Burgess's choices were, in turn, the Conservative Party; *The Times;* and finally, the BBC. Although none of these was overburdened with talent, they showed marked reserve about adding Burgess to the strength. He therefore acted on a classic Burgess precept, which had been reinforced by his contact with the Apostles. He canvassed his influential friends to pull strings for him.

The fact that Burgess craved institutional acceptance when he already possessed an assured background, evident social gifts and even a certain amount of private money, sometimes puzzled his acquaintances. (At a later stage in his life this craving reached almost obsessional proportions and for months at a time in the late forties he appeared to think—and talk—of nothing except his determination "to be established" on the permanent staff of the Foreign Office.) There was of course an obvious reason; one of his main concerns was to attain a position which would be most productive for his new masters. But this was not the whole answer. There was an irrational element in his pursuit of organisational security which a psychiatrist would probably ascribe to his fatherless late boyhood and adolescence. He revealed a similar insecurity in his personal relationships. There was the pattern of continual, manic seduction and a quality of possessiveness—one friend described Burgess's "ferocious tentacles" —which was invariably present even in his platonic relationships. One has the feeling that, like Maclean, he might, given a spark of religious feeling, have submerged himself in the Roman Church. As it was he had embraced Soviet Communism, the only alternative which also offered institutional grandeur and paternalist dogmatism.

Philosophically he had a solution to his needs, but there was still the question of employment. He tried an approach to the Conservative Party research department, which offered a wealth of inside information and contacts with the mighty. It had been founded only five years before by a political crony of Neville Chamberlain's, an enigmatic ex-intelligence man named Major (later Sir) Joseph Ball. Following an early twenties fashion which recurred again after the second war, Ball had joined the Tories straight from secret service work. He had been in MI 5 during the war, and left in 1927 to take over the

Directorship of Publicity, a curious job for a man whose previous work had involved keeping everything as secret as possible. In fact, Ball's strong suits were conspiracy and unscrupulousness, and he quickly alienated his new colleagues. One of them, who had run a particularly successful, and dirty, campaign during the 1924 General Election says brusquely of his new chief: "I hated him." Ball certainly never earned the nostalgic admiration which characterises the collective memory of another of Central Office's ex-spies, Vice-Admiral Sir Reginald Hall, who had been Tory Chief Agent in the early twenties.

Ball had been introduced to Central Office by Baldwin's most able Party Chairman, Lord Davidson. He developed into one of the most intriguing—and shadowy—figures of political life in the next decade. In 1928 Davidson delegated to Ball the embarrassing task of paying off at a cost of £5,000 another ex-MI 5 man, named Donald im Thurn, who had conveniently provided Central Office with information about the forged Zinoviev Letter (which incited the British Communist Party to revolution) in time for the Conservative Party to squeeze the maximum amount of political capital out of the affair during the 1924 election campaign.[1] Ball's discretion made him the ideal link man for a transaction which, possibly better than any other, justifies the view that the Conservative Party conspired to heat up the class war when occasion demanded. His discretion received its reward only three years later when he was chosen to be the Party's first Director of Research. It is not surprising that during the next ten years the Department acquired the reputation of being a convenient framework for Chamberlain's own personal intelligence organisation, nor that Burgess was attracted by what he heard of Ball's talent for intrigue. Ball was interested in Burgess, and they remained on quite good terms throughout the thirties. But the Conservatives studied Burgess's application and then decided, with some shrewdness, that he was not what they were looking for in the Research Department, certainly not in a full-time capacity. A similar approach to the Tory Central Office itself was equally unsuccessful, despite a careful publicity campaign mounted on Burgess's behalf by a well-placed

---

[1] Lewis Chester, Stephen Fay, Hugo Young, *The Zinoviev Letter.* Heinemann, 1967.

friend who made heroic efforts to win over Victor Cazalet, MP, then one of Baldwin's private secretaries. Cazalet sensibly objected that Burgess was a well-known Communist who had been prominent in left-wing affairs at Cambridge; not at all the kind of young man the Tories were after. The friend, revealing more loyalty than respect for truth, insisted that Guy was now a reformed character who had put all this childish nonsense behind him. This apologia too fell on deaf ears. Cazalet said: "Yes, I can see all that. But what about his *nails?*"

Burgess's insouciant undergraduate disregard for bourgeois standards of personal appearance had let him down. Like Evelyn Waugh's fictional Basil Seal, to whom he bears more than a passing resemblance, Guy throughout his life "never descended to the artifice of toilet." Many conventional, and influential figures echoed Cazalet's objections over the years, particularly in the Foreign Office. (It was one of Burgess's many natural deficiencies as a spy that he was too conspicuous, and in the wrong way.) But, he often found, women were frequently more sympathetic than men.

One of them, who now came to his assistance, was Mrs. Charles Rothschild, mother of his Trinity friend, Victor (now Lord). Invited to dine at Tring, the palatial Rothschild seat, Burgess talked at length about international affairs and convinced Mrs. Rothschild, who like lesser mortals had seen her investments diminish since 1931, that he, not some conventional figure in the City, was the man to keep her abreast of the latest developments in world economics. She had been impressed by an earlier meeting when Burgess, then an undergraduate, had correctly forecast that arms shares were on the way up. Burgess left Tring with an undemanding and useful source of income. He had been given a list of Mrs. Rothschild's impressive stock holdings; each month he was to send her a report commenting on them in the light of current developments and, in return, would be paid a retainer of £100 a month. As his friends who had gone into advertising and journalism were mostly earning less than five guineas a week, Burgess regarded this as a satisfactory start. He set himself up in a comfortable, though soon chaotic and rather disreputable flat at 28 Chester Square, and for a short period tried to acquire more clients for investment advice, citing his connection with the Rothschilds.

Burgess's capitalist activities and his attempts to endear himself to the Conservatives had confirmed the fears of his former Marxist associates at Cambridge. "Guy has turned fascist," they decided, a characteristic exaggeration which nonetheless soon seemed prophetic. Maurice Dobb, whose Marxist views had certainly influenced Burgess at Trinity, met him at this period and was left with the impression that the young man had moved some way to the right, perhaps into the Labour Party. Burgess was temperamentally unfitted for social democracy and Dobb must have caught him in the course of his transition from one side of the political spectrum to the other. Had the meeting taken place a few months later he would have been appalled to discover that his former protégé was now talking sympathetically about Nazi Germany.

There is no doubt that Burgess was constructing a new political persona for himself, probably following advice given to him in Moscow in 1934. There is no evidence at all to suggest that in 1934 and 1935 he was acting as an agent; the only explanation of his behaviour that squares with the facts is that he was preparing his ground. His main target was obviously the Conservative Party and this target accorded with his own predilection for good living and socially distinguished friends. He never became *déclassé* and his sympathy for the workers' cause did not mean that he had any contact with the manual classes after his Cambridge period, with the exception of the occasional proletarian boyfriend.

The direct approach to the Tories had been a failure so Burgess tried something more oblique; he became secretary, personal assistant and occasional travelling companion to his friend "Jack" Macnamara, a thirty-year-old former professional soldier who had retired with the rank of Captain and won the plum seat of Chelmsford for the Conservatives. The Captain, an energetic bachelor of pronounced right-wing views, was at this time advocating a series of hare-brained solutions "to save Britain and white civilisation." He was an important member of the Anglo-German fellowship, a pro-German body of considerable influence at this period. Veterans of this strange organisation disagree about the degree to which membership implied *approval* of the Nazi régime's murkier elements; they also differ on the precise point in the unfolding of the European tragedy at which membership of the Fellowship became impossible for a British patriot. However, there were one thousand members at the end of 1936, most of them prominent people in public life even though two years later many were beginning to drift away, and there was a flood of resignations in 1939 (the Association dissolved itself in some haste after Hitler invaded Poland on September 1st). In its hey-day Ribbentrop harangued the Association on such topics as the need to put down the "Komintern" and on one memorable occasion leading Fellowship members gave a dinner at Claridge's for General Tholens, deputy chief of the Nazi "Public Service Camps." Members were enthusiastic supporters of *The Times'* line on appeasement—it was the period when Geoffrey Dawson, editor of *The Times,* was "doing my utmost, night after night, to keep out of the paper anything that might hurt their (the Germans') susceptibilities"—and there was a strong House of Lords lobby. The following peers subscribed to the Fellowship: Aberdare, Airlie, Arbuthnot, Arnald, Barnby, Bertie, Douglas Hamilton, Ebbisham, Eltisley, Hollenden, Londonderry, Lothian, McGowan, Mottistone, Mount Temple (the President), Nuffield, Nutting, Pownall, Rennell of Rodd, Rice, Sempill and Strang.

The Fellowship provided Burgess with many useful right-wing acquaintances but by far his most important contact proved to be a foreigner and a radical, Edouard Pfeiffer, cabinet chief to the French Prime Minister, Daladier. Pfeiffer was a homosexual of arcane tastes and their first meeting in Paris, which Burgess recounted to his friend Tom Driberg, MP, in Moscow over twenty years later, was rather unconventional. Burgess arrived at Pfeiffer's flat for the appointment and noticed two silk hats in the hall; Pfeiffer and a companion would shortly be leaving for the Elysée. From an adjoining room Burgess heard the sound of a Ping-Pong ball and periodic guffaws. He discovered Pfeiffer and his colleague engaged in an energetic game, both of them immaculately attired in tailcoats and looking models of French political rectitude. Except for one detail, that is: instead of a net Burgess was amazed and delighted to see the athletic figure of a young man, stark naked. Pfeiffer gave the ball a last endearing flick at the young man's muscular thighs and broke off to talk business—the young man, he explained, was a professional cyclist, active in the Fascist-front Doriot organisation. Burgess was deeply impressed.

By the beginning of 1936 Burgess had constructed a basic network of contacts, but he still hankered for an institutional niche. He succeeded in getting himself a trial as a sub-editor on *The Times*—the standard method of entry in those days—and for a month he conscientiously travelled by tube from Victoria to Blackfriars station every afternoon to take his place at the very bottom of the subs' table. Burgess behaved impeccably for once, wearing a suit and staying sober, but again something went wrong and after four weeks in the frigid gloom of Printing House Square he was told that *The Times* considered him unsuitable. A fellow trainee was Oliver Woods, later a senior *Times* executive. He accompanied the unusually subdued Burgess on his daily tube trips, and recalls that the Printing House Square aspirant had done nothing wrong, "but he was obviously, you know, not quite the thing for *The Times*." The Burgess insititutional ambitions had suffered another setback, but there were consolations. He made three trips to Germany, including a visit to the Berlin Olympics (for which Macnamara had been handing out free tickets to members of his constituency association). Another German visit, the exotic details of which are unfortunately unknown, involved convoying a group of pro-Fascist schoolboys belonging to an odd organisation called Britannia Youth. With Burgess as their moral and political mentor the luckless children were taken to a Nuremberg Rally and shown some of the other highlights of National Socialist Germany.

But the most curious visit of all, again in 1936, was a "fact-finding" mission Jack Macnamara undertook, accompanied by the Venerable J. H. Sharp, a member of the Foreign Relations Council of the Church of England, who had acquired the unusual title of Archdeacon in South-Eastern Europe. The Venerable Sharp's sisters-in-law had shared in bringing Macnamara up as a boy and the Archdeacon, who had inherited a fortune from his family's jute-spinning business in Dundee, had also aided the Macnamara fighting fund at Chelmsford, which enabled the obscure young Army captain to win the seat with a sixteen thousand majority. The third member of the party was a young War Office official, Tom Wyllie, who was a favourite drinking companion of Burgess, noted for the wild parties he gave in the War Office during his period as Resident Clerk. (The Resident Clerk's perks included a flat on the premises.) This ill-assorted quartet made an extensive tour of the Third Reich gathering impressions which they later energetically disseminated in England. Burgess's right-wing *persona* was now firmly established but, the Foreign Office, the Tory Party and *The Times* having eluded him, he was now manoeuvring to get on the staff of the BBC.

Here the Apostles' network aided him again. Dr. G. M. Trevelyan, the distinguished Cambridge historian, had been inordinately impressed by Burgess's intellectual agility, so much so that he had tried unsuccessfully to persuade Pembroke College to offer him a Fellowship. Trevelyan now brought his influence to bear on the BBC and, to his delight, Burgess was offered an appointment in the Talks Department, which he took up on October 1, 1936.

By now Burgess had actually received payment from British Intelligence for several small jobs, or so he later claimed quite convincingly. The kind of material which Burgess had to offer was of most interest to Section One of the Secret Intelligence Service which dealt with political intelligence. Certainly one of Burgess's contacts was Mr. David Footman,[2] then number two in Section One of the SIS and later an emeritus Fellow of St. Antony's College, Oxford. One of Burgess's most useful items, acquired from the Ping-Pong devotee Pfeiffer, was the fact that after Hitler's occupation of the Rhineland the French cabinet had only decided not to resist Germany unilaterally by a majority of one vote. Burgess received a detailed account of the arguments advanced within the French cabinet, which would have been very different had the British Government offered any assurances to the French.

The BBC provided a whole new range of contacts—Burgess was producing talks, mainly on current affairs, and in those days when the radio attracted politicians in the same way that television came to at a later date, it was easy for a BBC producer to invite whomsoever he liked from the House of Commons and be sure they

[2] The names, functions and organisation of the British secret services of that time—chiefly SIS and MI 5—are explained in Ch. 8.

would be eager to broadcast. Later on he produced the very popular "Week in Westminster" programme, which meant he was dealing with MPs all the time and enjoyed the status of a kind of unofficial lobby correspondent. Most of his Communist friends had gone to Spain—Julian Bell's parents, Clive and Vanessa, tried to persuade Burgess to use his influence to prevent their son joining the exodus, but he failed and Julian was killed, like John Cornford, another Trinity friend. Though Burgess stayed at home he later claimed that he was able to inject pro-republican propaganda into his programmes. He also persuaded Macnamara to visit Spain with an all-party delegation; the Captain, now promoted to Colonel as he had become Commanding Officer of the London Irish Rifles, seemed like a natural Franco supporter, but Burgess believed he was able to use his influence in Conservative circles to promote the Republican cause. (Macnamara did make some surprisingly Republican noises, but to no great effect.)

Burgess was still active in small-time spying and Edouard Pfeiffer, who despite his eccentricities was secretary-general of the French Radical Party as well as chief of Daladier's cabinet, was again his main contact. Through Pfeiffer Burgess became a courier for letters from Daladier to Chamberlain, who distrusted and disliked the Foreign Office and by-passed it whenever he could. Burgess delivered the letters to Sir Joseph Ball, who in turn passed them to Sir Horace Wilson, head of the Civil Service, as well as to the Prime Minister. Burgess used to translate for Ball, whose French was minimal; in Moscow he told Tom Driberg that these were "the communications of a confused and panic-stricken patriot to an ignorant provincial ironmonger." Neither the patriot nor the ironmonger were aware that Burgess was also having the letters photostated for MI 5 by a man in St. Ermins Hotel, Westminster. Whether they were also finding their way to Ambassador Maisky at the Soviet Embassy in Kensington Palace Gardens is a question Burgess never answered. But at this period he did, for the first time, make a confession, in the course of trying to enrol a friend as a Soviet agent.

Goronwy Rees, a Fellow of All Souls, had met Burgess at Oxford five years before, and regarded him as the intellectual golden boy of the other university. They had been close friends ever since. Rees was a leftist though not a Party member. (Mr. Rees is one of those who believes that there was some homosexual element in the friendship between Philby and Burgess. But Burgess *was* capable of non-sexual relationships—his friendship with Rees himself was certainly not homosexual—so for the moment Mr. Rees's thesis must remain Not Proven.)

After 1937 they were virtually neighbours; Burgess was a constant visitor to Rees's flat in Ebury Street. One afternoon in 1938 he arrived fortified with a fair level of alcohol and announced: "I am a Comintern agent." Rees recalls that the statement was made "with a good deal of weight and seriousness, as if he wanted to impress on me the importance of it. I was shocked and surprised of course but this was the Spain period and the distinctions between Communists and non-Communists were much finer than they are now. It didn't seem immoral then to work for the Comintern." Burgess swore Rees to secrecy and attempted to recruit him to Comintern work. But when Rees declined the subject was dropped.

Rees was so amazed by this scene that he confided what had happened to a mutual friend, the novelist, Rosamond Lehmann. Burgess often stayed at her house, by the Thames in Oxfordshire, and she found the information a revelation. "For the first time I understood why Guy, whose views were obviously left-wing, had been spending so much time with Fascists. Previously I had just put it down to his paradoxical character—he loved turning intellectual somersaults." Rees thought a lot about this incident and over the years reached the conclusion that despite Burgess's wild and erratic character he was a much more serious and determined personality than was generally believed. (It is interesting that Guy was an extremely punctual man: he never missed appointments. It is one of the few clues suggesting a substratum of seriousness in his character.)

Certainly, the BBC job had not induced Burgess to tone down his behaviour; accounts of his social life during the period agree that he was as rumbustious as ever. His home from home was the Reform Club where he was such a regular and devoted figure in the area of the bar that a specially large glass of port was christened, in his honour, "a double-Burgess." He also had a weakness for the cosy, underground bar of the Travellers' next door and though he never actually became a Travellers' member he spent so much time there that most people thought he was. Burgess was also a devotee of less eminent institutions such as the Gargoyle, a drinking club in Dean Street then owned by the Hon. David Tennant, and other thirties meeting places like The Nest, the Boeuf sur le Toit, and the Bag o' Nails. (Some of these names remain part of London night life, but under different managements.) He was particularly fond of Frisco's, a club famous for its top-hatted Negro proprietor, a brick-voiced native of San Domingo, who liked to lead clients in a solemn chain-dance known as "trucking," the house's speciality. Burgess probably attended the famous party where the hostess shot her lover and the guests rapidly evaporated into the night with the exception of a well-known Chelsea lady who had passed out under the table. One of Burgess's set pieces was an imitation of her reply when the police brought her round, and asked whether she had heard the shot fired. "No, I couldn't hear anything except the clicking of the hypodermics." One of Burgess's friends was Jack Hewit, a seventeen-year-old from Gateshead who had been a dancer in the touring company of *No, No, Nanette*. Like so many of Burgess's friends Hewit found himself peripherally involved in the clandestine side of his life; in May 1938 the Czechoslovak quisling Henlein visited London where he met, among others, the indefatigable Macnamara. Henlein stayed at the Goring Hotel where Hewit, doing a temporary job as a telephone operator, was able to make a list of all the telephone calls that Henlein made.

But this was a minor operation compared to Burgess's main concern as the nation moved ineluctably towards Munich and Europe towards war. Chamberlain had organised, again through Sir Joseph Ball, a direct link with Mussolini which by-passed Eden and the Foreign Office. The system was similar to that used with Daladier and began in October 1937; one of the channels was Austen Chamberlain's widow, who lived in Rome. A supplementary contact was made via Count Grandi, the Italian Ambassador in London, who passed messages to Sir Horace Wilson, and hence to the Prime Minister, via the inevitable Joseph Ball.

On February 19, 1938, Grandi wrote a letter to Count Ciano, the golf-playing Italian Foreign Secretary, who had bolstered his diplomatic career by marrying Il Duce's daughter, Edda. Grandi referred to "a direct and secret link" with Chamberlain functioning since the previous October and added that from January 15, 1938, onwards the agent and himself had been "in almost daily contact." These contacts were crucially important because they gave Chamberlain an opportunity to manoeuvre while the Foreign Office and the Italian Embassy had reached deadlock. The Prime Minister was able to let Grandi know secretly, according to Duff Cooper's account of the affair, that he had determined to get rid of Anthony Eden. The Foreign Secretary was, in due course, furious to see press reports appearing in February 1938 that here were healthy prospects of a complete accord with Mussolini; he was all the more bitter when he discovered that this "leak" was attributable to Joseph Ball, who as usual denied all knowledge of the events.

Ball denied everything, on principle, throughout his life, and burnt most of his papers just before he died. After the war, Ciano's diaries were published in Italy, recording Ball's contact with Grandi: but Ball, by threats of legal action, managed to get the references expunged from the English version. (The references are also missing from later Italian editions.) When Professor Hugh Trevor-Roper revealed the suppressed facts in a letter to the *New Statesman*, Ball again seemed likely to sue. About this time, Trevor-Roper met Burgess for the first time, and Burgess offered to give evidence for him if the matter came to court, saying that he had actually carried the messages for Ball. Burgess was given to drunken boasting, but he was hardly fool enough to get himself involved in a court case unless he was on solid ground, so this claim seems likely to be more reliable than most he made.

Towards the end of 1938 Burgess was organising a series of talks on "Aggression in the Mediterranean," intended to be an exposé of Fascist territorial ambitions. Churchill had agreed to begin the series but withdrew when the Munich Crisis broke. Burgess went down to Chartwell to try to persuade him to change his mind and found him building a wall in the garden. Burgess told him how much he admired his stand against appeasement and they had a long, overcast conversation, which Churchill found more agreeable than it might have been otherwise because of Burgess's gift for flattery (when the occasion seemed appropriate). At the end of their indecisive talk Burgess was presented with an inscribed copy of Churchill's speeches, *Arms and the Covenant*. It was his most highly prized book and he liked to leave it lying about, open at the fly-leaf.

Politically, it was a depressing period but Burgess had other problems in 1938. In the words of a friend: "It had to happen eventually, I suppose. Guy met his Waterloo— it was either at Paddington or Victoria Station." Precise details of the events are now hard to establish but after an incident in the public lavatories it seems that Burgess was arrested by the police. They claimed that he had passed an obscene note to someone under the partition dividing the lavatories. Burgess insisted that nothing of the sort had occurred. He had been innocently passing a few minutes squatting on the seat immersed in *Middlemarch*—the detail was pure Burgess—when someone had passed *him* a note, containing various unpleasant suggestions. He had naturally passed it back and there was no more to it than that. In the end, after an examination of handwriting, Burgess was cleared but the squalid incident had been embarrassing. Burgess retired for a holiday in Cannes, as he put it, "under a cloud no bigger than a man's hand." Mrs. Bassett, his mother, went with him. It turned out to be a hilarious trip: Burgess, who never allowed events to dominate him for long, turned the contretemps to good advantage. They stayed at the best hotel they could find and there met a seventeen-year-old boy who impressed them all with his charm and good looks. Fresh out of school he in turn was taken by Burgess's brilliance and the fact that he seemed to know everybody. They became close friends and, when Burgess returned to London, the boy went with him; in due course he moved into Chester Square and the menage became more hilarious than ever.

In December 1938 Burgess's part-time secret-service chores were rewarded; he was offered a staff job. But there were snags. A new department, to handle propaganda and subversion, was being set up, but it was entirely experimental. Burgess could work there but, he was told, no one could guarantee that the job would last longer than six months. Despite this uncertainty he had no hesitation and began work in the third week of January 1939, clearly delighted with his new role. Obviously any Soviet agent would jump at the chance of working full-time for British intelligence but there was more to it than that; Burgess adored intrigue, undercover work and the possession of information debarred from ordinary men. He liked to imagine himself in the role of the man behind the scenes. Cyril Connolly acutely projected Burgess's fantasy as "Brigadier Brilliant, DSO, FRS. The famous historian, with boyish grin and cold blue eyes, seconded now for special duties. With long stride and hunched shoulders, untidy, chain-smoking, he talks—walks and talks—while the whole devilish simplicity of his plan unfolds and the men from MI this and MI that, SIS and SOE, listen dumbfounded. 'My God, Brilliant, I believe you're right —it could be done,' said the quiet-voiced man with greying hair. The Brigadier looked at his watch and a chilled blue eye fixed the chief of the secret service. 'At this moment, sir,' and there was pack-ice in his voice, 'my chaps are doing it.' "

Although his indiscretions would seem to have disqualified him from pursuing spying as a profession he was by no means as incompetent as many people have made out. The wildness and eccentricity also served as a kind of double-bluff. If Philby had confessed to someone that he was a Communist agent he would doubtless have been reported on the spot. Burgess saying the same thing merely convinced his confidants that he was trying to show off.

Reviewing his balance-sheet at the end of the 1930s, Burgess must have felt satisfied. He had made a shaky start in the couple of years immediately after Cambridge but had recouped in the end. The foundations of his spying career had been well laid; by far the most important stock in trade was the people he had got to know, from Edouard Pfeiffer and his cyclist to Winston Churchill, brooding in Chartwell over a world that was passing him by, if only temporarily.

What had Burgess been able to do for the Soviets by the end of the decade? The answer seems to be comparatively little, except to fill in odd tricky entries in the diplomatic crossword. His revelations about Chamberlain/ Daladier contacts, and, much more important, the similar communications between Chamberlain and Mussolini, must have helped to convince Moscow that Britain was too weak to resist the Third Reich. They would also have reinforced the traditional Russian nightmare that the Western Powers would reach an accommodation among themselves and turn on the new socialist society. It was the kind of thinking that led to the Nazi-Soviet pact. Burgess, despite some of his cloak and dagger pretensions, was a long way from being the fictional spy who steals documents at dead of night. He was more a para-diplomat and his role had been to provide the Soviets with a set of insights, some trivial and some crucial, into how the men who ran Britain were thinking. As time went by he became increasingly better placed to continue doing precisely this. There was no way that he could have served Moscow more usefully.

Guy Burgess had found the process of embarking on a career fitful and difficult, but for Donald Maclean it was all very straightforward. To start with he got his First in French and German in the summer of 1934 (an improvement on the previous year when he had been awarded a good second). The following October he began at a fashionable crammer's, Turquet's in Museum Street; with a group of other well-connected young men down from Oxbridge he set to work for the Foreign Office examinations. There was no more talk about Marxism or going to the Soviet Union as a teacher; Lady Maclean was pleased to see that Donald had got through what she had always regarded as no more than an adolescent stage. Her view was that he had put away childish things and was ready to come to grips with what really mattered. He worked phlegmatically though without any particular brilliance; he had no girlfriends—a fact he obviously felt sad about —and never appeared to indulge in any more exotic debauchery than an occasional lunch at Quaglino's with his fellow pupils. When the exams came round he did well enough on the written questions to receive oral interviews, but only just. On the written results alone he would never have passed but the examiners found his interview personality delightful.

The gangling young man of twenty-two was good-looking in a boyish way, diffident and charming. He had opinions but rather conventional ones; given the period, even his left-wing sympathies accorded with his priggish Presbyterian streak. He was clearly conscientious, malleable, and to use the expression applied to him by so many of his contemporaries, "rather wet." There was no likelihood, it seemed, of such a man ever letting the Foreign Office down or challenging them in any way. He was so evidently unformed that a few years in the Service would mould his personality into the image of the perfect diplomatist. But what about his Cambridge Communist period, which went some way beyond leftist sympathies? This obvious question was put to him by a close friend, Elizabeth Rea, daughter of the future Liberal peer, Lord Rea of Eskdale. There had been hopes, fondly nurtured by Donald's mother, that Elizabeth, a contemporary at Newnham, would marry her son. To Lady Maclean's chagrin, however, the much-wooed Miss Rae had become engaged to a graduate of King's, the future chairman of ICI, Sir Michael Clapham.

These children of the Liberal Establishment had remained on good terms, despite this dynastic setback, and they met to have tea together immediately after Donald emerged from his Foreign Office interview. Lady Clapham recalls that Donald was elated and claimed, quite correctly, that it had gone off brilliantly.

"But what about the Party?" his friend wanted to know. "Didn't they ask anything about politics at Cambridge?"

"One did," Donald told her. "He asked if I'd been a Communist as an undergraduate. I said I had been and, of course, I still was. They all laughed."

Presumably the eminent board of examiners either thought Maclean was joking, or assumed here was yet another example of his youthful, high-minded conscience.

There is only one other recorded comment of Maclean's dating from this period on the subject of his curious *volte-face*. A Cambridge Marxist asked him, in the jargon of the time, why he had suddenly ceased to be "active." Maclean looked slightly abashed and then laughed the questioner off: "I have decided," he said, "that my future lies with the oppressors rather than the oppressed." It was a flippant and silly remark but he was probably happy to turn the conversation in any direction.

Maclean was confident and clever when it came to semi-academic undergraduate chit-chat but he had yet to lose all his public school *gaucherie*, particularly with women. Despite his size and very considerable physical strength he gave many people, women included, an impression of effeminacy. A friend recalls an evening when he and Donald attended a dance given by the girl students at the Slade School of Art. The girls apparently embarrassed Maclean deeply by collapsing in fits of giggles every time he went on the dance-floor. They eventually discovered that the joke was a remark one of the girls had made. "Look at that tall boy—he's got hips like a girl." This incident did not increase Maclean's sexual confidence and neither did another which occurred during a house-party in Devon. Maclean spent the weekend pursuing every woman in sight like an oversized and hyperexcited spaniel. His fellow guests reacted by putting a Victorian figure-head in his bed and, after he had found it, singing an unkind song which began: "Oh, Lady Maclean. . . ."

After he had finally got into the Foreign Office in 1935 the exam pressure was off and Maclean took a small flat in Oakley Street, Chelsea. His social life looked up a bit and he began to appear at parties around the King's Road; the ambience was artistic and intellectual, but not so frenetically bohemian—or snobbish—as that favoured by Guy Burgess. A friend of the period, Mark Culme-Seymour, used to spend two or three evenings a week with Maclean. They would have a few bitters at the Commercial—Maclean was not yet a heavy drinker—and afterwards favoured a game of billiards at the nearby Temperance Hall. Maclean was always inquiring whether there were any parties in the hope that he might meet a girl. Culme-Seymour was sexually a lot more successful and proficient than his friend, and Maclean seems to have hoped that some of it would eventually rub off on him. Politics appeared to be a long way from his mind—"He never talked to me about anything except people in general and girls in particular," Culme-Seymour recalls. "I didn't think of him as a political person, rather the reverse." Occasionally, when feeling rich, they would go to a Soho club, such as Frisco's, and they probably came across Burgess and his set—they were hard to avoid. But there is no evidence that Burgess and Maclean had any important contacts with each other at this stage. A constant companion of Burgess's over a decade beginning in 1938 has no memory of Maclean's name ever having been mentioned. Socially Maclean did not seem to be enjoying any considerable success but the Foreign Office evidently found his probationary work satisfactory because his first posting, in 1938, was to Paris, a "Grade A" Embassy.

It was a fortunate posting for Maclean, as well as a prestigious one. The Ambassador was Sir Ronald Campbell and his son Robin had been a contemporary at Monsieur Turquet's (Robin, unfortunately, had failed the Foreign Office exam). Campbell immediately took to Maclean, whom he found charming, and he also made a friend of another important figure in the Embassy, the Minister. Confusingly his name was also Ronald Campbell, like the Ambassador. He too thought the new Paris recruit had a brilliant future and ten years later, when he became Ambassador in Cairo with Donald Maclean as Head of Chancery, he was able to play an important part in helping his protégé, though this time it was not so much a question of furthering his career as preventing it falling apart.

Maclean's personality was at last slowly maturing; he had an impressive capacity for work and though he was now leading an extensive social life he still arrived at the Embassy in the Faubourg St. Honoré early every morning and got through his allotted amount of paper-work with commendable speed and precision. He attended all the diplomatic corps parties punctiliously but seemed happier on the Left Bank where he made friends in the Boulevard St. Germain café society which was not dissimilar to the King's Road life he had led in London. He became a habitué of the Deux Magots and Café de Flore in St. Germain where he met the sculptor Giacometti and Tristan Tzara, the surrealist poet who had founded the Dada movement. They used to spend long evenings drinking, playing chess and talking; despite the fact that both Giacometti and Tzara were men of the extreme left none of the people who knew them can remember politics figuring large in the conversations. There were, however, certain indications of the pattern Maclean's life was to follow in the future. Again many friends found him slightly effeminate and wondered whether he might be a suppressed homosexual, though he showed no overt tendencies in this direction. For the first time there are stories of his getting drunk and behaving destructively and wildly. And finally he seemed to lean heavily on the company of two older women, both of them married to distinguished journalists. His relationships with both these women were evidently platonic which could have been a disadvantage as far as the development of his personality was concerned—an *affaire* with a knowledgeable older woman might at that point have been the making of him. But these two friends, both of whom found him delightfully ingenuous, were the people he automatically turned to for advice and reassurance. He was revealing a certain maternal need that was to recur later. Some of his Left Bank friends were amused to have such a proper young diplomat in their group—with his double-breasted grey suit and long blond hair Maclean always *looked* exactly as laymen thought someone in the Foreign Office should.

They also noticed that his life was divided into compartments separated symbolically, as well as geographically, by the River Seine. On one side of the river he was charming his superiors and laying the foundations of a diplomatic career which should logically have ended with the coveted "K"—Maclean often used to joke about "Sir Donald," a wry projection of his Foreign Office self. In St. Germain he was rather different, a bohemian young man who might have been a student or a budding novelist, an anarchist or a Communist. Was Maclean acting as an agent at this period? No one has been able to advance a scintilla of evidence to suggest he was, even though his Cambridge convictions may well have become submerged rather than discarded.

Maclean's overriding concerns were to work his way up through the Foreign Office and get his sex life sorted out. He found the first easier than the second. Although few of his friends regarded him as exceptionally talented his success in the Paris Embassy was quite remarkable; by 1939 he had acquired a reputation as a coming man, one of those young third secretaries, and there were very few of them, who had already made their mark. Only a couple of years later in London he was being talked of as a future head of the Foreign Office. It is difficult to define the qualities which made Maclean so highly regarded; all they really seem to amount to is a facility at handling paperwork and a brand of public school diffidence combined with good looks—in Paris he lost the podginess which had afflicted him since late adolescence—which exercised a considerable appeal for ambassadors. One has to assume that Maclean projected a brilliance on paper that was not apparent in his conversation. In the end it seems that he simply "fitted" unusually well; the Foreign Office was made for him in the way Cambridge had been for Guy Burgess.

All he needed was a wife to settle him down and complement the social end of his duties. Here his friendship with the suave Mark Culme-Seymour finally paid off. Culme-Seymour had left London for Paris shortly after Maclean to live as a broadcaster, translator and freelance journalist. One night the two friends from the King's Road were sitting in their usual Café de Flore when two young American girls sat down at the next table. Maclean still retained enough of his adolescent shyness to be inhibited from beginning a conversation but Culme-Seymour's practised charm removed the difficulty. He manoeuvred Maclean and himself on to the next table and soon established that the girls were Americans "studying" in France; like so many of their compatriots who had read the works of Hemingway and Fitzgerald at an impressionable age they regarded Paris as their spiritual home. Mark was more interested in the elder girl, Harriet Marling; the second sister, Melinda, was considerably quieter. "She was quite pretty and vivacious but rather reserved," Culme-Seymour recalls. "Frankly, I thought she was a bit prim." The primness which put Culme-Seymour off enchanted Maclean from that first meeting onwards. In a matter of weeks it was evident that he was in love at last.

PENETRATION

7. The Spanish Decoration

Kim was, above all, sincere.
   —FRANCES "BUNNY" DOBLE

Kim Philby during the early thirties appeared about to settle down to a life of middle rung journalism. He had been introduced to Sir Roger Chance, editor of the *Review of Reviews,* by a journalist named Wilfred Hindle. It was a Liberal monthly with offices in King William Street. Philby was engaged as a sub-editor-cum-feature writer at four pounds a week. It was an undistinguished job and Philby filled it in an undistinguished manner. He shared a small office with a woman journalist, Alison Outhwaite, did a competent scissors-and-paste job on other people's articles and occasionally wrote one of his own. They are remarkable for their colourless anonymity—"Lawrence of Arabia, the work behind the legend"; "Three Years of Protection, weights in balance"; "Japan's Pacific Islands"; "The Balkan Tragedy"—all professional, readable prose, but carrying no hint of the real Philby.

Chance, who dined with the Philbys once or twice in their Hampstead flat, thought Philby was a "liberal democrat, middle of the Labour Party, but definitely anticommunist." Alison Outhwaite assumed he was Labour even though he never discussed politics with her. Both were a little puzzled why a man of Philby's ability should stay in the job—Chance because the magazine was slowly dying and the salary was obviously not enough to maintain Philby's free-spending standard of living, and Alison Outhwaite because she considered Philby brilliant and the job mundane. She eventually asked him why he was there. "What's the point in leaving?" he replied, "I'll be in the trenches in a few years anyway." He later regretted this rare moment of candour and managed to make an opportunity to tell her that he was proposing to leave and was only hanging on until something better turned up.

What was Philby *really* doing all this time? According to accounts he gives to people in Moscow he was meeting his communist controller, at regular, usually weekly, intervals and, apart from being told to continue to rid himself of all his left-wing associations, was told time and time again: "Wait. Do nothing. We'll tell you when to move!" This can only be seen as a means of testing Philby's resolve. If he was prepared to keep a set of fruitless appointments over a two year period without losing interest then it could be said that he was a serious recruit.

In the meantime, in the long dull hours in the office, he learnt Arabic, filling exercise books with immaculate translations and careful exercises in grammar. It was a period of re-orientation, a planned remoulding of his image. In the summer of that and the following year, instead of taking Litzi home to holiday in Vienna, with the risk of renewing his Communist associations, Philby took her to Spain. The transition from committed Communist to Establishment Conservative leaning to Fascist could not be too abrupt (he did not have the flamboyance to carry off a Burgess-style conversion) so Philby affected a dilettante attitude to politics and gathered around him a group of liberal friends who tended to find his disinterest annoying—"It was impossible to discover his politics. We assumed he was a liberal like the rest of us, but occasionally he'd let something slip that indicated he was somewhere to the right of the Conservative Party."

This view was backed by Philby's association with the Anglo-German Fellowship, the same pro-German organisation which had earlier attracted Guy Burgess through his friendship with Colonel "Jack" Macnamara, and which kept up a staunch anti-communist line until its dissolution on the outbreak of war. The swastika-decked dinner the Fellowship gave on July 14, 1936, and which Philby attended, was a fairly routine demonstration of Aryan solidarity. Given to honour the Kaiser's daughter, the Duchess of Brunswick, and her husband, the guest list included Admiral Sir Barry Domvile, the founder of an altogether more sinister pro-German organisation called The Link (he was imprisoned in 1939 under the 18b regulations), Lord Redesdale (Nancy Mitford's ferocious father), Earl Jellicoe, General J. F. C. Fuller, the military historian; Prince and Princess von Bismarck, Dr. Fritz Hesse, Baron Marschall von Bieberstein, Count Albrecht

Montgelas, Dr. Gottfried Roesel and Baroness Bruno Schroder.

Philby swallowed what must have been his contempt for the Fellowship and its members, edited its magazine (explaining to his liberal friends that he only did it for the money) and began to establish himself as a quiet admirer of Hitler and the Third Reich. It is fascinating to reflect how far his German fraternisation could have progressed had it not been brought to an early end by the outbreak of war in Spain.

Philby went to the war in February 1937, choosing the Fascist side deliberately. He went as a freelance journalist with some loose unrecorded connection with *The Times* and carrying a letter of accreditation from a Mr. F. L. Towers, director of the London General Press, a news and syndication agency. According to his own account, Philby also went on an assignment for Soviet intelligence: to get firsthand information on all aspects of the Fascist war effort. It nearly cost him his life. His Russian superiors provided him with a code set out on a tiny piece of rice paper which Philby kept in the ticket pocket of his trousers. He had been in Spain only a few weeks when he decided to travel from Seville to Cordoba to see a bullfight. He had barely settled into his hotel in Cordoba when he was arrested and taken to the headquarters of the Civil Guard. There a major told him that he had committed an offense by travelling to Cordoba without a military permit and ordered the guards to search him. Thinking quickly, Philby took out his wallet as if to help them and threw it on the major's table. When the major and the guards grabbed for it, Philby quickly took the code paper from his pocket and swallowed it. The incident gave him, he said, a "whiff of the firing squad."

As in Vienna, Philby found himself in Spain in the middle of what appeared to be a trial of strength between the Old Order and the New. The theories he had discussed in Cambridge, the portents he had seen in Vienna, the ideological rifts of Europe, were now set out in the cruelly dramatic form of civil war. On one side stood the rebel generals, the right-wing traditionalists of an ancient Spain, an alliance of bankers and landowners, of Monarchists, Fascists and passionate Roman Catholics, backed by men and arms from the governments of Hitler and Mussolini. On the other side stood the Republican Government, an unhappy alliance of the parties of the Left—supported by Russian arms and military advice—claiming to be dedicated to those ideals of equality and brotherhood propounded in the French Revolution.

Though riven by factionalism and undermined by savage excesses, the Republican cause as it struggled for survival commanded the unquestioning support of all those young men of Europe and America who had come to believe in freedom and justice for the masses. Workers, intellectuals, writers, artists and artisans filtered into Spain to serve in the militia and the International Brigades. Many made their commitment and all were affected by it for the rest of their lives—Hemingway, Orwell, Koestler, Bessie, Capa, Cockburn. It was a time for heroism, a time for sacrifice.

The month Philby arrived Franco took the offensive on the river Jarama south-east of Madrid, and on a single day the British battalion of the 15th International Brigade lost 375 of its 600 men.

> Death stalked the olive trees
> Picking his men
> His leaden finger beckoned
> Again and again.

Many of those who died were Philby's contemporaries at Cambridge. They had made their commitment openly. Philby had made his in secret. While they died for a cause they passionately believed in, he dissembled and deceived for the same cause. Philby no doubt felt that he saw a broader spectrum. Others could fight for the workers' state in Spain. His mission was more important. (Only Burgess divined this. "Kim wouldn't have gone to Franco," he told Jack Hewit, "unless he had a very good reason.")

The reason is now eminently clear. Philby saw Spain as a natural opportunity for an initial attempt at penetrating British intelligence—providing he was on the "right" side—and he knew that journalism would provide him with both his cover and his means of making contact. (The editor of *The Times* might not have known, but it was no secret in the trade that since the First World War a number of *Times* foreign correspondents had been drawn into British secret-service work. They had an ideal cover. They were well-placed to gather information, and because they were schooled in sorting rumour from fact they were reckoned to be reliable.)

Philby weighed all this and his first moves in Spain were concerned with getting the loose and unwritten arrangement with *The Times* on to firmer footing. He submitted a string of articles "on spec" and succeeded in getting one of the better ones accepted. On May 24, 1937, at a youthful twenty-five, he succeeded James Holburn as the newspaper's special correspondent with Franco. This was an important job by any reckoning, and to prepare himself for his new responsibilities he returned to London and spent a few days in *The Times* office. Here his father's reputation carried him high. When Deakin, the foreign news editor, described him to strangers it was: "H. A. R. Philby, son of St. John Philby, the Arabist." (Philby was to enter the secret service with similar recommendations.) Salary and expenses arranged, Philby returned to Spain, now wearing the full protective panoply of the British Establishment. It is hard to imagine any more perfect cover.

In 1937 Franco's headquarters were at Salamanca, the incomparable Renaissance capital of a tawny western province. Here among splendid monuments of an ample age, the contingent of foreign correspondents reported the war, passing most of their time in bars and cafés, as journalists tend to do. At intervals they made a sortie to the front, but always under the supervision of Spanish escorting officers, who drove the press cars and acted as interpreters. Each morning at about eleven the correspondents were briefed in the airy first floor gallery of the university quadrangle. This was their principal source of news. Pablo Merry del Val, whose father had been Spanish Ambassador in London for many years, conducted these sessions with more charm than frankness. He also censored the dispatches of his audience.

Philby never gave him any bother. The copy he filed was eminently acceptable to the Nationalist cause and Philby himself was obviously a gentleman sharing the normal conservative reflexes of a ruling class. Luis Bolín, another anglophile of the old school, spent one long Salamanca evening talking to Philby and remembers him as a "decent chap who inspired confidence in his reports because 'he was so objective." During the long hot summer of 1937 Philby went on establishing his credentials. Again and again Spanish officers concerned with the foreign press echo the judgment of Merry del Val and Bolín. "Philby was a gentleman. Philby was objective."

On his personal front Philby lost no time in finding himself a replacement for Litzi—Frances ("Bunny") Doble, the divorced Canadian wife of Sir Anthony Lindsay-Hogg. Lady Lindsay-Hogg was a middling bright star of the London stage, ten years older than Kim, gay, passionate and an ardent Royalist. Nine years earlier on a trip to Spain she had fallen in love with the gracious ways of the aristocracy, and was now determined to share their war and their agonies. She had used her friendship with a Spanish diplomat to get into Spain across the Portuguese border and her influence to persuade the Spanish press officers to allow her to stay. She soon became Philby's close friend; "It's hard to say why. There was nothing exceptional about him, but he was attractive and above all, very sincere."

In fact, of course, Philby made Lady Lindsay-Hogg his dupe. He never talked politics with her but let her understand that his views accorded with hers. When they discussed the war he gave her the impression of an impartial observer, correcting her own emotional appraisal with hard fact. He spoke little about himself but often, and with apparent deep affection, of his father, making such an attractive picture of St. John that Bunny regrets to this day not having met him.

Philby fooled Bunny, but he maintained a protective attitude to her which only confirmed the Spaniards' conclusions that he was an exemplary gentleman. For example, on one occasion a Spanish press officer had a message for her. Knowing she was with Philby in Burgos, he telephoned her there. Philby was furious, insisted that Lady Lindsay-Hogg was not with him and demanded to know why the officer imagined she would have been.

While all this was going on (to the annoyance of other journalists) Philby was professionally occupied with the crucial fighting in the north. Though cut off for many months from the rest of the country the industrial cities of the north were still in Republican hands and, under the autonomous control of the Basques, played a vital part in the Republican war effort. To win the war, Franco had to get control of the steel industry which flourished there. On

April 26 the German Condor Legion bombed Guernica, destroying the centre of the town and indiscriminately machine-gunning the streets: the first mass air attack on civilians and an event which was to become an indelible symbol of Fascist barbarism. On June 19 Bilbao fell and by August the Nationalists had fought their way to Santander.

When the city fell on August 26, Philby sent *The Times* a dispatch which illustrates the Nationalist slant of his copy: "Santander fell to the Nationalists today, and troops of the Legionary Division of the Twentieth of March entered the city in triumph. Its columns, headed by a young general on a chestnut horse, were followed by a detachment of Spanish cavalry and part of the column was formed of captured militiamen who added a Roman flavour to the triumph. The enthusiasm of the populace lining the streets was unmistakably genuine." The article continued with a gay description of how Philby had entered the town with a press officer ahead of the Nationalist troops. "Our progress was considerably hampered by the fact that your correspondent's escort was wearing the first Nationalist uniform seen in Santander, by virtue of which he was regarded for a short space as the paramount authority in the city."

Once Philby had made it clear that he was willing to accommodate himself to the Nationalist cause his real aims were easier to conceal. In retrospect many of his actions now take on more significance than was apparent at the time. He always seemed to be the journalist who asked the last question at the press conferences. He was never content with knowing the general details of troop movements. He insisted on numbers, divisions, regiments —information far more detailed than any of the readers of *The Times* would have required. What was he doing with it? Samuel Pope-Brewer (later to lose his wife to Philby) thought that Philby was working for British intelligence. And Pedro Giro, one of the Spanish press officers, recalls an odd incident at a café. While talking to some friends, a man Giro knew to be a German agent slipped him a note warning him to be careful what he said because two men sitting at a nearby table were British agents. Giro looked hard at the men to remember them, and was rather puzzled to note that on two subsequent occasions the men had long and serious discussions with Philby.

So we think that there is little doubt that it was in Spain that Philby made his first careful, tentative contacts with the intelligence service he was later to dominate, even though Philby himself dates his first contact as being in the summer of 1940 "to the best of my knowledge." It is, however, possible that Philby was trying to look like a suitable recruit for British intelligence, and the appearance was taken for reality. Certainly Karl Robson, of *The Daily Telegraph,* who shared a room with Philby for a time, noticed a tendency to "over-correct," to be more pro-Franco than necessary. In their long conversations over endless games of poker dice Philby set out for Robson an elaborate upside-down version of his real convictions. Communism was the coming world power, he argued, and must be fiercely resisted. Unless something was done China would turn communist, uniting with Russia to become the most important political factor in the world. Robson listened but was too occupied with the war to take much notice.

A second oddity was noted by Enrique Marsans, one of the Spanish press officers who worked a lot with Philby. For a top war correspondent, Philby seemed strangely uncompetitive. "He never fought for his own way or resorted to ruses to obtain good copy like the others," Marsans says. This could have been due to Philby's idea of how a *Times* reporter should behave. It is more likely that he was experiencing one of the rewards of being a secret agent—being relieved of the need to compete in the open world. Already he had "honour and respect in the mouths of the chosen few."

As the autumn of 1937 brought its first chill to upland Spain, the pace of the fight slackened. Franco's foreign journalists were now often in Burgos, a cold Northern town less welcoming than Salamanca. They were a hard-drinking, convivial group and although Philby drank as much as any of them he usually did so alone and was generally regarded as "rather stand-offish." The procedure at the front had also changed. Manuel Lambarri, a painter who had been a professional army officer in his youth, was in charge of field excursions and saw his duty in bold, primary colours. With casual disregard for maps or personal safety he led the journalists into the heart of the action. "I did not care for Philby," says Lambarri, "because I felt that he kept a barrier between himself and other men."

The foreign journalists were now gaining battle experience. At dawn on New Year's Eve, 1937, in sub-zero temperatures, a convoy of journalists' cars left Saragossa for the battle at Teruel, a grim, walled town on the high inland plateau. Franco had launched a counter-attack to try to relieve the Nationalist garrison which had been besieged for nearly two weeks.

Mid-morning the convoy stopped in the main square of a village called Caude, a few kilometres from Teruel. The Spanish officers lit a small fire on the cobblestones and stood huddled over it. The journalists strolled for a few minutes in the village but were forced back to their cars by the bitter cold. In one of the cars Philby sat talking with Dick Sheepshanks of Reuter and two Americans, Ed Neil and Bradish Johnson. A shell fell half a mile away but no one paid any attention. Suddenly there was a violent explosion and the Spanish press officers were knocked to the ground. They staggered up to see that the car in which Philby had been sitting had caught the full impact of a shell. They forced the front door open. Johnson fell out dead, a gaping hole in his back. An eye was hanging out of someone's face. Sheepshanks was unconscious, badly wounded in the head and face. Neil's leg was broken in two places and riddled with shrapnel.

Philby was stunned, had a cut on his forehead and wrist, but was otherwise unhurt. His cuts were treated in a field hospital and he rejoined the group "sad but serene and certainly with no sign of panic." Sheepshanks died that evening without regaining consciousness; Neil two days later from gangrene.

Philby returned to Saragossa and sought out Bunny in a restaurant. His head had been heavily bandaged. His own clothes had been nearly blown apart so he was wearing an old pair of sandals, a woman's coat with a fur collar, pale-blue, moth-eaten and too long. Everyone in the restaurant stopped talking to look at him. He sat down and the waiter rushed over with a drink. "His hands were shaking," Frances remembers, "but his mind was absolutely clear."

On January 2, the day Neil died, Philby filed a cool

dispatch to *The Times* describing the death of his companions. "Your correspondent who was in the same car," he wrote, "escaped with light wounds and has recovered." What he did not write was that the shell which had nearly killed him had been fired from a Russian 12.45 cm, known in the war as "a quarter to one" and that the real story should surely have been how a rising Russian agent had nearly been blown to pieces by one of his own guns.

The sequel, surely the ironic height of Philby's Spanish imposture, came on March 2 when Franco personally pinned to Philby's breast the Red Cross of Military Merit (there were posthumous decorations for the journalists who were killed). Philby was breathless when he came back from the ceremony. "Exhausted with emotion because of the high honour done him," Frances said. (It is much more likely that Philby's exhaustion was due to the effort of repressing his real emotions when he found himself congratulated and embraced by the Fascist leader.)

But he was condemned in private, as in public, to the deceptions of a double life and he had to maintain his act for Frances as much as for the outside world. In fact it had become so much a part of his life that he felt he had to keep it up even when it was no longer necessary. Years after their separation at the end of the war, Lady Lindsay-Hogg looked up Philby in London, obtaining his address from *The Times*. He had just returned from his stint in Washington in the wake of the Burgess-Maclean scandal. He told Frances how Burgess had lived in the Philby house and then went on: "I was in my office and my secretary came in and told me that Burgess had defected. You can imagine how horrified I was." Philby continued at length about his shock and surprise. It was only after Philby himself had defected that Frances realised the significance of this story. She was totally uninterested in the Burgess-Maclean affair and had scarcely read the newspaper reports about it. Yet Philby had felt compelled to continue the duplicity he had started with her in Spain.

For a few days after the accident at Caude, Philby retreated to France under orders from *The Times*. He stayed with Edgar de Caux, *Times* correspondent with the Republicans, but de Caux could not talk him into taking a long rest. He returned to Burgos to cover the formation of Franco's first regular cabinet. There was a year of fighting left. At the beginning of 1938 Franco's armies swept eastwards on the Aragon front and reached Catalonia and the sea before they could be stopped. The Republicans fought back. Through a burning summer and into the autumn the two armies were engaged around the River Ebro. The outcome was still unclear when Chamberlain went to Munich, but as Communist supplies to the Republicans dwindled, their resistance collapsed, and they were overwhelmed.

Among the hundreds of members of the International Brigades taken prisoner in the war were two Englishmen, Dr. Isidore Konigsberg and Donald Eggar. They were held in a monastery near Burgos and one morning were brought out, filthy and louse-ridden, to receive a visit from a press party. Philby came up to them. "I'm Philby of *The Times*," he said, and spent twenty minutes talking to them. Before he left he took both men's British address and agreed to write to their relatives. He never did so. With his close attention to detail he reasoned that even a simple humanitarian act like this could endanger his Fascist image.

Philby may, as Karl Robson suggests, have gone further than necessary in aping the attitudes of the Nationalists. His own view is clear. Years later in Moscow he said: "I wouldn't have lasted a week in Spain without behaving like a Fascist." But was he using these assumed attitudes only as a cover for penetration of the British secret service or was he also passing information to the communists? There is nothing to suggest communist contacts in Spain itself, but the foreign journalists frequently crossed the border into France. There they gathered at such agreeable spots as the Bar Basque at St. Jean de Luz. But Philby, more often than not, was conspicuous by his absence. Over and over again colleagues recall that he used to "vanish" in France. These disappearances may have simply reflected a desire to get away on his own from the strain of his double life; equally he may have used them to pass information to the Comintern network.

In January 1939 Franco took Barcelona and the war was all but over. Philby, in a car driven by Enrique Marsans, and with Bill Carney of the *New York Times*, reached the heart of the city before it was fully under Nationalist control. "Your correspondent's car," he wrote, "which was the first to cruise down the great *Diagonal* and enter the Plaza de Cataluña, was surrounded by crowds of madly-excited people who with red and gold bunting in their hands mounted the mudguards, footboards and bonnet, cheering with arms upraised. Tears mingled with the shouting and laughter. People seemed torn between hysterical abandon and unbelief."

At this moment of disaster for the Left, Philby's Spanish cover reached perfection. The Republican Embassy in London, stung by Philby's articles, accused *The Times* of carrying "falsehood and propaganda." *The Times* replied saying it regarded Philby as a trustworthy correspondent and that it had every intention in its own interest as a newspaper to watch the work of its correspondents and prevent it as far as possible from taking on propagandist form.

The Nationalists entered Madrid. The war ended and there was a slightly tetchy exchange of memos when *The Times'* management tried to take away Philby's car—"If Philby is going to be domiciled in Madrid is there any reason why he should still retain a car? . . . It is necessary for us to prevent more travelling than news and liaison would justify"—and succeeded in terminating his allowance of fifty pounds a month which had covered "special expenses while acting as a correspondent with General Franco's army."

By late July 1939, Philby was obviously fed up with Spain, the aftermath of war, censorship and his reduced circumstances. He had been in Spain some two-and-a-half years, longer than almost any other reporter. He wrote a memo saying that the stream of news had dwindled since the end of the war and that it was no longer worthwhile keeping two resident correspondents (himself and de Caux) there. He said goodbye to Lady Lindsay-Hogg with sentiment but no deep regret and reported back to London, the first stage of his life-long plan successfully completed.

8. The Phony War

*Once you are inside the front door, a sale is
virtually assured.*
—HANDBOOK FOR VACUUM-CLEANER SALESMEN

When Neville Chamberlain croaked his announcement of
war to the nation on September 3, 1939, he raised the
curtain on one of the strangest interludes in recent
British history: the Phony War, which lasted the better
part of a year. The organisation of life was, for the moment, dislocated rather than altered radically. Nobody
quite knew what was coming, or what they were going to
do. People nervously scanned the skies for Nazi bombers
which did not arrive. Schools and swimming-baths were
made ready to receive corpses from a new and massive
Guernica. There were blackouts, air raid alerts, and,
later, the Home Guard parades with broomsticks. Queues
formed outside registry offices; a million resentful urban
women were evacuated to the country; and chorus girls
practised milking cows on canvas udders equipped with
simulated teats. Those who disliked the prospect of being
shot at (and were not yet mobilised) used the interregnum to try to manoeuvre themselves into a safe and
agreeable occupation for the duration. The winter of 1940
with its uncertainty and government inanition was ideally
designed for those who, like Waugh's Basil Seal, had decided their *métier* was to be hardfaced men who did well
out of the war.

It was a fruitful period for Burgess who was able to
exploit his talent for intriguing, making use of powerful
friends, and giving the impression that he was a power
behind the scenes. For Donald Maclean it was exciting.
The drama of the fall of France finally made Melinda's
mind up for her; at the eleventh hour she and Donald
contracted a marriage which was to be a source of unhap-
piness to them both over the next twenty-five years. For
Kim the last months of the Phony War were crucial; it
was then he succeeded in gaining a job in the British
intelligence organisation. And it was this event which

92

ensured that the careers of these three Cambridge Communists, instead of working themselves out as individual stories of penetration—and probable capture—would eventually be woven together into a kind of public classic of espionage.

Maclean's progress through the Phony War is the most easily and swiftly charted of the trio. His work, like that of everyone else at the British Embassy in Paris, passed through fiercer and fiercer levels of effort throughout 1939 and 1940. It reached a climax in June 1940 when Maclean's Ambassador, Sir Ronald Campbell, was trying desperately to brace the failing resolve of Paul Reynaud, the French Premier.

Reynaud was under great pressure to negotiate with the Germans. Within days of the invasion of Paris on June 14 diplomatic negotiations were still going on, with Reynaud pleading for British fighter squadrons to be sent south of the Loire and Campbell explaining that this was impossible; Britain needed all her airpower to stave off the imminent Channel invasion. In the middle of all this, on June 10, Donald Maclean and Melinda Marling decided to get married.

Their life together since the night in 1939 when they had met at the Café de Flore had not been without its problems. Donald was keen to marry Melinda but, as her letters at the time show, she herself had considerable reservations. Melinda's mother, Mrs. Dunbar, had divorced Melinda's father, a minor Oklahoma oil baron and remarried. There was no shortage of money in the family. Melinda was rather spoiled. She tended to be shy with strangers, but once they had got to know her members of Maclean's Paris set noticed that she was stubborn and self-willed. Melinda seemed to have decidedly set opinions about everything and her pretensions, reinforced by a rather mediocre intelligence, did not appeal to most of Maclean's friends. They thought her dull and provincial but he remained completely infatuated; the fact that she complained angrily about his periodic bouts of drunkenness and delivered long lectures about how he ought to conduct his life only increased her appeal. Melinda's ambivalence shone through her letters to her mother and sister Harriet, who had returned to the States. She was entranced by the idea of marrying such a fine looking English diplomat from a titled family but she was shrewd enough to see that when it came to it Maclean might well turn out to be a rather difficult husband. The imminent German invasion made up her mind.

June 10 was the last possible day for getting out of Paris. Maclean was helping his colleagues to pack up the Embassy papers and Mark Culme-Seymour, who was cutting his departure rather fine, rang Maclean before breakfast to get the latest news. Maclean was very excited but unhelpful. Everything was chaotic, he said; the Embassy was evacuating to Tours that afternoon. Before they left he and Melinda were going to get married. Culme-Seymour offered perfunctory congratulations, but was more concerned with making an escape. (By that afternoon he was heading south in an enormous Packard containing himself and five English ladies from a refugee committee.)

Largely because many of Maclean's friends thought his wife was beneath him, intellectually anyway, the story became current in later years that he had only married Melinda to get her out of France. There was no truth in this; even at the last minute, with the sound of gunfire just audible and getting closer all the time, she hesitated. But finally the urgency of the situation overcame her doubts and forebodings about what she called "Donald's drunken orgies."

After the ceremony they set off south aiming for the port of Bordeaux where they hoped Melinda might be able to take a boat for America, which was, of course, still neutral. But the roads were so crowded with other evacuees from Paris that they only reached Chartres on the first day; they spent their first night as man and wife in a field. It was nearly two weeks before they were able to leave Bordeaux on a French destroyer and the journey was by no means over then. They were transferred to a trawler and eventually reached England after a nightmare voyage of ten days avoiding U-boats and dive-bombers. The beginning of their marriage had not been auspicious and things continued to go rather badly in London. They were bombed out of two flats and Melinda, who had never managed to hold a job down for any length of time in the past, was not very happy working at the gloomy Times Bookshop in Wigmore Street. Even so it gave her something to do in the daytime because Maclean, once again back at the Foreign Office, was working extremely hard. He was also drinking much more than he had in Paris and those who knew them were not confident about the future of the marriage. Things looked up for a brief period in 1941 when she became pregnant and sailed for the States so that she could be with her beloved mother, Mrs. Dunbar. Sadly the baby was still-born and Melinda returned inconfidently to the London blitz and Donald Maclean.

When war was declared Guy Burgess had already been a minor British secret-service officer for nearly a year. Some of the inadequacies in that service which partially explain how it came to recruit so radically unsuitable a person are set out in the next chapter: for the moment, what matters is that Guy had been having a rather quiet time until the war began. He had been used for odd jobs such as trying to organise the European trade-union movement as a vehicle for anti-Fascist underground organisations. He travelled a fair amount in Scandinavia, and arranged for a series of programmes extolling the British way of life to be broadcast, in German, on Radio Luxembourg.

It was rather small beer, but horizons widened dramatically when the secret departments began a vigorous expansion in early 1940. Burgess was well placed to exploit this. Much of the recruiting for secret work was done in the better-padded clubs of the West End: an ambience with which this Comintern agent was thoroughly familiar. He was a member in good standing of the raffish and eccentric element of the British ruling orders, who not only found themselves powerfully attracted towards secret work, but were generally thought to be suitable people to perform it. The spirit of the times was perfectly summed up in a conversation one of the present authors, David Leitch, had with an amiable gentleman who passed the war excitingly in a series of very clandestine occupations. They were discussing the quality of the intake in those hectic days of the early forties, and the exchange was as follows:

Leitch: "An amazing amount of crooks seem to have got into SOE, SIS and all those outfits during the war, don't you think?"

Veteran: "Well—have to take what you can get in wartime, don't you?"

Leitch: "They seem to have got most of these chaps out of the bar at White's, so far as one can see."

Veteran: "Yes, well you wouldn't find anything except crooks there, would you?"

Leitch: "Where were you recruited?"

Veteran: "Boodle's."

Burgess was by no means the most grotesque adventurer to be washed up on the hospitable shores of the secret world. The prize probably goes to another Old Etonian homosexual named Brian Howard, one of the originals of Ambrose Silk in Evelyn Waughs *Put Out More Flags*. Waugh (quoting Byron on Lady Caroline Lamb) once said that Howard was "mad, bad and dangerous to know"; another judge described him as "the leading arrogant swine of his generation." Something of his character can be gathered from an incident when he and Guy Burgess were in a Soho night-club which was raided by the police for serving drinks after hours. A policeman checking names and addresses stopped in front of Howard, a tall and elegant figure with a Roman nose and an air of bored *hauteur*. "My name is Brian Howard and I live in Berkeley Square," he said. "I presume that you, Inspector, come from some dreary little suburb."

Howard's work for MI 5 was supposed to be detecting potential Fascist sympathisers among his upper-class acquaintance, an assignment which he interpreted as a licence to blackmail his many enemies. Another of his night-club evenings with Guy Burgess provides perhaps as perfect a vignette of the period as one could ask for. The details are supplied by Mrs. Marie-Jacqueline Lancaster, who was then working in the War Office. She found herself at a table in the Gargoyle with Burgess, Howard and Dylan Thomas.

Mrs. Lancaster was wearing leg-paint, because stockings were in short supply. Thomas, gargantuanly drunk, insisted on licking the paint off "in time to the music of the rather old-fashioned band the Gargoyle affected." When the band ended the evening with a limping version of the National Anthem, Burgess refused to stand up (not, as it happened, out of ideology but because he had lumbago and was very drunk). In an unexpected fit of patriotism Thomas, applauded by Howard, leant across the table and knocked Guy out.

Peter Pollock, a friend of Guy's, also had an MI 5 job which consisted of living on generous MI 5 expenses at the Dorchester, with instructions to "keep an eye on aliens —particularly Hungarians." The routine of this work was varied from time to time when Guy would hire a suite at Claridge's for a weekend-long party. (Around this time Burgess was arrested for drunken driving, but was let off after his counsel told the court a moving story of how his client was working round the clock at the War Office to beat Hitler.) It was all too good to last, of course. Pollock went back to his regiment, fought with distinction at Anzio, and was blown up and captured. Howard was sacked by MI 5 because of his habit of going up to people in bars, telling them he worked for a "very secret organisation," and accusing them of being Fascists. He joined the RAF as an AC 2 and passed the rest of the war in richly deserved obscurity.

Even Guy had a set-back. He had a plan for going to Moscow to negotiate with the Russians an agreement about support of anti-Nazi resistance movements in Europe. Sabotage and resistance were indeed supposed to be one of the concerns of Burgess's department, and it was just the sort of thing Brigadier Brilliant might have been expected to do. The deal would be that the British would support Communist as well as non-Communist resistances in the East. Even though Burgess proposed to take his considerably more respectable friend Isaiah Berlin—a fluent Russian speaker—the idea did not meet with official favour. In July, one of Guy's highly-placed friends, Harold Nicolson, told Burgess to forget the idea. (Nicolson was the Parliamentary Under-Secretary to the Ministry of Information, which had marginal secret-service interests.) Nevertheless, Guy set off shortly afterwards for Moscow, with Berlin. They were travelling via America, and when they got to Washington the trip was abruptly cancelled. Berlin was left in Washington to write his famous political newsletters to Churchill, and Burgess was brought home.

Burgess's life at this time revolved around his new home, a large flat at No. 5 Bentinck Street, near Harley Street. (Being Burgess, Guy did not inhabit the place regularly, but he spent more nights there than anywhere else.) The flat was, says Kenneth Younger who was then in MI 5, "a bit of a standing joke in intelligence circles."

It accommodated, in various ways, a remarkable sample of the staffs of British secret departments. It received at parties and dinners a wide assortment of the minor hangers-on of those occupied in secret work: some of the minor hangers-on were homosexuals, and one or two at least were mighty drinkers. Burgess was both, of course, as well as an outspoken Marxist.

The flat had formerly been occupied by Victor Rothschild, who was in MI 5. He still came to dinner from time to time. A fairly continuous resident was another Apostle and old friend of Guy's from Cambridge, Anthony Blunt, the art historian. Blunt had just left the staff of the Warburg Institute to work for MI 5. Teresa Mayor, Rothschild's present wife and his assistant in secret counter-sabotage work, visited from time to time. Guy Liddell, one of the most important permanent executives of MI 5, was a visitor, as was Desmond Vesey, another MI 5 official. Two of Guy Burgess's friends, Peter Pollock and Jack Hewit, spent time at Bentinck Street, and Hewit also did odd-jobs for the intelligence men. Although the whole outfit would have thrown J. Edgar Hoover into a delirium, it of course did not in any sense hinder the assault on Nazidom. It was, however, the sort of phenomenon which could only be part of a relatively leisured and amateur approach to espionage and counter-espionage. And just after Dunkirk, another part-time resident arrived who carried a secret in his head which, once it was out, would make such casual trust and tolerance an impossibility. This was Guy Burgess's old friend Kim Philby, back from reporting the battles of the British Expeditionary Force for *The Times*—and about to take up a newly-offered job in the same branch of the secret service as Guy Burgess.

When he arrived at Bentinck Street, Philby had been out of the country almost continuously since early 1937. Between leaving the Spanish War in July 1939 and setting off with the BEF as *The Times'* No. 1 war correspondent, aged twenty-eight, Philby had only a little time to arrange the details of his amicable divorce from Litzi. (Obviously, he could not endanger his new right-wing image by remaining married to a Communist.) By October, he was at British HQ in Arras, and experiencing, like most other journalists involved with the Expedition, a rather frustrating time.

Here was one occasion when the famous Philby charm did not quite come off. At the sepulchral Hôtel du Commerce everyone's nerves appear to have been frayed; the central heating broke down, communications were erratic and, worst of all, there was no news. The reporters were bored, frustrated and drunk. *The Times'* number two, Bob Cooper, thought Philby a boozy and rather brutal young man—he was addicted to a curious bar game which involved demonstrating his superior reflexes by busting other people's knuckles. Willy Forrest, the *Daily Mail* correspondent (a former Communist who had just left the Party and a veteran of the Spanish War which he had covered from the Republican side) thought Philby was offensively pro-Fascist. Philby had obtained permission to wear his Fascist-given decoration on his war correspondent's uniform.

After rushing 158,000 men, 25,000 vehicles and 140,000 tons of stores to the Belgian border, the British did not as much as see the enemy for nine months. While the phony war dragged on—the French called it *drôle de guerre*—the troops were put to work building pill-boxes, digging anti-tank trenches, wiring, draining and plumbing. The results of these activities did not prove very much use against Guderian's blitzkrieg when it came in the following year but at least the troops were occupied. The journalists had no such diversions. They fell naturally into two groups.

There were the reporters from popular papers who broke their hearts trying to produce stories about inconsequential skirmishes round Metz and the arrival of the first ATS girl. As usual on such occasions the press camp, swelled to forty by the arrival of a tough bunch of American correspondents, buzzed with unlikely rumours. To tease Paul Bewsher of the *Daily Mail* the group round the bar at the Hôtel du Commerce invented a story about a woman who had masqueraded as a soldier after joining up out of patriotism. As a contemporary reporter, F. G. H. Salusbury of the *Daily Herald*, recalled afterwards: "For one glorious day his reporter's curiosity made him stalk into circumstantial details like a cat."

But alas there was no woman-soldier for Bewsher and precious little material for the serious papers either. Most of their correspondents were reduced to consulting the Thesaurus to vary their ways of saying nothing and one original despatch of Philby's that has survived is so scored with blue pencil marks from the Press Censor that he must have despaired of getting a story to London even if he discovered one. (This particular piece, written on December 21, 1940, is highly innocuous. There are long descriptive passages about fog and ice and a reference to the guns of the Maginot Line, which he called "The Mistress of the Great Divide." His prose style, perhaps in deference to *The Times*, tended towards anachronism.)

Despite the difficulties Philby formed an alliance with the *Daily Mirror* man Bernard Gray, a tough reporter nicknamed "Potato" because of his bucolic appearance. Between a lot of serious drinking they passed the hours trying to track down grotesque rumours and writing to their offices explaining the lack of news. Finally, in an inspired attempt to find out what was happening, Philby, Douglas Williams of the *Telegraph*, and Alan Moorehead of the *News Chronicle* set up a mess in a house owned by a French wine merchant who was away serving in the Maginot Line. The idea was that the army top brass, seduced by the high quality cuisine and the impressive contents of the merchant's cellars, would tell the reporters all. Unfortunately it did not work out that way. With a discretion that Philby must have admired, the generals dined magnificently, but said nothing.

Philby continued his policy of carefully cultivating a right-wing connection. He moved on terms of equality and friendship with the aristocratic and horsey set of conducting officers, many of whom exemplified the more eccentric traits of the British upper classes as richly as any of Burgess's London friends. Charles Tremayne, for example, bid 28,000 guineas for a yearling, though Tattersall's —considerately, in view of Tremayne's condition at the time—knocked the horse down to the Maharaja of Baroda. Sir Arthur Pilkington was so fond of racing and drinking that, his friends said, he smiled as he died of a chill caught in a racecourse bar. Philby managed to get to Paris now and then and was seen escorting Lady Margaret Vane-Tempest-Stewart on a round of restaurants and bars.

A study of Philby's correspondence with *The Times* office during his periods in Spain and France shows that he exercised almost superhuman self-control with the accounts department which was constantly querying his very modest expenses.

He was ultra-careful not to offend *The Times*, and answered painstakingly the most pinpricking complaints from the accounts department—which most journalists of comparable stature would have dismissed with a blast of rage. Both in Spain and France Philby was paid fourteen guineas a week, hardly a princely salary. Yet the office was always trying to make economies and when on May 19, 1940, Philby lost all his kit in the frenzied retreat from Amiens the accountants demanded a detailed list. Philby's letter to them began, "I fear certain misapprehensions exist in London about the conditions of life here. . . ." He attached a list of nineteen items lost with their values: "Camelhair overcoat (two years' wear) fifteen guineas; Dunhill pipe (two years old, and all the better for it) one pound ten shillings; hat one pound . . ." and the total came to one hundred pounds sixteen shillings. As Philby added rather acidly he had judged the prices by consulting the Army and Navy Stores catalogue.

It was virtually his last communication to *The Times*. As soon as the Germans had swept through the Lowlands Philby and the other correspondents were bundled back to Britain via Boulogne. They sailed as the first Panzer scouts moved cautiously into the outskirts of the port and arrived back on the south coast of England in time to see the armada of small ships massing to take off the battered BEF at Dunkirk. A fortnight later six correspondents, Philby among them, were allowed back into France. Their stay was short-lived. Paris fell and within ten days they were all evacuated to Britain.

Back in London, Philby found himself a minor lion at parties: he was one of the few people about who had been "over there," and seen what was happening. St. John, who was in London, began taking his now rather distinguished son on a tour of his still-prolific Establishment contacts, the people who, St. John said, "had their fingers on the pulse." Behind the stammer and the reserve, inside his decorated uniform, Philby must have been experiencing a strange political and emotional turmoil. St. John was not far away by now from his internment under Regulation 18b as a potential Nazi sympathiser, and he was fresh from fighting his Parliamentary campaigns at Hyth and Epping on the platform that Hitler was a peace-

lover and Churchill an alarmist, crying wolf to revive a
failing political career.

It was at this time that Alison Outhwaite met St. John
and heard his outburst about the "new Romans" who
would sweep away the decadence of Europe. Kim, condi-
tioned by his Viennese experience, presumably had very
little faith in the capacity of liberal democracy to resist
Fascism; during the Phony War there were still important
people in Britain who believed that an accommodation
could be reached with Hitler, which would lead to a joint
confrontation with the Bolsheviks, who were the real enemy. Seeing London society partly through his father's
eyes, Philby probably saw his life-work as an attempt to
penetrate the intelligence services of a capitulated and
pro-Fascist Britain. There is enough substance in the idea
for it to have made a genuine nightmare in 1940. Conceivably, Kim imagined himself involved in a secret fight
with his own father on the other side.

But he had a substantial reason for pleasure. The years
of patiently suppressing his feelings, of cultivating a conservative appearance, had at last paid off. On July 15,
1940, he was writing to *The Times* about his departure:
they understood that he was being taken on by Lord
Gort, commander of the BEF, to write up the official record of the campaign. But so far as we can tell from talking to officers who served on Gort's staff, this was never
anything more than a cover-story. In August 1940, Philby
became a member of Section D of the British Secret Intelligence Service, which was then expanding rapidly.
Possibly he was first introduced via Guy Burgess, who
had been in Section D since January 1939 (and was
about to be fired). In his own book Philby says he *was*
introduced to SIS by Burgess, but he also mentions a
telephone call to Ralph Deakin, the Foreign News editor
of *The Times,* from a Captain Leslie Sheridan of the War
Office, who asked if Philby was "available for war work."
At least one of Philby's colleagues in secret work recalls
that Sheridan, a lawyer with numerous journalistic contacts, "did have something to do with Kim's entry." Sheridan, however, is now dead. It was a confusing period,
during which a great many people were temporarily
taken on by branches of the SIS, and its rival MI 5. No
one seems to precisely remember how Philby got in, and
in any case the entry to Section D was only a first step,

which was to lead to a much better-recorded breakthrough into the inner chambers of the SIS a year later.
But Philby was on his way. How could the defences of
the British "secret world" have become so decayed that
they were open to penetration in this way? At this point,
a story of espionage becomes a kind of social document.
It is an account of a great breach that opened up in the
defences of a class, and therefore in the defences of the
nation whose interests that class conceived itself to be
protecting.

9. The Secret World

*In a secret department the greatest temptation
in the world is to use secrecy not in the national
interest but in the departmental interest . . . to
cover up.*
—R. H. S. CROSSMAN in the House of Commons

What was the nature of the British "secret world" that
Kim Philby penetrated, as a minor employee of "Section
D" in August 1940? There is a clue to be found in the
dispute over the origins of the code-initial "C" which traditionally cloaks the identity of the secret world's most
important denizen, the chief of the Secret Intelligence
Service.

According to much expert evidence, this official is
known as "C" because the founder of the service, Mansfield Cumming, took the initial of his surname as his
code-letter—successors whose names began with different
letters nevertheless inheriting Cumming's code as a kind
of heirloom of office. According to other people, "C" is
merely one letter in a code-series in which the Permanent
Secretary to the Treasury is "A" and the Permanent
Under-Secretary at the Foreign Office is "B." ("Z," perhaps, being the chief executive of the White Fish Authority?) And there are other explanations: recently the
Evening Standard declared that all other theorists were
mistaken. "C," said the *Standard,* stood for "Control," as

revealed in the spy-novels of John le Carré. (Another version is that "C" stands for "Chief.")

As in all discussions about secret services, the contending explanations are put forward by their protagonists with the uniquely vivacious dogmatism of men secure in the knowledge that chapter and verse can scarcely be produced one way or another. Formally, the Secret Intelligence Service does not exist. Formally, none of its operations have ever taken place. While Foreign Office, Treasury and Cabinet papers can be scrutinised at the Public Record Office after fifty years, the files of the secret world remain forever secret.

It is a nerve-racking task to verify the facts about an officially non-existent organisation which is devoted by its nature to subterfuge and deception. One produces half-a-dozen ex-officers of the SIS who maintain that "C" stood for Cumming. . . . Ah, but suppose they are maintaining a clever deception? Conceivably, one might find some documents of the First World War initialled "A" from the Treasury "B" from the Foreign Office, and "C" in the bright green ink that Mansfield Cumming used. . . . Ah, but the inner beauty of the code-plan was naturally not revealed to other departments, on the "need-to-know" principle of secret work. (Tell no one anything he does not need to know to perform his task.) Cumming, it will be argued, was maintaining an elaborate pretence for the sake of security.

The trouble is that a man can hold almost any theory he cares to about the secret world, and defend it against large quantities of hostile evidence by the simple expedient of retreating behind further and further screens of postulated inward mystery. Secret services have in common with freemasons and *mafiosi* that they inhabit an intellectual twilight—a kind of ambiguous gloom in which it is hard to distinguish with certainty between the menacing and the merely ludicrous. In such circumstances, the ever-present affinity of the human mind for myth and legend easily gets out of control.

Certainly the British secret world at the time Kim Philby joined it was a place of legend—in the sense of the sixth definition of the word "legend" offered by the OED: "unauthentic story, handed down by tradition, and popularly regarded as historical." The legend had its origins in administrative reality, of course: the British government has had secret departments at least since Elizabethan times, when Mr. Secretary Walsingham was supposed to run the best intelligence network in Europe.

The administrative reality has been overlaid by thick, fictional and semi-fictional accretions. The vogue for books about espionage is today at such a point that the spy ranks as one of the most potent images of mid-twentieth century life; but the stream of works in English about espionage, intrigue and secret service goes back at least to the latter part of the nineteenth century, and there is a curious inter-relationship between secret service work and literature. Not only does one encounter in the secret world characters and actions which might have been invented by novelists: one may well encounter novelists acting out, in what for want of a better term must be called real life, situations which might easily have sprung from their own imaginations. The list of writers of fiction who have worked in one way or another for British secret organisations includes some of the most widely read of our time, like John Buchan, Compton Mackenzie, Somerset Maugham, Graham Greene, Dennis Wheatley, Ian Fleming and John le Carré (and even, perhaps, Rudyard Kipling). People often say that fictional espionage bears little resemblance to the real thing. On the contrary, espionage is one of the human activities where truth and fiction are most closely interwoven.

The British secret world at the beginning of the Second World War carried the flavour of Buchan and Kipling. It was presided over by tight-lipped military men who, consciously or unconsciously, were stamped with the mould of Buchan's Brigadier-General Sir Richard Hannay. The quality is perfectly caught in Bickham Sweet-Escott's description of the circumstances of his entry, which took place at about the same time as Philby's. Sweet-Escott was confronted [1] in a bare room at the War Office by an officer in civilian clothes "closely resembling Sherlock Holmes." The officer said: "I can't tell you what sort of a job it would be. All I can say is that if you join us, you mustn't be afraid of forgery, and you mustn't be afraid of murder."

In 1940, the secret world consisted principally of two

[1] Bickham Sweet-Escott, *Baker Street Irregular*. Methuen, 1965.

rival bureaucracies, which hated each other bitterly.
These were the Secret Intelligence Service, otherwise
known as MI 6, and the Security Service, otherwise
known as MI 5. Both of them still exist today, although
the antipathy between them is now greatly tempered: in
fact, the story of Kim Philby's career in British espionage
is to a considerable extent the story of the resolution of
the rivalry between SIS and MI 5. The debacle he
brought about for the SIS was in large part responsible
for the final victory of MI 5 over the SIS in the drastic
reforms of British intelligence in the mid-1950s.

Despite the length of the secret tradition in Britain,
neither of these departments is very old. MI 5 is slightly
the senior, having been founded in 1909 by the Committee of Imperial Defence. Its first director was a young
Army officer, Captain Vernon Kell, a veteran of the
Boxer Rebellion. It was designed as a counter-espionage
organisation; that is, its task was to frustrate the attempts
of foreign powers to obtain British secrets. Two years
later in 1911, another department was set up to handle
offensive espionage—that is, to gather other countries' secrets—and this was named at first MI 1c. Its first director
was Captain Mansfield Cumming, RN, and it fairly soon
became known as the Secret (or Special) Intelligence
Service. After the First World War, in the thirties, its alternative designation was changed from MI 1c to MI 6.

Before the establishment of these two departments,
British espionage affairs had been conducted in a more or
less *ad hoc* fashion. The Diplomatic Service, and the
armed Services, had collected information, and even established spy networks, as and when information was required. But it was a very haphazard process. Admiral
Lord Fisher described British intelligence during the Boer
War as "a wretched failure," and the exploits of the operatives often sound like short acts from a fevered musical comedy.

It seems somehow inevitable that one of the nation's most revered amateur spies at this time—of the
sketchbook-and-woodcraft pattern—was Baden Powell,
founder of the Boy Scouts. (The Scouts' activities to this
day bear traces of this interest of the founder's: most intriguingly, the mnemonic "Kim's Game," with its powerful
overtones of Kiplingesque espionage.) Baden Powell's
own greatest exploits seem to have been with either

butterfly-net or fishing-rod in hand. Once, it is reported,[2] he was ordered to obtain information about the position and power of ordnance in the fortress of Cattaro in Dalmatia (Yugoslavia). His disguise was that of an entomologist. Armed with his butterfly net, he strode up the slopes beneath the fortress and deluded the onlookers by sketching the outlines of the fort and its armament in the wings of the drawings he made of the local insect life. He was dismissed, according to the report, as an eccentric Englishman, which he unquestionably was.

This colourful period when various arms of government commissioned freelance operators more or less haphazardly was the heyday of agents like Sidney Reilly, the Russian Jew who became known as "Britain's Master Spy." According to his biographer Robin Bruce Lockhart[3] Reilly began operating around the turn of the century, and performed such amazing deeds as securing the Persian oilfields for Britain, almost single-handed. But the foundation of MI 5 and MI 1c represented the halting beginning of a new bureaucratic approach, made necessary by the increased importance of national security in a power-hungry world.

The function of MI 5 and MI 1c was therefore to specialise in espionage, to provide a new dimension to work which the Army and Navy intelligence departments, and the ordinary police, could only perform in a limited fashion. The two secret departments had much in common: chiefly, that they were both recruited from the military cadres of the British middle class. These respectable people were leavened, in the case of MI 5, by a few ex-Special Branch policemen, and in the case of MI 1c, by a sprinkling of adventurers in the swashbuckling Reilly manner.

Both organisations differed from the Armed Services in that, although the work was precarious and unreliable for junior operatives, if offered considerable job-security to senior executives. Most of the senior men in MI 5 and SIS were, until recent times, men who had held their chairs almost for a lifetime. But unlike the normal Civil

[2] Winfried Ludecke, *Behind the Scenes of Espionage*. Harrap, 1929.

[3] Robin Bruce Lockhart, *Ace of Spies*. Hodder, 1967.

Service, the secret departments did not impose intellectually rigorous entrance qualifications. How could they?— the jobs could hardly be advertised. Both departments therefore recruited via the ramifications of personal introduction, and John Bulloch writes of MI 5[4] that "under Kell, the department never lost that air of being a family concern." This meant that the two departments were to have difficulty in matching up to the demands of modern espionage work. The armed services compensated for the flexibility of their entrance qualifications by the tradition of "get promoted or get out," applied with varying degrees of vigour throughout the first half of the century. The Civil Service compensated for its security by its entrance standards. Lacking either civilian or military self-discipline, it was easy for the upper echelons of the secret departments to become havens of mediocrity.

Mansfield Cumming, the man who founded MI 1c/SIS, and whose character profoundly influenced its development, was a tough, one-legged sailor. He wore a gold-rimmed monocle, refused to write with anything but green ink, and pursued frequently eccentric policies of staff selection. He appointed Paul Dukes, one of his best agents in post-Revolutionary Russia, not because of his mastery of Russian and considerable knowledge of the country— he was about to reject Dukes, despite that—but because the young man fortuitously admired Cumming's collection of firearms.

Cumming inhabited a bizarre headquarters on the roof of a block of flats, which Dukes[5] has described: "I had always associated rabbit warrens with subterranean abodes, but here in this building I discovered a maze of rabbit-burrow-like passages, corridors, nooks and alcoves, piled higgledy-piggledy on the roof. Leaving the lift, my guide led me up one flight of stairs so narrow that a corpulent man would have stuck tight, round unexpected corners,

---

[4] John Bulloch, *MI 5*. Arthur Barker, 1963.

[5] Sir Paul Dukes, *The Story of ST 25*. Cassell, 1938.

very recently absorbed in feuding with each other; this is something which crops up in the recollections of virtually every veteran of the British secret world. Much of this enmity sprang from the uncertainty of the demarcation between their tasks. There is no clear-cut and obvious line

[6] Compton Mackenzie, *Water on the Brain* (footnote to novel), 1951.

and again up a flight of steps which brought us out on to the roof. Crossing a short iron bridge we entered another maze until just as I was beginning to feel dizzy I was shown into a room ten feet square where sat an officer in the uniform of a British colonel."

Cumming's own room was even more startling. "From the threshold the room seemed bathed in semi-obscurity. Against the window, everything appeared in silhouette. A row of half-a-dozen extending telephones stood at the left of a big desk littered with papers. On a side table were maps and drawings, with models of aeroplanes, submarines and mechanical devices, while a row of bottles suggested chemical experiments. These evidences of scientific investigation only served to intensify an already overpowering atmosphere of strangeness and mystery."

The inhabitant of this strange room was the subject of perhaps more legends than any of his four successors in the role of "C"; legends generated chiefly by his intense secretiveness about his work. "He could be as silent as the grave. Even his intimate friends thought he was doing little more than keeping the War Office informed on Indian conspiracies" wrote his obituarist. Perhaps the most remarkable story about him is that he severed the remnants of his own leg with a pen-knife when trapped in his overturned motor car: a feat he performed in order to crawl to his dying son.

The overriding consideration in MI 5 and SIS was a mania for secrecy, which extended to the use of masks and pointless rules about never taking taxis directly to the headquarters. Compton Mackenzie, who operated for Cumming in Athens in the First World War, and was offered the post of second-in-command, made clear in 1933 his feelings [6] on the real reason for this secrecy. It was to make sure that the men of the secret world "should not run the slightest risk of the unpleasant experience that the Emperor underwent in Hans Andersen's tale, in which, it will be remembered, a small child among the spectators called out that the Emperor, so far from wearing a beautiful new suit was walking in the procession with nothing on at all." And indeed there is little evidence that Cumming's spies contributed anything very much to the war against Germany, although MI 5 did some useful police work against some rather moderate German spies.

Much of the energies of the two departments was until

very recently absorbed in feuding with each other; this is something which crops up in the recollections of virtually every veteran of the British secret world. Much of this enmity sprang from the uncertainty of the demarcation between their tasks. There is no clear-cut and obvious line between espionage and counter-espionage. To take an over-simplified case, a man might be sent into an enemy country to find out what he can about that country's administration. His task in that case is espionage. But suppose the enemy happen to offer him a job in *their* organisation spying on *us?* He is then engaged, automatically, in counter-espionage. Should he transfer from SIS to MI 5?

The division between MI 5 and SIS was formally made by giving MI 5 exclusive rights on British territory, and giving SIS exclusive rights on foreign territory. This meant that SIS was responsible not only for espionage, but for counter-espionage undertaken on foreign soil. There were further complications in that MI 5 was responsible for counter-espionage in colonies and dominions; as may be imagined, the espionage efforts of foreign powers did not always respect these neat departmental frontiers, and there were endless possibilities for friction in vital places like Gibraltar. In the event, SIS and MI 5 during the Second World War appear each to have handled a number of operations which might as logically have been handled by the rival department. For instance, the German intelligence officer Otto John was handled by MI 5 when he defected to Britain. But other German defectors, like the diplomats Eric and Elizabeth Vernehren or the intelligence officer described as "Kuno" in the memoirs[7] of a wartime SIS man, were handled by the SIS.

The friction caused by demarcation disputes was aggravated by the oddly-contrasted departmental moralities of SIS and MI 5. William Skardon, perhaps the best operator MI 5 ever had, was once taxed with the fact that he did not seem friendly towards the men of SIS. He justified himself by saying that "you have to be a bit of a villain for that work." Essentially, MI 5 are the guardians of national purity and the upholders of law and order, while the organisers of espionage are at best patriotic brigands, gentlemanly destroyers of other people's law and order. SIS

---

[7] "John Whitwell," *British Agent.* Kimber, 1966.

men, naturally, repaid the disapproval of the MI 5 men by regarding them in turn as elaborated policemen.

Each department deeply distrusted the other's idea of security. MI 5 believed that the SIS, operating overseas, often hiring agents who had betrayed their own countries for money, was hopelessly insecure. SIS, on the other hand, merely thought that MI 5 failed totally to understand the real nature of espionage. The result was that the two departments rigidly resisted any exchange of information, even to the point where this became an operational liability. In fact, their theories of security were based on very similar premises: chiefly, the idea that the interlocking connections of the British middle and upper classes provided checks on people through their public schools, clubs, regiments and—when relevant—universities.

The old SIS had its greatest days in the melodramatic chaos of Russia after the Revolution. The Service failed in its aim of overthrowing the Bolsheviks, but did succeed in implanting in the Russians a lasting fear of the machinations of Western intelligence organisations which may have had a good deal to do with the subsequent operations of Philby and his successors. In retrospect, the Russians were clearly mistaking the ludicrous for the menacing; but incidents like the "Lockhart Plot" would not have inclined them to take chances. (On August 31, 1918, a Social Revolutionary named Dora Kaplan shot Lenin twice. The design was that Lenin's assassination should coincide with risings in Moscow and Petrograd organised by Sidney Reilly. But Reilly was late, and she shot too soon. Lenin, however, nearly died.) The Russians, who are nothing if not paranoid, probably reacted melodramatically to the news that there was an SIS dining circle called the "Bolo [for Bolshevik] Liquidation Club."

During all this time the SIS was under the control of the Committee of Imperial Defence. But the Foreign Office was fighting to gain control of all secret intelligence. Perhaps the FO was worried by the ambitions the SIS was demonstrating in Russia—if not, it certainly should have been. Two years later Cumming died, and was succeeded by Admiral (later Sir Hugh) Sinclair, under whom the SIS went into relative quiescence.

Sinclair's activities were strictly limited by his resources; whereas Compton Mackenzie as a young captain in 1917 had had £12,000 *a month* to spend in Athens alone, the Secret Vote in 1927–28 was only £180,000 altogether.[8] (It was not until 1936–37 that it was increased to £350,000, reaching £1,500,000 in 1940–41 before figures were suppressed as a wartime measure.) The Foreign Office, presumably, were not unhappy about the SIS living a quiet life, as vigorous and active secret services make life very difficult for ordinary diplomats, and just before the Second World War the SIS survived a Foreign Office inspection.

The SIS worked in a relatively leisurely manner, sending young men, usually with City or Service connections, out to cover European countries.* They worked mostly under business cover, or were given jobs as passport control officers in British embassies. There was no very elaborate training for agents, who were expected to set up their networks of sub-agents more or less in their own way. They purchased tit-bits of information in the same manner as newspapers: £10 here, £25 there for some details of troop movements or a picture of a new aeroplane. Military and political intelligence seem to have been pretty thoroughly mixed up, and one wartime recruit from the universities declared that the whole SIS network was just "a mechanism for gathering up the gun-room gossip of Europe."

The worst weakness of the system was, interestingly, its paramount obsession with security. This meant that there could be almost no serious assessing of intelligence according to reliability or importance, because this would have involved discussing the sources of the information. Not only did the SIS resolutely refuse to tell the "consum-

---

[8] In the same year 1927–28 the Foreign Office and Diplomatic Service cost £1,886,168, and Government hospitality cost £13,000. However, in the days before social engineering, the SIS did get more money than the Ministry of Transport, which got only £126,500. The Secret Service vote, virtually the only official documentation available on the SIS, is easily examined in Whitaker's Almanack. In 1978 (the most recent figure available) it was £31.4 million. It does not represent the true total, because large amounts of expenditure can be "buried" in Service accounts, etc. But it is a guide to the rate of increase of expense.

* The number that could be sent abroad at any one period was strictly limited because of SIS's small staff. At the outbreak of war, there were not more than twenty regular officers in SIS, and in counterintelligence no more than six.

ing" departments in Britain anything about its sources, even discussion of sources within the organisation was much discouraged. Great security was obtained, at the price of making much of the information gathered virtually meaningless.

As the shadow of the Second World War moved closer and Admiral Sinclair aged, the Secret Intelligence Service fell more and more under the influence of three men: Stewart Menzies, Valentine Vivian and Claude Dansey. The Service which Kim Philby devastated was in large measure their service.

Of this trio, Menzies was the most important, because he was Sinclair's deputy, and when the Admiral died in November 1939, Menzies took over as "C." Menzies remained in the post throughout the war and the period of the Burgess and Maclean defection, so it was under his command that the Service recruited and promoted Philby. He died in 1968: Major General Sir Stewart Menzies, KCB (1951), KCMC (1943), DSO (1914), MC.

His *Who's Who* entry was explicit about his breeding and connections, but reticent about his career. It recorded that he was born in 1890, son of Lady Holford, was educated at Eton and Sandhurst, and served with the Grenadier Guards and the Life Guards. He was married three times, once to an earl's daughter, once to a baron's granddaughter, and once to a baronet's daughter who had been married to the son of a viscount. The entry revealed that he served in the First World War, when he won his DSO and MC, besides being mentioned in dispatches. But it gave no clue to why, in addition to his elevated British decorations, he should be a Grand Officer of the Legion of Honour, a Grand Officer of the Order of Leopold, Crown of Belgium, a member of the Legion of Merit (USA), a Grand Officer of the Order of Orange Nassau (Holland), a member of the order of Polonia Restituta (Poland), and a Commander of St. Olaf (Norway). There was not even the customary euphemism—"attached to the Foreign Office."

It would be possible to caricature Menzies as an upperclass figure of fun in the manner of Graham Greene's wickedly funny portrait of the secret-service chief in *Our Man in Havana*. (Greene served under Menzies in the SIS during the war.) And some of Menzies' remarks after his retirement seemed almost calculated to aid such a process, such as his reaction when Montgomery Hyde revealed for the first time, in his book *The Quiet Canadian*, that Menzies had been head of the SIS during the war. The General told the *Evening Standard* that he did not think the revelation affected national security. But he said he was fairly prominent in the Hunt in his county, and he wondered how people would take it. When we wrote to ask about Kim Philby, Menzies replied courteously that he could not discuss the matter with us. But he vouchsafed one comment: "What a blackguard Kim Philby was!" It was an understandable comment, but somehow irrelevant to a case of ideologically-inspired espionage—as though someone had described one of the frequently dangerous Catholic infiltrators with which Elizabethan England had to deal as a "blackguard."

But Menzies was not a buffoon. It is fairer to describe him as a perfectly efficient intelligence officer of the old school, who was unlucky enough to retain high office in a period when espionage had changed dramatically from the relatively gentlemanly business he had known as a young man. He had many good qualities—the most famous of which was his ironclad discretion. According to a story told by ex-SIS officers, he was once pressed, jokingly, by King George VI to reveal details about the Service. "Menzies," said the King, "what would happen if I were to ask you the name of our man in Berlin?"

Menzies replied: "I should have to say, Sir, that my lips are sealed."

"Well, Menzies—supposing I were to say, 'Off with your head?' "

"In that case, Sir, my head would roll with the lips still sealed."

Menzies was said to have access to the King whenever he wished. He certainly had an excellent introduction to Court circles through his mother, who was Lady-in-Waiting to Queen Mary. Whether his Court links were particularly useful or not is hard to say, but it seems clear enough from the accounts given by people who served with him that Menzies' general connections in high quarters were extremely useful both to Menzies himself and his department. It was a time when social connections mattered more than they do today.

Nowadays intelligence officers, particularly in America, tend to have intellectual pretensions. (These are not nec-

essarily unjustified: you can find men like Lyman B.
Kirkpatrick, formerly Assistant Director of the CIA, who
is now Professor of Politics at the distinguished Brown
University.) Menzies' approach to his work was conscientious, but he certainly did not bring intellectual pretensions to it. According to colleagues, he relied on his
instinctive judgements of men and situations, rather than
detailed reading of cases, and his relaxations centered on
an uncomplicated interest in hunting and racing. "He
could be disconcerting to work with, because of this reli-
ance on hunch," says an officer of the wartime Special
Operations Executive who handled liaison with SIS. "But
his instinct—it was almost feminine—hardly ever let him
down."

He was not the showy sort of administrator. Lord Swinton, the great Tory grandee who was chairman of the National Security Executive in between numerous other
appointments of power and influence, once said: "Whenever I ask Stewart about something on the telephone, he
invariably says he must check up and ring me back. I
have ninety-nine business interests, and I have the details
of them all at my finger-tips." But he *was* a canny administrator—"the great thing about Menzies," Churchill said,
"is that he runs his service on pennies." He was sensible
about finance, and about relationships with other departments and with the politicians. "He was very good at in-
terdepartmental manoeuvring," says an officer who served
during the war at the SIS headquarters, then at 54 Broadway, near St. James's Park Underground station.

Menzies possessed the one really essential qualification
for a British secret-service chief: he inspired a feeling in
his political masters that he was unlikely to do anything
silly. This is crucial because the shadowy, mysterious—
but always potentially explosive—work of espionage and
security makes politicians, and "straight" civil servants,
intensely uneasy. They have no desire to be familiar with
the details of the business. All they want is a feeling that
the man in charge of these unpleasant affairs can be relied on not to do anything that will get them into trouble.
Naturally they will exchange a lot of potential brilliance
or originality for that kind of reliability.

A secret-service chief cannot, of course, confide in
many people—and this, no doubt, is why Menzies
preserved correct, but somewhat frigid and distant rela-

tionships with most of his officers in SIS. This he compensated for by leaning heavily on Dansey and Vivian, and
on one or two wartime assistants who came from similar
moneyed, clubbish backgrounds as he did himself. The
most noticeable of these wartime assistants seems to have
been a fellow-Etonian of Belgian descent named Peter
Koch de Gooreynd.

Koch de Gooreynd had been, before the war, a minor
hero of the London gossip columns, who were still retail-
ing to suburbia the rather threadbare legend of the Bright
Young Things. One of his achievements was to own one
of the first home cinematographs in Britain, with which
he used to show Mickey Mouse films after dinner. Later,
he launched a personal crusade against the tide of imported music which was swamping the British popular-
song market. Undaunted by the fact that he did not read
music, and had only a skeletal command of the piano, he
set out to write and publish what he described as "good
British songs." Up to the time that this campaign was cut
short by his recruitment into the Secret Intelligence Service, his greatest success had been a song called "Silver
Hair and Golden Eyes," which was sung by Richard
Tauber.

Both Menzies and Koch de Gooreynd belonged to
White's, the club which is usually bracketed with the Turf
at the top of the subtle hierarchy of London clubland.
During the war, an etiquette grew up among members of
White's, that one was not to bother Menzies and Koch de
Gooreynd when they were together at the bar, because it
was understood that they were "running the secret service,
or something." It would hardly have struck anyone at
White's as odd that the club should occasionally be a sort
of partial, alternative headquarters of the secret service:
rather the reverse, in that the major clubs of the West
End are, quite unselfconsciously, citadels of the British
ruling orders. It would have seemed odd at that time if
men at the bars of White's, Buck's, Pratt's and similar establishments, down to the Athenaeum (to which Kim
Philby belonged) and the Reform (to which Guy Burgess
belonged), had *not* been running the secret service, and a
good deal else besides.

It is not hard to see why Menzies would have felt the
need to have someone like Koch de Gooreynd around.
His two principal executives, Dansey and Vivian, nur-

tured a passionate distaste for each other which was entirely in the tradition of clandestine bureaucracy—but which would have made it difficult for Menzies to have spent much time with one of them, at the expense of the other, without splitting the Service.

Philby was to some extent a counter in the struggle between these two men, in that he was the most important of several bright young champions of Vivian's side of the service against Dansey's. It almost seems unjust that Dansey should have died in 1944, when Philby's star was in the ascendant, and not lived to see the discomfiture of his enemies on the denouement of Philby's betrayal. But few people who knew both men would have relished the spectacle of Dansey's triumph over Vivian—who is generally reckoned to have been a man who was honourably, if unluckily, trying to introduce some new blood into the service.

Colonel Sir Claude Dansey, as he was when he died shortly after D-Day, bore a good deal of resemblance to those fictional spymasters compounded of chilled steel and intrigue. "A man who thinks nine ways at once" was one colleague's description of him. He was responsible for offensive espionage networks, while Vivian was responsible for counter-espionage and was Director of Security for the SIS.

Dansey had been a Territorial officer in the First World War, when he got into Intelligence work in France. After the war, he attempted a number of unlucky business ventures: at one stage he ran an English-style country-club in America, complete with footmen in wigs and knee-breeches. After that, he worked for the SIS in Italy and Switzerland, and was eventually brought back to London to organise a mysterious intelligence service called the "Z" organisation. For some reason, a curious air of danger and slight disrepute still attaches to his name: he was described to one of the present authors, amid the Victorian rectitude of the United Services Club, as "something of a bounder."

Likely enough, this sprang from nothing more than the mystery which consistently surrounded his life and his vitriolic way of expressing his many powerful likes and dislikes: one of which seems to have been university graduates. "I would never willingly employ a university man," he is reported to have said. A representative Danseyism was his marginal note on a file which discussed the question of a colour-code for Vivian's beloved counter-espionage section, in which Philby worked. "I suggest yellow would be a suitable colour for this section," wrote Dansey. At another time he described Vivian's staff as "a lot of old women in red flannel knickers." After the death of Admiral Sinclair, Menzies appointed Dansey his deputy, and Colonel Vivian made a habit of always being on leave when Menzies was on leave, so that he would not have to take orders from Dansey as acting chief of the Service.

Colonel Valentine Vivian, known as "Vee-vee" to his staff, was an altogether more amiable man. Physically, he and Dansey were contrasting types: Dansey rugged and bear-like; Vivian lean and elegant, with crinkled hair and a monocle. Vivian embodied one of the most solidly established traditions of British intelligence-work, in that he came from the Indian Police. Until the European conflicts of the twentieth-century became all-dominant, Britain's chief need for intelligence, security and counter-espionage work was naturally in her overseas empire. The Special Branch, the section of Scotland Yard which acts as the executive arm of MI 5, was originally the Irish Special Branch, formed to combat the Irish nationalists (and drawing a number of recruits from a group of policemen who had been put together to control nationalists in Egypt after the British assumption of control there). India was the arena of greatest effort, since only by maintaining an effective intelligence operation could the British maintain the amazing trick of controlling the sub-continent with scarcely more than a few thousand men.

This huge espionage task is the "Great Game" of Kipling's novel *Kim*. The Indian Police therefore provided a pool of reasonably experienced officers on which the SIS and MI 5 found it convenient to draw: contact and recruitment being made all the easier because the Indian Police between the wars had a London staff whose task was to keep tabs on the numerous Indian nationalists in residence in London. The availability of the "Indians" must have seemed a real blessing to departments which were too hard-up to train large numbers of officers themselves. But this kind of recruitment had a good many disadvantages attached.

The intellectual qualifications for entry into the Indian

Police were a good deal lower than, for example, those for the Diplomatic Service. Yet the Indian Policemen who were recruited to the SIS and MI 5 were expected to perform tasks at least as complex as the diplomat's task—perhaps more so. It may be doubted whether the "Indians'" suitability for work in the complex ideological jungles of modern Europe was much increased by the fact that they had spent their formative years in colonial administration.

Colonel Vivian, as it happened, was one of those who saw that the SIS needed some more sophisticated recruits. It seems clear that he was largely responsible for the influx of dons, journalists and writers at the beginning of the Second World War. "My intellectuals," he sometimes called them. But ironically, the Indian connection pursued Vivian even in this campaign to change the mental climate of the Service—and with deadly results. For according to his conversation at the time, one of the reasons for his recruitment of his star "intellectual," Kim Philby, was the fact that Kim's father, St. John, had been a friend of Vivian's when they served together in India.

The combination of privileged amateurism at the top with parsimonious makeshift below was common enough in British government service when the Second World War began. It derived from essential deficiencies in British society, many of which are still with us, but some of which were remedied during the war by heavy expenditure of blood.

In most of the services there was at least some saving grace. However much advantage there might be for social eminence in the Diplomatic Service, there was at least a powerful tradition that recruits should be well-educated. Certainly in the Air Force and the Navy the unavoidable demands of technology did a great deal to maintain standards. And in ordinary departments and services, there is the marginal disciplinary effect of public scrutiny. None of these things, of course, applied to the SIS.

There are people, it is true, who maintain that the SIS was really a brilliant organisation, fully worthy of its legend. And of course it is not easy to refute them categorically, because they tend to retire behind a screen of mystery when asked to support their assertions. There was, for instance, a period in 1940 when according to at least three published accounts one of SIS's subsidiaries was in a considerable tangle. When one of the present authors made the point to a distinguished General that very few of the officers involved in the episode seemed to know, even today, what was going on, he replied: "Ah! Good security, you see." There is something in the argument that a secret service cannot readily discuss its triumphs. But a quarter of a century later, this argument wears a little thin.

A noticeable fact about the SIS is that most of the intellectually distinguished people who worked for it during the war, or who came into contact with it, are very caustic indeed about its efficiency. The most ferocious critic is Mr. Malcolm Muggeridge, who has more than once referred in print to his belief that it would be impossible to over-estimate the stupidity of the Secret Intelligence Service he knew during the war. As Mr. Muggeridge is known to be a man of caustic views on almost every subject, it might be possible to discount his opinion of the SIS. But they are corroborated, if not in detail at least in general spirit, by numerous other people we have interviewed.

Whatever may be the merits of this sort of evidence of opinion, it can hardly be denied that the war began with a major disaster for the SIS. This was the "Venlo Incident," in which the Germans captured two important officers of the SIS—and with them a huge amount of information.

An important European network of the SIS was run from Holland, under the command of Major H. R. Stevens and Captain S. Payne Best. In November 1939 the Gestapo captured both of them at Venlo, a small town on the Dutch-German border. The operation was run by SS Group-Leader Walter Schellenberg (an "intellectual gangster," as Edward Crankshaw called him), and together with Gestapo assistants he lured the two luckless SIS men to Venlo on the promise that they were to meet a German general, and other officers, who were anti-Nazi and anxious to make peace. The Germans claimed to have gained a great deal of information by interrogating Stevens and Best, who survived the war in concentration camps. However much they got from Stevens and Best precisely, the Abwehr[9] obviously had fairly thorough

[9] The Abwehr was the German equivalent of the SIS.

tabs on the British operation in Holland. Hermann
Giskes, an Abwehr staff officer, wrote after the war that
the Germans had filmed the British SIS officers in Sche-
veningen regularly enough to be able to identify all, or
virtually all, British agents working against Germany.
These agents, he says, were naturally all taken in, unless they agreed to "broadcast the messages England
wanted in the way the German counter-espionage branch
wanted." [10]

It was presumably because of this German coup that
by the summer of 1941 Churchill was complaining bitterly about the paucity of information coming out of
occupied Europe. He even went so far as to ask the
subversion-and-sabotage service, Special Operations Executive, to try to produce information. This must have
been especially galling for the SIS—because the very
existence of SOE represented a failure on their part. This
failure occurred, however, on the battlefields of Whitehall, not of Europe.

It had become plain during the latter thirties that in the
coming war there would be another secret function to perform, apart from traditional espionage: that is to say,
subversion and sabotage in enemy-occupied territory.
Late in 1938, the SIS set up a sub-department to handle
this task, which they christened "Section D" (from one of
the alternative names of the SIS, "C Department"). It
may be that this move was due entirely to martial zeal;
but it seems likely that a substantial motivation was the
desire to make sure that the new function came firmly
under SIS control, and did not lead to the incursion of another rival organisation into the secret world. Whatever
the motivation, the new group did not have an entirely
happy history—quite apart from the fact that in January
1939 it recruited Guy Burgess. A basic and unavoidable
problem for Section D was the inevitable clash of interest
between espionage and sabotage. Bickham Sweet-Escott,
who served in Section D, wrote in 1965: "A fundamental
conflict . . . arose from the start. For the man who is
interested in obtaining intelligence must have peace and
quiet, and the agents he employs must never if possible
be found out. But the man who has to carry out opera-

[10] Hermann G. Giskes, *Abwehr IIIF*. Amsterdam, 1948.

tions will produce loud noises if he is successful, and it is
only too likely that some of the men he uses will not escape." [11]

In this conflict, the interests of the SIS itself were almost invariably paramount because, as Sweet-Escott also
says, "they controlled our communications, whether by
letter or cipher telegram."

Possibly Section D might have overcome this difficulty,
but before it could do so the Government abolished it,
and took the subversion-and-sabotage function away from
the SIS empire. The step is very understandable, in view
of the confusing manner in which sabotage organisations
were proliferating while Section D was under C's control.
On the armed-operations side, D was supposed to have
links with an organisation called MI(R). But in September 1939, MI(R) broke away to work on its own. It was
responsible for supporting any guerilla operations which
seemed likely to aid the British cause, and although theoretically there were demarcations between MI(R) and
Section D, in practice, says Sweet-Escott, there was "confusion and friction." This was not lessened by the fact
that MI(R) itself produced another off-shoot, operating
in the Middle East called G(R). "In one capacity or the
other MI(R) had sent people all over the world just in
case," wrote Sweet-Escott, "and were afterwards to find
that they had men in such unlikely places as the Canary
Islands and Buenos Aires."

Section D had also acquired some terribly complicated
connections in the area of propaganda and broadcasting,
which was simultaneously inhabited by bodies like the
BBC, the Ministry of Information and the newly-created
Ministry of Economic Warfare.

At least two propaganda organisations appear to have
come under Section D control: the Joint Broadcasting
Council, accommodated secretly in a house near Eridge in
Sussex, and the "Hexton" group, at another country
house in Hertfordshire. The JBC, in which Guy Burgess
worked for a time, was supposed to arrange for ordinary
BBC programmes to be recorded and distributed throughout the world as exemplars of the British Way of Life.
"Hexton" (this was a cover name) was a place where
rather filthy kinds of propaganda material were produced.

[11] *Baker Street Irregular.*

There were postcards, designed for distribution throughout Europe, of Hitler licking Stalin's naked hindquarters, and similar gems.

Section D's immediate rival for control of these units —and perhaps there were others—was the "Electra House" organisation, which took its title from the name of its headquarters building on the Embankment. "EH," as people called it, was run by Sir Campbell Stuart, an elderly newspaper executive and veteran of First World War propaganda. Sir Campbell, who had retained a fascination for propaganda technique, had started up his own informal discussion groups of Electra House in the late thirties, and on the outbreak of war had acquired official status under the Foreign Office.

A BBC man who worked for Electra House was given the dismal task of visiting Hexton and the JBC to find reasons why they should be brought under control of EH rather than Section D. He came across Guy Burgess, "bull-like and opinionated," as more or less the guiding spirit of the JBC. And Sweet-Escott has another glimpse of Burgess at "what for want of a better word I suppose should be called inter-departmental meetings on propaganda," which he says took place at frequent but irregular intervals during June and July 1940.

"There were no minutes, there was no agenda, and no chairman . . . there never seemed to be less than twenty-five people in the room. Besides the heads of 'D,' innumerable other departments were represented—Terry Harman from Electra House, Hilda Matheson from the BBC, and a floating population from the Ministry of Information, and occasionally the Foreign Office and the Ministry of Economic Warfare. What generally happened was that somebody would throw a bright idea into the arena and let the others tear it into pieces, a process which was often amusing, but generally unprofitable. . . . On the few occasions when it was agreed that action should be taken, it usually seemed to be obscure who was expected to do the job, and I never discovered that any of the ideas really led to action. There was one boiling July afternoon when, with dogfights between the RAF and the Luftwaffe going on over our heads, Guy Burgess, who I believe was then employed by Electra House, nearly convinced the meeting that the way to end the war was to wait for a westerly wind and then send off large numbers of balloons in the direction of central Europe, hoping that incendiary bombs attached to them would set the cornfields of the Hungarian *puszta* on fire and starve the Germans out."

Very probably the immediate nemesis of Section D was the series of absurd contretemps surrounding the "leave-behind" operation which it mounted in the late summer of 1940. This was based on the assumption that German invasion was imminent: it was decided to establish secret stores of arms and ammunition up and down the country to provide the warlike sinews of a putative yeoman resistance behind the German lines. Officers were dispatched around the country to establish these stores and find suitable local recruits to command them. Time was held to be short: too short, it seems, properly to inform other branches of Government what Section D was doing: Kenneth Younger, late Director of the Royal Institute of International Affairs, was then in MI 5, and described to us the alarm which was felt in MI 5 as reports came in of what were not unnaturally taken to be potential German agents touring the countryside with munitions for subversion. Several emissaries of Section D were arrested before the tangle was sorted out. Guy Burgess's ill-fated attempt to reach Moscow in July 1940 (described in the previous chapter) was one of Section D's last spasms of activity. When Burgess arrived back in London, he found that Section D was being brutally dismantled.

Not before time, the diverse and mutually antagonistic bureaucracies of subversion, sabotage and propaganda were being rationalised. In the process, the SIS parent lost its Section D offspring and a new organisation did make its appearance in the secret world. This was the Special Operations Executive, created by a Cabinet directive of 22 July 1940.[12] It absorbed the role and most of the personnel of Section D, but it was independently responsible (with its own communications) to the Minister of Economic Warfare, Dr. Hugh Dalton. SOE, which was dissolved at the end of the war, remains to this day a highly controversial organisation. Some people maintain that it was little better than an agglomeration of talented roughnecks, crooks and eccentrics, with poor security and

[12] J. R. M. Butler, *Grand Strategy*, Vol. II, HMSO, 1957.

irresponsible ideas on policy. Others claim that it was effective and aggressive, and certainly SOE got a lot of
agents into Europe and blew up a lot of things. Its history has already been amply enough described elsewhere
for readers to make up their own minds. [13]

It is hard to see how SOE could have been worse than
the extraordinary tangle of departments which preceded
it: anyway, all that strictly matters to the progress of this
narrative is that the advent of SOE did a good deal to increase the acidity of SIS's relationships with the rest of
the secret world. The senior SIS officers regarded SOE
with the same unblinking hostility they had previously reserved for MI 5. According to Captain Henry Kerby, MP,
who served in SIS during the war, there was a brief rap-
prochement at this time between SIS and MI 5, as the
two groups of "professionals" combined to protest about
the powers being entrusted to the "amateurs" of SOE.
But it did not last long—indeed, relations between the
two departments soon became, if anything, even more
hostile. This was due to a change in the nature of MI 5.

Up to 1940, MI 5 was an organisation of smiliar character to the SIS, in that its operations and philosopy were
dominated by the attitudes of the Regular Army and the
Indian Police, from which, like SIS, it drew most of its
officers. The main difference appears to have been that it
was not so rich in colourful and romantic characters, or
in upper-class connections. The nature of its work was, of
course, a good deal more pedestrian than the work of the
SIS. Much of it was simply filing work.

When the Second World War began, MI 5 was still
commanded by the man who founded it in 1909. This was
Major-General Sir Vernon Kell, who was sixty-seven in
1940. MI 5 had done reasonably well in the First World
War (although it failed to capture the unknown saboteur
who is assumed to have been behind the destruction by
magazine-explosion of four British warships in harbour
between 1914 and 1917). But its system seems to have
been a little overwhelmed by the huge demands of the

[13] Chiefly, in M. R. D. Foot, *SOE in France* (Official History, HMSO) and E. M. Cookridge, *Inside SOE* (Arthur
Barker, 1966), apart from Sweet-Escott's distinguished personal account.

new war. The core of MI 5's operation, of course, was its system of records: the files had to preserve in orderly and swiftly-accessible detail a vast amount of information collected by Special Branch policemen, about people who were potentially of danger to the State.

Without its records system, MI 5 was nothing. And a disaster overcame the files in 1940: they were stored at Wormwood Scrubs Prison, and a bomb unfortunately set them on fire. This was one of a series of disasters which overtook the lurching MI 5 organisation: an examination of its condition in the early part of the war indicates that it was in no condition to handle Britain's resistance against Soviet penetration. The organisation had been hastily enlarged and reinforced, in the forlorn hope that it could easily be prepared to cope with the exigencies of a wartime situation. Sadly, things did not work out. The first of the MI 5 people moved into their forbidding new home in the dismal Victorian Gothic of Wormwood Scrubs while the last of the prisoners were still being bundled away. It was an appropriately comic beginning; wartime employees of MI 5 at this period recall the period as an interlude of almost unalloyed farce, conducted in an atmosphere of inconsequential surreality.

In the rush to shift the prisoners an elderly chaplain was forgotten and left behind. He held weekly services at which—not realising his congregation had drastically altered—he would instruct the MI 5 staff in their civic responsibilities after "they had paid their debts to society," and entreat them to go straight after they were released. One MI 5 employee said: "I never missed a service."

A woman who served under Kell comments: "I doubt you will be able to believe the absurdity of it all. Lots of the people were totally unsuitable. The Scrubs was crawling with hunting and fishing types—what we needed was typing and filing types."

The aristocratic intake of MI 5 at the beginning of the war was not accidental, but was the result of a deliberate recruiting policy instituted by General Kell. "I want all my girls to be well bred and have good legs," the General once remarked, as if he were discussing stud mares. But it was more than an aesthetic preference. Kell believed as an article of faith that members of the upper classes were *ipso facto* more "secure," to use the jargon, than repre-

sentatives of humbler social echelons. It was the same principle which led his counterparts in SIS to assume that Kim
Philby could hardly be a communist because he was a
member of the Athenaeum.

It proved to be an equally disastrous assumption in MI
5, though for rather different reasons. The essence of MI
5's operation was meticulous filing and administration.
Unfortunately the General's social prejudices ensured that
the place was staffed with girls from impeccable families
—they were asked in the application forms whether or
not they had a title—who had not the faintest qualifications for the job. "The standard of typing, spelling and filing was beyond belief," one of their number remembers.
"We treated the whole thing as a joke." (The typists fell
into the habit of bringing shooting-sticks and hampers
with them; they would picnic in the meadows outside the
prison walls as if parodying an upper-class day in the
country. It was not a good security move.)

In the circumstances such irresponsibility is understandable. The girls were very young and their superiors in the
main fossilised regular officers of Kell's vintage and perception. The men in between, young officers, many of
whom had legal backgrounds, were in the course of the
war to oust the blue blood and thunder Great War war-
riors, but the process took time. In the interim the reactionaries tried to run the place like a cavalry regiment in
the pre-tank era.

Naturally, the girls dined out on their stories of life in
the Scrubs and soon every polite drawing room in London
was tittering about "Five's" new HO.[14] When the number 72 bus drew up outside the prison each morning to
disgorge its debby passengers there would be delighted
giggles as the conductor bellowed: "All change for MI 5."
Kell was not the bus-riding type so he was spared the
trauma of hearing his security turned into a joke. It would
have broken his heart.

Apart from the top officers only one person really tried
to get the girls to work properly. She was a ferocious ex-

[14] The typists composed a lament which ran:
"*I'm just a girl at MI 5, and heading for a virgin's grive
My legs it was wot got me in—I'm waiting for my bit
of sin.*"

shop detective in charge of registry, who soon adopted the
military tradition of referring to lower ranks by their surname alone. Sadly her zeal only increased the atmosphere
of dormitory feast hysteria that prevailed; one of the girls
had an unfortunate name. A bellow of "Smith, come
here," was all right. When she tried "Pigg, I want you,"
the whole typing pool fell about unrestrainedly.

All this had bad effects on MI 5's chief claim to fame,
the enormous register of names and addresses of "suspect" people. It was widely thought that MI 5 could turn
up the record of any political activist or subversive organisation within minutes. The staff tell a different story.
One of our informants said that the files were voluminous,
but quite meaningless. One night, for example, she was
working on a late shift and decided to thumb through the
cards of some of her friends. Quite by accident she discovered that her mother was listed because she had once held
a musical evening, and among the guests had included an
Austrian couple, who were refugees from the Nazis. Another "dangerous" person was a woman living in the English fishing port of Lowestoft who was recorded thus:
"She is always gazing out to sea and has a German
friend" (sic).

Official naiveté and lack of humour was apparently
bottomless. Under "B," for example, there were three suspicious characters, whose names had been gleaned from
the attendance book at a left-wing political meeting. The
trio were "Mr. Fred Buggery," "Miss Nora Borlzov," and
"Mrs. Maisie Bigtitz." Our informant swears that all had
been entered solemnly without any question. One wonders
what ever happened to Maisie . . . (Obviously, the idea
that dangerous leftists had the wit to invent pseudonyms
had not penetrated MI 5.) Then there were the fascinating accounts given of witchcraft *soirees* held by Mr.
Aleister Crowley. MI 5 agents who attended these functions disguised as witches and wizards, wrote long memoranda about the consumption of goat's blood.

Girls sorting through information of this quality soon
became cynical and disheartened. One girl said, "We
would be asked for the card on someone or other. You
could spend hours plodding patiently through card after
card and finally discover it said: 'Once signed a petition
against book censorship.' It seemed worthless to pass on

such frivolous information. Most of the time I didn't bother to hand it in." She was not the only secretary to become bored and disillusioned. It became common practice for girls to stamp inquiries for cards with the initials "N.L.T." which meant "No likely trace." As a veteran explained: "It was always better to write N.L.T. than just N.T. which meant no trace. If the file was found after you had written N.T. there was trouble. With N.L.T. you were perfectly safe because the file could have been anywhere." For an unexplained reason all suspects with the surname Smith were filed under Schmidt, which would seem to indicate advanced xenophobia among the filing supervisors. There was another classic file of considerable volume headed "Suspect servants in the U.K." This contained dossiers on butlers and footmen in aristocratic homes. Most of the information, however, seemed to refer to indolence or insubordination.

The incendiary bombs, which landed with uncanny accuracy on the registry building, finally did for Kell. Almost all the records went up in flames but for a while no one worried. After all, such a contingency had obviously already been envisaged. About a month before the attack a group of agents had been given the tedious, yet crucial job of photo-copying every single file. Kell suffered a stunning blow when it was discovered that the agents had succeeded in botching the job. Some of the film negatives proved impossible to print. With others, the information had been copied successfully but the names to which the note had been attached were left off. The General was promptly summoned to 10 Downing Street.

When he returned Kell gathered the staff together, as if for a parade. He told them, with no visible emotion, that he had to bid them farewell. And the summer of 1940 was marked by a drastic shake-up in the MI 5 leadership.

The shake-up was the work of a powerful and effective body called the National Security Executive, which had been set up to take central supervisory powers over all British agencies concerned with security. Clearly there was a serious risk of German invasion, and a risk of internal subversion. The situation was far too dangerous to take any chances, and the Security Executive exemplified the real power and effectiveness of the British ruling caste; something quite different from the imitation to be found in the secret world.

Its chairman was Lord Swinton, a tough and experienced Tory administrator who had been in and out of the Cabinet and the upper levels of the business world since the twenties. Its joint secretaries were two brilliant young men named William Armstrong (later Sir William, and a Joint Secretary to the Treasury) and Kenneth Diplock (later knighted, and Lord Justice Diplock). It combined a man who was used to the exercise of real power with the energy and competence of the administrative orders at their best. The result of its enquiries into the workings of MI 5 was that Kell relinquished the directorship of MI 5 and a number of ex-Indian henchmen accompanied him into retirement.

Kell was at first replaced by an ex-policeman named Harker. Harker, however, did not stay long himself. The next director of MI 5, who remained until the end of the war, was Sir David Petrie. Under his rule, something of a revolution overcame MI 5. Petrie was an "Indian," but he recognised, like Colonel Vivian at SIS, that men from other backgrounds were needed to handle the new complexities of secret work. And unlike Colonel Vivian, Petrie was fortunate—or shrewd—in the men he relied on. Some remarkably talented men worked for Petrie during the war: Victor Rothschild (later Lord Rothschild), Herbert Hart (later Professor of Jurisprudence at Oxford University), Anthony Blunt (one-time Keeper of the Queen's Pictures), Helenus Milmo (later Mr. Justice Milmo), Patrick Barry (later Mr. Justice Barry and a knight), Kenneth Younger (a minister under Attlee) and Henry Pilcher (also a judge, but now dead).

The brilliant "amateurs" were organised for Petrie by two "professionals" who had been in the peacetime Service, and had long been pressing for reform. These were Dick White and Guy Liddell. Liddell was the elder, a quiet, cool man who had been in MI 5 since 1919. He had intended to be a cello-player, but the First World War had interrupted his studies. Liddell was the man of experience: White was generally regarded as the dynamo of the organisation. Then thirty-four, he had been to Christ Church, Oxford, and then to the Universities of Michigan and Southern California. Essentially, he was not a military man, but a civilian intelligence specialist, and more or less the first example of such a thing in recent British administrative history. Except for his rather unusual specialisation, he was not much different from any other bright young Civil Servant on his way up. Eventually, White and the reformed MI 5 were to destroy Kim Philby's career as a Soviet agent—but not before many mistakes had been made, and much blood spilt.

10. The Rise of Kim Philby

Aren't double agents always a bit . . . tricky? You never know whether you are getting the fat or the lean.

　　　　—GRAHAM GREENE, *Our Man in Havana*

Philby's role in the secret departmental battles of 1940 was at first that of a pawn, for he was a new recruit. He is first remembered by veterans of the period as a lecturer in methods of preparation of propaganda leaflets for distribution in enemy territory, a task he was presumably given because of his journalistic experience. He was, of course, somewhat hampered by his stammer; one pupil remembers that Philby developed a technique of slapping his thigh suddenly when he struck a particularly formidable "block" in his speech. The violent gesture seemed to release the faculty of speech again. When Section D was destroyed, Philby survived the purge which removed his friend Burgess, and continued briefly into service with the newborn Special Operations Executive.

He was posted to the SOE agents' school, which inhabited several country houses on the Montagu estate at Beaulieu in Hampshire. Each house contained agents of different nationalities being trained for sabotage and subversion in their occupied homelands. The houses were labelled with rather ridiculous code-names—the "House on the Shore" contained Frenchmen, the "House of the Rings," Poles, and so on. Philby, it seems, took the agents' course himself—and might well have been dropped into Nazi Europe, because he is reported to have performed well in the physical side of the training. Had he gone, much embarrassment might have been saved, for at that time the mortality among SOE agents was dauntingly high. But he was rejected for a combination of reasons. His French was insufficiently idiomatic; his stammer made him conspicuous, and his time in Spain with the Fascists had presumably made him well-known to awkward numbers of German officers.

He became an instructor, which at this time was a job with considerable political overtones. For example, the Polish recruits were often more anti-Russian than anti-German. "They wanted to get their fingers around Russian necks, not German," says one of Philby's colleagues. "Kim was very successful at persuading them to concentrate on the Germans and leave the Russians out of it." One of his specialities was printing. There was a scheme for suborning Linotype operators in occupied countries; the idea being that they would be persuaded to surreptitiously set lines of type for subversive pamphlets at their workshops, and smuggle them out for secret printing. Trips were arranged to *The Times* office in London, so that agents could become familiar with printing machinery.

Philby was then twenty-nine, with a good deal of worldly experience behind him. His seniors in SOE made considerable fuss about his reputation as a war correspondent, and he was admired by his pupils. To the Continental recruits Philby, with his pipe, flannels and old tweed jacket, must have seemed the epitome of English reliability. Some of the anti-Communist Poles may have died later because of what Philby knew about them, but at the time no one divined his real political affinities.

Once, he said a curious thing about the Spanish medal Franco had given him. Paul Dehn, the scriptwriter, then in SOE, asked Philby about the medal, and Philby said: "It's no use unless Hitler wins. Then I can infiltrate the British Nazis. There are plenty of them who will vouch for me." Was this the nightmare of Fascist victory again?

According to Dehn, Philby was restless as an SOE instructor and was casting around for something more exciting. His opportunity was created by the problems of the Secret Intelligence Service, which badly needed some new administrative strength if it was to recover from the martial and bureaucratic reverses of the first year of the war. Philby's opportunity matured, as near as we can place it, in the early summer of 1941, when he was offered an executive post in Section V, the counter-espionage section of SIS. After some twelve months on the fringes, Philby had reached the central citadel of the secret world. It was the crucial penetration.

Philby went to take over command of the Iberian subsection of Section V. This dealt with counter-espionage in Spain and Portugal, and was more important than it might seem at first glance. The reason was that the Straits of Gibraltar, and the British shipping that plied in the Straits and their approaches, were enormously important targets of German espionage. The Germans needed accurate shipping intelligence to pass to their submarines fighting the Battle of the Atlantic, and few readers will need reminding that it was in the submarine division of the war at sea that Germany came nearest to real victory.

There were further reasons why the Iberian peninsula was a major arena of Second World War espionage battles; chiefly, that Spain was a neutral friendly to Germany, while Portugal was a neutral friendly to Britain. And the jurisdiction of the Iberian subsection of Section V did not end with the peninsula, because agents were dispatched at least as far as Mozambique in Portuguese East Africa and Freetown in West Africa, to deal with German shipping spies. The Iberian sub-section, then, was important; but it is reported that the arrival of Philby was awaited with great expectation.

Section V inhabited a neighbouring pair of country houses near St. Albans, named Prae Wood and Glenalmond. The buildings were of the kind which might easily have been made over into a private school. The head of Section V was Major Felix Cowgill,[1] an ex-Indian Policeman, who had succeeded Valentine Vivian, his fellow "Indian," not long before the war. Vivian was now Vice-Chief of the Secret Service (VCSS) while his old rival Dansey was Deputy Chief of the Secret Service (DCSS). The security traditions of the SIS led to a belief that it was bad practice to entrust information to MI 5: it was also felt that it was necessary to be extremely careful of the offensive-espionage side of his own service. This was

---

[1] Later Lt. Col. Cowgill.

no doubt good security policy, but it exaggerated the tendency, present in every organisation, for the right hand to be in the dark about what the left hand might be doing. On one occasion, the offensive side of the SIS sent a group of six agents into the field in Spain, and when nothing was heard from them after three weeks, became somewhat alarmed. They were about to send another agent to investigate, when they discovered that Section V had been aware for some time that the men had been captured. The British counter-espionage man in the area had intercepted a German message recording the capture of the British spies, but the philosophy of security made it impossible to pass the information on.

The problem, not an easy one to solve, was to unite into a cohesive organisation two very disparate groups of people. On the one hand were the tight-lipped, close-cropped, middle-aged men from the Army, Navy and Indian Police who had run the peacetime service. On the other hand were the rather younger academics, writers and professional men who were being drafted in and encouraged by Colonel Vivian. This was the section in which Graham Greene and Malcolm Muggeridge served —and with which Hugh Trevor-Roper was briefly connected—together with less well-known figures who still had very little in common with the "Indians," such as Richard Comyns-Carr, later a financial journalist, Rodney Dennys, later Somerset Herald at the College of Arms, and Roland Adams, later a QC. The irreverence and loquaciousness of some of the recruits horrified the old guard, and produced a reaction in them which turned their natural caution and security into an extreme secretiveness on most matters they handled. The important Iberian sub-section, which was more or less the heart of Section V, had its problems.

The situation was an awkward one for the SIS, which could scarcely afford more failure in the wake of the Section D debacle, and the crippling of the offensive networks in Europe resulting from Venlo and the German's successes in the Netherlands. In the early part of 1941 Lord Swinton, the butcher of MI 5, began to make some private inquiries about the SIS which much alarmed its leadership. The SIS did not come, formally, within the brief of the National Security Executive. But there could be little doubt that obvious disorganisation in the counter-espionage section would lead to real trouble.[2]

The anxiety of the SIS to discover a saviour is the background against which the mystery of Philby's recruitment must be considered. And it is something of a mystery, for there can be scarcely any doubt that a reasonably determined examination of his past would have revealed the depth and seriousness of the Communist commitment in his Viennese period. (Apart from anything else, his Communist first wife, Litzi, was still in Britain.) The first question is: did the SIS know about his past, and ignore it, or did they simply not know?

A point which should be made immediately is that there would obviously have been a case for excluding Philby from SIS work in 1941—because of his ostensible history of pro-Germanism and pro-Fascism. This, far from needing to be uncovered by determined search, was obvious and inescapable, for Philby had gone to some trouble to make it so. He had been attacked by the Spanish Republicans for writing "Fascist propaganda." He had worn, while with the British Army fighting the Germans, a medal given him by Franco. Was this a suitable man to entrust with the secrets of British counter-espionage?

It must be said that such leniency towards the Right was far more characteristic of the SIS leadership than any leniency towards the Left. Indeed a senior officer of the SIS of that time, who was subsequently involved in the investigation of Philby after the flight of Burgess and Maclean, has told us: "It is simply inconceivable that Kim would have been allowed in if anything like Communism had been known against him." Another man who joined the SIS at this time as a wartime recruit has told us that "of all anti-Communists, none were more dedicated then ex-Indian policemen like Colonel Vivian and Major Cowgill."

[2] The amount of information the Germans had obtained about the SIS is demonstrated by an incident in neutral Istanbul during the war. The SIS had a symbol system for foreign countries, in which Germany was "Twelve-land." One night some SIS men from the British Embassy dined in a restaurant which also contained a party of Germans. Towards midnight the Germans, very drunk, began singing: "Zwoelf-land, zwoelf-land über Alles!"

Unless the British Government were to so alter its policy on disclosure of secret service archives as to produce Philby's personnel-file (which must be a remarkable document) it is scarcely possible to be quite sure what happened. But of course, the official "trace" system which checked the backgrounds of recruits to secret work might well have missed Philby's Communist links. The system was operated by MI 5, and that department, as we have shown, had until recently been in a state of confusion. Also, MI 5 dealt exclusively with events occurring in Britain: indeed, they were jealously prohibited by the SIS from working on foreign soil, and so their knowledge of Viennese Communism in the early thirties was presumably non-existent.

MI 5 must have known something about Communist organisation in Cambridge during the thirties. But that does not mean they would have known anything about Philby, because he went down in 1933, which is generally recognised as the year in which the University Left finally metamorphosed from a small network of private commitments to an obviously noticeable political movement. And by the time Philby returned to Britain in 1934 he already had committed himself to underground work.

It may be that the failure on the part of the MI 5 "trace" system to produce any left-wing evidence against Philby would not have been very relevant. Firstly, it is not certain that a senior SIS man in 1941 would have turned away a much-desired recruit merely because the much-distrusted MI 5 reported adversely on him. And indeed, the "trace" system at the time made some ludicrous errors: we have been told of a case in which the conservative academic, Michael Oakeshott[3] was "traced" as a left-winger due to an absurd misreading of the title of a Cambridge undergraduate society of just the kind described in the previous chapter.

The real tests against Philby would have been social and personal, and these he passed with ease. He had been to an ancient public school, Westminster, to which his father had also been. He had been to a very good college at Cambridge—Trinity—to which his father had also been. He was a member of a most respectable, if slightly intellectual, club, the Athenaeum. Again, his father be-

[3] Professor of Political Science, London School of Economics.

longed to the Athenaeum. He was unmistakably a gentleman, as Franco's officers had noted four years before in Spain. The fact that he had been a journalist might have raised a few hackles—except that he had worked for *The Times*, which was regarded as a special case. (Even when the young Claud Cockburn was being criticised for joining *The Times*, his family's friends could not say anything stronger than that *The Times* was tantamount to going into journalism.)

In the social context of the time, the institutional labels alone would have been sufficient to virtually guarantee the quality of the man within. But in addition, two SIS executives were acquainted with Philby's family: and the important one, of course, was Valentine Vivian, then fifty-five, who had known St. John Philby when St. John was in the Indian Civil Service and Vivian was in the Indian Police. Several people remember the enthusiasm with which Vivian announced: "I've got a bright young man for us—Philby, the *Times* war correspondent. Used to know his father in the old days."

Vivian's faith was that Philby could rescue Section V by bridging the gap between the "Indians" and the intellectuals. It was a faith which was brilliantly justified: and this no doubt accounts in great part for Vivian's subsequent powerful patronage of Philby within the Service. His excitement about his new recruit seems uncannily like that of the fictional *sahib* Lurgan in the novel *Kim*—the taciturn intelligence officer who promotes the talented youth into a romantic conception of espionage. *"Even Lurgan's impassive face changed. He considered the years to come, when Kim would have been entered and made to the Great Game that never ceases day and night. . . . He foresaw honour and credit in the mouths of the chosen few, coming to him from his pupil."* And indeed, there was honour and credit, until the dreadful nature of Kim Philby's true allegiance became plain.

Philby's other connection was with David Footman, the head of Section I[4] of the SIS, which distributed political intelligence to the Foreign Office. Footman was unusual among the SIS hierarchy in that he was a considerable scholar, a veteran of the Levant Consular Service who

[4] The Sections were I (Political); II (Military); III (Naval); IV (Air) and V (Counter-espionage).

had written several books before the war about the Soviet
Union and the Middle East. He had known St. John since
the twenties, when they met at a seminar on Middle Eastern affairs, but he knew the son immediately through Guy
Burgess. Burgess had made Footman's acquaintance during the middle thirties—and although Footman, later a
Fellow of St. Antony's, Oxford, declines to discuss this, it
seems not unlikely that it was Footman's Section I to
which Guy was peddling items of intelligence before he
entered Section D.

Burgess introduced Philby to Footman just after Philby's return from Spain: Burgess, the BBC man, had just
been interviewing Philby, the *Times* man, on the radio.
(It would have shattered most of the listeners on that day
in 1939 to know that both men were dedicated undercover agents of the Soviet Union.) Might Footman have
guessed what Guy and Kim really were? He was one of
the few people in the SIS, perhaps, who was equipped to
do so, for he was an expert on Russia.

Remarkably enough, there was a means at hand within
the Service by which Philby's European Communist past
might have been discovered. It so happened that just before Philby joined Section V, another of Vivian's intellectual recruits arrived who had been a school friend of
Philby's at Westminster. This man's name we give as
"Ian" because of official claims that to give his full name,
in view of later aspects of his career unconnected with the
Philby affair, would be against the national interest. "Ian"
went to Christ Church, Oxford, when Philby went to
Trinity, Cambridge. But they maintained their friendship,
and travelled together during the vacations in Central
Europe and the Balkans. "Ian," it seems, rather hero-
worshipped Kim, and talked a good deal about him at
Christ Church. One of the things he said about Philby
was that he was a Communist.

By another remarkable chance, there was an SIS officer already there who had been at Oxford with "Ian." He
remembered "Ian's" talk well enough to look forward
with some eagerness to meeting at last the tough, glamorous Kim Philby "Ian" had described. When he did so, it
did not occur to him that he was meeting any but a recently active Communist, even if he was now a "burnt-
out case."

Had all the connections been made, had the available

leads been followed up, Philby's career as a Soviet penetration-agent would have been drastically shortened. But there are reasons why the connections were not made—the first having been already set out, which is that the social attitudes of the older SIS men were such that they would probably have thought it absurd, a waste of time, to closely scrutinise a recruit with such perfect credentials as Philby's. In the abstract, no doubt, men like Footman or Vivian would acknowledge that such a man *could* be a ruthless Communist, but ten years before the flight of Burgess and Maclean to Russia it seems doubtful that the idea could mean much to them in concrete terms.

Younger men, like "Ian" and his Oxford contemporary, ignored the clues for a somewhat different reason. This was because they regarded Communists merely as the most radical opponents of Fascism. Many of their friends had been Communists a few years before the war, especially at the height of the Spanish crisis. But the conviction, in most cases, had not bitten anything like as deep as Philby's, and that was not surprising. As we have tried to show, his background was deeply unusual. (Apart from any other consideration, how many young Englishmen had seen anything like the Right slaughtering the unresisting Left in the streets of Vienna?)

Many young men abandoned or modified their Communism after the Nazi-Soviet Pact of 1939: so many, in fact, that a mistaken assumption arose that there was nobody left maintaining any serious commitment to the Soviet Union. Once Russia was in the war, therefore, the general anxiety of young, politically-aware Englishmen was to eliminate the frequently lunatic anti-Communism of their elders in order that attention might be concentrated on the fight against Fascism. Certainly the elders of the SIS would have been seen by their younger aides as men all too prone to lunatic anti-Communism, and the last thing any of Kim's contemporaries would have done would have been to draw attention to Kim's sinister history.

It is therefore unrealistic to blame the SIS for admitting Philby to the citadel in 1941. The real accusation against the Service is that three years later, in 1944, he was appointed to run a newly-created section designed to operate against the Soviet Union—that, by anyone's standards, was a grotesque mistake to make. But by then, Philby had long got past the dangerous corner, and was firmly entrenched in the administration of the Service and the affections of his colleagues.

The prime reason for his rise was his brilliance at doing the thing Vivian recruited him for—bringing together the warring elements in Section V. The intellectuals welcomed him as a refreshing breath of oxygen. ("The first able man to get a powerful job.") And just as important, he avoided refrigerating the climate for the Indians. The great thing was that he was able to handle the intellectuals without himself displaying any of the attributes of an intellectual which the clubmen and ex-policemen found so distasteful. He did not talk about incomprehensible abstract ideas, make incomprehensible jokes, or humiliate people by referring to works of literature. He was not irreverent.

It does not seem to have occurred to anyone that Philby, intelligent, patient, industrious and even-tempered (his strongest reprimand was "I say, you shouldn't really have done that") was, literally, too good to be true. Nobody asked *why* Philby worked so hard, and went so far to be pleasant to everybody. The most general reaction was simply to idolise him, and those who did not actually idolise him relied on him. Among those who relied on him was Major Cowgill, with whom Philby spent numerous weekends discussing policy while other officers were relaxing. There is every reason to think that until Philby was strong enough to intrigue against Cowgill, Cowgill imagined Philby to be his friend—one of the few men in the organisation who, like Cowgill himself, lived for the work.

The work in which Section V was then engaged, foreign counter-espionage by means of agents, is the most complex and mysterious extension of the entire business. Counter-espionage of the type practised by MI 5 consists primarily of watching communications, checking for leaks, analysing the histories of people who hold vital information. But working directly against the enemy spy networks themselves involves the most esoteric of variations upon ordinary human deceit. A case in point is the work Muggeridge was sent to do in Portuguese East Africa as an agent of Philby's Iberian sub-section. There was, it seems, a particularly good German agent in the port of Mozambique, who was believed to be feeding useful information about British shipping to the Abwehr. Muggeridge's brief was to destroy this agent's credit with the Abwehr by feeding him false information.

Getting into contact with the man would have been reasonably easy: this would involve working out who his possible informants could be among the port workers, and paying them a little money. (He already would be paying them for pieces of information.) Going on from there, the technique would be to pass information to the German via his own sub-agents.

But in order to "hook" him it would be necessary to pass him, at first, perfectly sound, true information. Indeed, if one sent him anything else, he would obviously reject it, and perhaps break off contact. But the weakness of an agent's position is that he cannot reject real information, even if it comes fairly obviously from an agent on the other side. He must drink from the poisoned chalice. He cannot divine, at second and third remove, the motives of the man from whom the information comes: the man may be a brilliant counter-espionage agent, or he may be a perfectly genuine traitor. The spy must accept what he is given.

On the other hand, the position of the counter-espionage agent at this time is also curious and exposed. He is supplying real information to the enemy—some of which may cause the deaths of his own compatriots. In the most extreme forms of the game, he may be so exposed that other agencies of his own government may shoot him out of hand if they catch him, for his actions may be quite indistinguishable from those of a traitor. However, his superiors in turn are in one way as exposed as he is himself, for once they have granted him permission to pass information to the enemy for counter-espionage purposes, they must protect him to the last against accusations of treachery. It is an obvious point that in the final analysis a spy has no protection but the faith of his friends, who must believe that no matter how far he has gone with the enemy, he remains in the end loyal. In these situations, the relationships of espionage services with their enemies are even more morally hazardous than the relationships detectives have with the criminal underworld—in which the best detectives are often those who are nearest to the criminals themselves.

It is easy to see that operations of this kind can swiftly get altogether out of control. A counter-espionage department using agents can maintain itself only by the most efficient administration at the centre, in which every case is followed in minute and accurate detail. Only then can accurate judgements be made of such a delicate sort as the selection of the moment at which an enemy agent has become so dependent that if he is fed "poisoned" information he will be forced to go on accepting it until he is destroyed. Philby was a superb counter-espionage administrator: he combined a meticulous grasp of detail with a degree of flair. He handled the paper-work which is, unromantically, so vital to espionage, with ease. The clarity of his mind was much admired: this admiration was based on his ability to write out a report in one process, without a draft.

Whether Philby did any more than improve the organisational functional capacity of the Iberian sub-section, and its capacity in general, is hard to say. Under him, the Iberian operations certainly gave an impression of reasonable efficiency, and the bizarre incidents inseparable from espionage and counter-espionage were held to a minimum. (There is a story of earlier Iberian days which sounds very much like the origins of *Our Man in Havana*. The SIS men in Tangier wanted to keep an eye on German submarine movements from Barcelona, and so they hired a Spanish marquis who had advertised himself as a suitable agent, furnished him with money, and sent him to the town for a month. The marquis, a man of taste, established himself at an excellent hotel, and, being a homosexual, amused himself copiously with the local boyhood. On the day before the deadline after a number of cables of reminder, he suddenly produced a fat wad of information about submarine sightings in the most circumstantial detail. The SIS dispatched this with great excitement to Naval Intelligence in Britain, where sadly it was found to correspond with no single item of information already known, and to include quantities of U-boats whose numbers were plainly fictional.)

Even with all the operational files of Section V available, it might be hard to judge with accuracy how effective its work was during the war. Counter-espionage is in its nature a negative thing. But the Germans did *not* win the submarine battle against Britain's shipping, and had they been able to pass better intelligence to the U-boat wolf-packs they might have come closer to victory. For Philby, what mattered was that the work prepared the way for his most remarkable coup.

Kim Philby

Guy Burgess

Donald Maclean

Anthony Blunt

The honorable schoolboys

Litzi Friedman on her honeymoon with Karl Friedman.
She was later to become Philby's first wife.

Philby's second wife, Aileen. (1955)

Kim Philby holds a press conference at his mother's house
in London regarding missing colleagues Burgess and Maclean.
(AP photo, November 8, 1955)

Opposite: Eleanor, Philby's third wife.

Kim Philby, shown here in Red Square in a photo
taken by his son John. (1967)

Opposite, above: Kim Philby with Melinda Maclean in the
countryside outside Moscow. (By John Philby)

Opposite, below: Kim Philby with wife Nina in 1971. (By John Philby)

Kim Philby in Moscow, 1967.

Guy Burgess

Mr. and Mrs. Donald Maclean
at the funeral of Guy Burgess
in Moscow.
(By Peter Keen, Camera Press)

Anthony Blunt, the Fourth Man.

The masters of deceit

EXPLOITATION

11. The New Enemy

A ruling class which is on the run, as ours is, is capable of every fatuity. It makes the wrong decisions, chooses the wrong people, and is unable to recognise its enemies—if it does not actually prefer them to its friends.

—MALCOLM MUGGERIDGE, *Tread Softly for You Tread on My Jokes*

Life at Prae Wood was probably as pleasant as the conditions of wartime England would allow. On summer evenings, the staff of Section V used to play pick-up cricket games on the broad lawns belonging to the house; and there was time for some enjoyable pub-crawling in the pleasant countryside.

Curiously, in view of his lifetime fascination with cricket (today, in Moscow, he keeps up with the game via the airmail *Times*) Philby did not play. He usually hurried off to the house near St. Albans where he had established his new wife. This was a strikingly pretty, dark-haired girl named Aileen Furse, who had spent occasional nights with Kim at Bentinck Street. She came of a prosperous and well-established West Country family—"bristling"—as one friend put it, "with bishops and admirals." Josephine, the first of their five children, was born in 1942, and Philby, if not uxorious, was obviously much moved and delighted by the advent of the children. Presumably he was aware—even if dimly—that his relationship with them in adult life would be complex, and perhaps unhappy.

During the next few years, at Prae Wood and in London, Philby was cautious about mixing socially with his colleagues. For instance, in the forties the SIS maintained a country house (perhaps it still does so) complete with swimming-pool and tennis-courts, in which the London-based staff could relax and expand without the risk of indiscretion. Philby was rarely a member of the weekending parties. Despite this, he was much liked—indeed, he was popular to a degree which cannot be entirely ex-

146

plained simply by the fact that he had done a great deal
to get the Section working properly. It is clear from the
recollections of the people who worked with him that he
possessed a remarkable charm which, in the slightly
claustrophobic conditions of a secret-service office, came
fully into its own.

Charm is a difficult quality to analyse. But in Philby's
case it appears to have derived from a certain sense of
remoteness, of disengagement, which he carried with him.
At the simplest level some people, especially women, were
moved to sympathy by his stammer, which was frequently
appalling. (He was also good-looking in a conventional,
blue-eyed English way.) If he was somewhat inarticulate,
that was of course no offence to the blunt and military
element of the SIS—quite the reverse. Yet he did not
strike his more sophisticated colleagues as silent and un-
congenial, for where the soldiers and policemen saw only
a proper reserve, these people detected what they took to
be a distant and economical irony.

There were, of course, good reasons for Philby to be
careful about the amount of time spent socially with his
colleagues. He must sometimes have felt the strain of
constantly dissembling his political views and real feelings, of suppressing even the bitter jokes that other people
could make about the crusted reactionaries who dominated so many organisations in wartime Britain. Clearly,
it would have been dangerous to pretend to some specific
non-Communist political creed: sooner or later, he would
have been found out, or at least incurred distrust. Instead,
he said as little as possible, and allowed people to project
their own ideas onto him.

In later years, people who thought they had known him
well looked back and realised that he had allowed them
to *assume* many of the things they thought they knew
about him. But even at that time, some people did notice
the odd remoteness. "It was rather as though his personality was wrapped up in a very well-packed eiderdown,"
one man told us. Hugh Trevor-Roper describes a slight
sense of frustration in speaking with Philby—as though
somehow his mind did not really engage with one's own
mind. "One had the sensation of a tough, flexible and
active set of defences constantly at work, and which
formed a barrier around him." However, no one had any
reason to think that there was anything dangerous behind

the reserve: Malcolm Muggeridge claims to have detected "a quality of suppressed violence," but it did not occur to him that this quality, if it did exist—and no one ever saw it burst out—had any political significance. Another man, one of Philby's subordinates, sometimes felt a slight unease in his company. But this man could not formalise this beyond saying that somehow Philby gave the impression of "a sensitive man trying to make himself out to be tough." Even today, this acquaintance cannot penetrate further into the mystery.

The occasions when Philby did mix with his colleagues were drinking occasions: he was by now a voracious and rather indiscriminate drinker. (He was known, in Prae Wood days, for throwing down the most appalling mixtures of alcohol.) Not infrequently, he drank with the plain intention of getting speechless drunk. He obviously possessed one of those fortunate constitutions which resist the ravages of alcohol extremely well, and even twenty years later in Beirut he remained more or less unscathed. But far more important than the physical resistance was the way in which his personality resisted the impact of alcohol. Most people's tongues are loosened to some extent by drinking. Donald Mclean, to take a case in point, could be almost pathetically unmanned by drink, and a few years later was telling people in Soho clubs that he was a Soviet agent. (Nemesis might have overtaken him sooner but for the fact that most of his confessors were too drunk themselves to understand what he was confessing to.) Philby, however, found that no matter how drunk he got, he did not become indiscreet, and he could relieve his inner tensions in this way without fear of self-betrayal. This is so extraordinary a facility to most people that it probably stood in his favour when he eventually came under suspicion. Most of those who knew him know that he was an habitually heavy drinker, who often and happily surrendered to the obvious effects of drinking. Surely so reckless a drinker could not be hiding a great secret?

Such resistance is, of course, remarkable—but not in retrospect inexplicable. After all, by this mid-war period, when he was moving into his thirties, Philby had been "underground" for the best part of a decade. He had had plenty of time to erect, consciously a strong set of inhibitions, and to temper them under conditions of some danger and unpleasantness in the Spanish war. And he was, clearly, erecting these conscious inhibitions on a strong layer of subconscious inhibition which must have dated back to his early childhood. His stammer is evidence of this, and without trying to apply long-range psychoanalysis to Philby, it is worth recounting what is known, clinically, about the phenomenon of stammering.

It is seen as a consequence of suppression of childish rage in the early years of life: rage against frequent frustration, usually in the parental relationship. In adult life, it is manifested as a mechanical inhibition against spontaneous intercourse at an individual level, and the inhibition is present because such spontaneous intercourse may spark off a burst of rage, which must not be let out. The stammerer is, literally, afraid of what he might say. And so it was no doubt extremely acute of Malcom Muggeridge to notice a quality of "suppressed violence" in Philby when he knew him.

This does not mean, of course, that stammerers are, underneath, any more violent than anybody else. They have merely acquired an inhibition against spontaneous expression because it *may* be violent. Significantly, they do not normally suffer from their inhibition when making a set speech: that is, when they have worked out in advance what they have to say and are making a public performance rather than trying to communicate at an individual level. And Philby conformed to this pattern, in that he had been quite able to make election speeches at Cambridge in 1931. And in 1955, when he held a Press conference to deny that he was the "third man" in the Burgess-Maclean affair in 1951, he managed to speak without a stammer. (We have played the soundtrack of the television newsreel, and Philby's voice scarcely flickers once.)

The combination of conscious and unconscious inhibition may have placed the inner secrets of his personality beyond the reach of alcoholic dissolution. Just possibly, though, he might have been cracked open by another force: that is, intellectual pressure. Again, Trevor-Roper has an interesting story, of a conversation with Philby in which there was for once a sense of intellectual engagement. He and Philby were chatting one day in a pub about the comparative analytical merits of various historians. It was perhaps rash, and certainly uncharacteristic, of Philby to pit his modest history degree against the future Regius Professor of Modern History at Oxford. As the two young men talked, the conversation flared in a sudden and unpredictable manner, which seemed to provoke Philby. He blurted out: "Of course, every attempt at historical analysis is nothing once you compare it to Marx's *Eighteenth Brumaire!*"

Trevor-Roper had a sharp, momentary impression that he was talking to Philby on a serious level, and that there were no defences between them. But it was very brief. Philby, as though embarrassed at his own uncharacteristic vehemence, changed the subject and returned to his normal pose of amiable, disengaged worldliness.

One might easily assign, in retrospect, too much intrinsic importance to this conversational incident. But it makes an interesting general point: suppose Philby had been forced to spend more time than he did in first-class intellectual company? Almost the only time in his career when he did have to was in this two-and-a-half year period at Section V. From 1944 onwards, when he went to higher things, he no longer had to work with the bright young amateurs. He was then in the undemanding company of the unreconstructed upper echelons of the SIS, few of whom could have mounted any very elaborate conversation on modern history or politics. (Muggeridge mentions that at the end of the war, it was felt necessary to educate SIS people in the mysteries of Marxism, and to this end an article on the subject was clipped from *The Spectator* and circulated until it disintegrated.) Apart from Guy Burgess, Philby's friends were nearly all politically right-wing. (We know nothing about the political stance of the admiring former school-friend "Ian.") For instance, at this time in Section V, he founded a life-long friendship with the late Richard Brooman-White, a distinctly High Tory who later, as MP for Rutherglen, used his political influence on Philby's behalf.

There is also an interesting case from this period of Philby's political alignment showing up, faintly, in his work—the trace being minimised by Philby's careful refusal to be drawn into discussion about what he had done. During the summer of 1943, a brilliant "temporary" SIS analyst specialising on Germany produced a paper arguing, from straws of evidence but nevertheless persuasively, that there was a serious split in Germany between the

Nazi Party and the Army High Command, which was beginning to lose faith in Hitler and the war. Further, this
paper said, the Abwehr shared especially strongly in this
disillusion. The paper provided a background against
which peace feelers from the Abwehr—attempting to discover an accommodation for Germany short of uncondi-
tional surrender—might be taken seriously rather than as
a ruse. It was generally thought to be a brilliant paper,
opening up exciting possibilities about the way the war
might be going. Indeed, this is the sort of feat which secret services are really for. And of course the paper was
magnificently prophetic. The disintegration it detected became manifest a year later in the Officers' Plot against
Hitler's life, and Otto John's arrival in Lisbon as personal
emissary of Admiral Canaris of the Abwehr.

Naturally, there was an immediate suggestion that this
paper should be circulated to all SIS departments. But by
this time Philby was sufficiently important in the SIS hierarchy for his *imprimatur* to be necessary before a paper
could go into general circulation.

Resolutely, and without offering any explanation,
Philby blocked the circulation of this paper.

Looking back, of course, one sees his reasons at once.
The nightmare of his Soviet masters was the same as it
had been when Guy Burgess was feeding them information about the diplomatic manoeuvrings of the appeasers
in the latter thirties: the fear that the Western powers
might resolve their differences with the Axis and turn their
united might against the Soviet Union.

The intention of most anti-Nazis in Germany, after all,
was not to stop the war against Russia. Rather, they
wanted to eliminate Hitler, make peace with the West,
and complete the invasion of the Soviet Union in which
they stood on the brink of success.

Philby's job as a Soviet agent in Britain was, in this
context, blindingly clear: to resist, in every way, the
growth of a feeling in Britain that there was any practical
way of dealing with Germany—short of destruction.

To do this, he would clearly take some risk of exposure, although he was clever enough to minimise it by refusing to discuss his reasons for the suppression of the
prophetic paper. He merely said that it was "speculative"
—had he tried to counter it with reasoned arguments, he
might easily have betrayed his true feelings, and he would

certainly have enlarged the whole incident in people's memories, with possible dangers to himself accruing in later days. Philby continued this pattern of resistance to Abwehr peace-feelers: and when in 1944 Otto John finally did defect to the British Philby did his best to minimise John's importance.

During the winter of 1943–44, Section V moved back into London, to a house in Ryder Street between Pall Mall and Piccadilly. Many of the staff were sorry to leave their country mansion with its pleasing grounds, but not Philby. "I'll just be glad to get away from all this damn green," he said. He said this to one of the American officers who were being attached to the SIS in increasing numbers: the extraordinarily intimate association between the two major Western intelligence organisations was beginning and Philby was in on the ground floor. Some of the Americans came from the Federal Bureau of Investigation, this being the American organisation responsible for counter-espionage. (One of them, as it happened, was Melvin Purvis, the man who killed John Dillinger.) But the larger contingent came from the Office of Strategic Services, Roosevelt's newly-set-up offensive secret service, and the American opposite number of the SIS.

In this relationship the OSS men regarded themselves very much as the junior partners. They had come to learn from the British, and in fact they modelled themselves so closely on the British, and formed so close a relationship with them, that for many purposes the OSS and the SIS could be regarded as the same service. This was a relationship which was, of course, of crucial importance to Philby and his Russian masters, for it gave him access to the American secret world almost as freely as to the British.

The wartime relationship was to survive, to Philby's great profit, into the peace and the Cold War. For although the OSS was closed down in 1946, the Central Intelligence Agency which succeeded it in 1947 was essentially a re-creation of the older body, and leant on the British SIS as heavily as its predecessor had done.

The mistake the Americans made in taking the penetrated SIS as an admirable and brilliant secret service was to cost them heavily in the years ahead. But there were several understandable reasons for the mistake, of which the first and most obvious was that the United States, the nation which liked to talk about "open covenants openly arrived at," did not have any experience of secret service work of the kind possessed by the British—and indeed by most European nations. The SIS itself might be only thirty years old as a department, but it was the heir to a tradition. And the OSS, anyway, was only eighteen months old.

This feeling of respect for people who had been in the business longer was enhanced by the fact that many of the early OSS administrators, such as General "Wild Bill" Donovan, were strongly Anglophile. They had many friends in Britain, and in the secret world: they were impressed by the ceremonies of clubland and the mysterious shorthand of upper-class speech. The British seemed so much better-equipped for the clandestine and the secret than the Americans. And on top of this the British had just disclosed a shattering and remarkable intelligence success which appeared to the Americans as the latest and most amazing coup of the silent empire ruled by the man named "C."

This achievement was the breaking of the machine-codes used by the German Navy, and which were crucial to the progress of the submarine war in the Atlantic. (The Americans, now, were also involved in the Battle of the Atlantic.) Although many of the details of this operation remain, even today, shrouded in secrecy, there can be no doubt that it was a truly war-winning stroke of intelligence—altogether more important to the shipping war than the counter-espionage with which Philby himself was involved. The Americans, who had just been told about it, were quite right to regard it as a stunning exhibition of British originality and application. They were wrong, however, to focus their almost awed respect upon the SIS hierarchy, whose connection with the operation, although sufficient to attract much of the credit at the time, was in reality little short of fortuitous.

The British tradition of cryptographic skill extends back at least to the First World War. In those days, it was a Naval monopoly, suitably enough because the Navy clearly had a direct functional interest in telegraphy. The operation fell under the control of a remarkable Director of Naval Intelligence, Admiral Sir Reginald (Blinker) Hall, and was responsible for one remarkable coup which traces back intriguingly to St. John Philby's old opponent in the Middle East, Wilhelm Wassmuss. This was the affair of the "Zimmerman Telegram" in February 1917. This story is too well-known to be recounted in detail: essentially the Navy code-breaking team (known as "Room 40" from the number of their room in the Admiralty) intercepted and decoded a radio telegram from the German Foreign Secretary, Arthur Zimmerman, which offered Mexico the return of its lost territories, Texas, Arizona and New Mexico in return for Mexican help against America in the event of America entering the war. Not unnaturally, when the British published the decoded telegram, it merely helped to precipitate American entry into the war.

The British were able to read the Zimmerman telegram because they had captured the book of the relevant code (No. 13040, the German diplomatic code) from Wassmuss[1] in 1915, during the Wassmuss's attempts, mentioned in Chapter 3, to promote a Holy War against the British. Hounded by the British, allegedly including St. John Philby, Wassmuss only escaped by leaving his baggage behind—which included a book of code 13040. Presumably Wassmuss never informed the Germans of his loss, and they continued to use the code.

"Blinker" Hall, originally a ruthless fighting sailor, was one of the most effective intelligence chiefs Britain ever produced. But he was also very ambitious, and he tried to extend the tentacles of his Naval Intelligence empire into the Special Branch of Scotland Yard (the detective body working for MI 5), the War Department, and MI 1c, as the SIS was called in his time. The Foreign Office were naturally alarmed at the spectacle of his spreading power, and this seems to have been the rationale of their struggle, successful in 1923, to bring secret intelligence work firmly under Foreign Office control. At the beginning of the Second World War the chief of the SIS was responsible, as he is today, to the Prime Minister—but via the Permanent Under-Secretary at the Foreign Office and the Foreign Secretary. And in the Second World War, Menzies also had formal control of the British code-breaking operation, carried out extremely secretly at the Government Code and Cypher School in Bletchley.

[1] Barbara W. Tuchman, *The Zimmerman Telegram*. Constable.

But for most practical purposes, GCCS was a separate enterprise. During the first part of the war, when the vital breakthrough was made, it was run by an RNVR veteran of the 1914–18 Room 40. This was Commander Alastair Denniston, aided by an ex-RN navigator, Commander Eddie Hastings. The naval flavour of the personnel involved was, however, only part of it: the vital clues upon which the code-breaking depended were supplied by the regular Navy. The key to the problem, naturally, was the German coding device, known suitably as the "Enigma" machine. One was carried in every U-boat—with instructions that it must be destroyed on the appearance of any risk of capture. (The Enigma was also used, with modifications, in most other German codes.) During 1941, the British obtained at least two Enigma machines: one during a Marine Commando raid on the Lofoten Islands in mid-March, and the other on May 9 when the U-110 was captured. The GCCS cryptographers constructed a working model of the German codes by the end of 1941, and it appears that by the end of 1942 the German naval code at least was thoroughly exposed. Eventually the British code-breaking success seems to have covered most of the German machine-codes, and the information from the intercepts—often of crucial importance—is referred to from time to time in Churchill's writings as "Most Secret Sources."

As few people as possible, of course, were told about the origins of the remarkable intercept information which Menzies took, never less than twice daily, to Churchill. It was hardly a case where the niceties of departmental credit could be taken too seriously, for the coup would have become worthless had the Germans even suspected it.[2] The Americans seem to have been filled in on the full extent of the British success some time in late 1942 or early 1943, and they were quite properly not told enough to decide which section of the British "secret world" had really done the job. They naturally assumed that the ami-

[2] According to the American cryptographer and writer Ladislas Farago, the British even went to the length of sending out aircraft to pretend to look for targets, like the *Bismarck,* which had already been located by decoded intercepts.

able clubmen of the SIS were just as brilliant, beneath
their crusty patina, as the legends said they were.

Philby was not one of those people who complained
that the privileged upper echelons of the SIS were getting
away with credit which was not strictly their due. Quite
the reverse: according to a man who saw a good deal of
him at this time, he gave the impression of being "a com-
plaisant passenger in a racketeering upper-class world."
Secretly, of course, the passenger was trying to move
steadily and unobtrusively towards the driver's seat—and
this, rather than revulsion from the delights of nature, was
why Philby was glad to get away from that "damned
green" and back to town. Certainly when he got back he
initiated an intrigue designed to enhance his standing in
the Service. He decided to attack his boss, Felix Cowgill.

Up to this time, Philby's advancement in SIS had been
the almost effortless consequence of social and personal
advantages. Now he decided that the time had come to be
altogether more determined in the pursuit of office. And
he was, of course, wonderfully equipped for the business
of intrigue in bureaucratic corridors. People felt that Kim
was not interested in mere personal ambition and, of
course, they were right. Perhaps the hardest thing for an
ambitious man to dissemble is lust for office, for it shows
in so many tiny details of behaviour. Nobody detected
such telltale signs in Philby. He was dissembling something
altogether less familiar.

Cowgill, we can justifiably suppose, would hardly have
felt any danger from Philby. Kim, after all, was one of his
closest advisers. But Kim, clearly, was merely acting in
accordance with Machiavelli's instruction to make no
move against an enemy until you have the power to destroy him utterly, and until that time to preserve a
friendly appearance towards him.

Philby's power lay, on the one hand, in his grasp on the
affections of the staff, most of whom could remember an
occasion when Philby had preserved them from damage
in one of the frequent and mysterious battles which still
shook the secret world. Graham Greene, for instance,
once contrived to compromise the SIS with the great and
continuing enemy, MI 5, by forgetting to send an SIS man
to appropriate the intelligence role in the Azores after the
British take-over there. In the end, the belated SIS emissary was only able to send his arrival report back to Lon-

don through the courtesy of the MI 5 man, who had been there some time and had established radio communication. Philby, in the resultant row, defended Greene against fierce and serious threats which might well have resulted in dismissal.

On the other hand, Menzies and Vivian found Philby invaluable in their dealings with the other departments of the secret world. In Whitehall committees he defended SIS departmental interests coolly, politely and with reassuring command of detail. Bickham Sweet-Escott, who attended meetings in a similar capacity for Special Operations Executive, told us: "Philby gave the impression always that he was a man of integrity, a man who could be trusted."

Philby's plan of campaign against Cowgill had its elaborate aspects, but it began with the simple move of telling Colonel Vivian, quite untruthfully, that Cowgill was not loyal to him. In the atmosphere of habitual intrigue in which the SIS existed, this false accusation from the admirable Kim was unfairly damaging. Although this was not the immediate cause of his departure, it was not long before the entirely loyal and devoted Cowgill had left. (Happily, Felix Cowgill found a niche shortly afterwards. In 1966, he retired from the task of liaising between the British Army and the local citizenry in München-gladbach, West Germany. On retirement, he was given the rare award of the Golden Ring of München-gladbach.)

The next part of the plan seems to have been a bid by Philby, with the backing of the staff, to take over the directorship of Section V. This depended on "Ian," by now No. 2 in the Iberian sub-section, taking over command of the sub-section, and Graham Greene stepping into "Ian's" place. Greene, however, seems to have rather upset the plan by declining to take the promotion. He did not care for the atmosphere of intrigue that he saw in the affair. So although Philby had certainly gone a long way towards his goal, he still had not attained major office. But presumably by this time, at the start of 1944, he knew well enough that things were going his way. He showed no distress when a glamorous career opportunity *outside* the SIS came to nothing.

This was a chance to go back to journalism in a most prestigious job with *The Times*. It was something most of

Philby's disillusioned colleagues in Section V would have leapt at. The correspondence with *The Times* indicates an enthusiasm to retain Philby's services, on the part of his superiors in the Service, which no doubt still causes occasional painful twitches of memory. It began on January 31 when Ralph Deakin, the Imperial and Foreign News Editor, wrote to Philby inviting him to come to lunch and discuss "important new appointments" at *The Times*, adding that "the tasks to be done are after your own heart." Philby replied from his club, the Athenaeum, that as he was now stationed permanently in London, he would very much like to meet Deakin. They duly lunched at the Reform Club on February 17. A few days later, Deakin wrote to the Foreign Office, addressing himself to Frank Roberts, later Sir Frank and British Ambassador in Moscow and Bonn.

February 23, 1944.

Personal

My dear Roberts,

I wonder if I may have a word with you in the near future in the following matter?

During the early stages of the war *The Times* had as its War Correspondent attached to Lord Gort in France an excellent young man in H. A. R. Philby. Lord Gort became so well disposed to Philby that he took him away from *The Times* (Philby being then about 28 years of age) to do work upon the record of the Expeditionary Force before Dunkirk. Thereafter Philby was moved into an intelligence job, about which, I think, you are well informed. *The Times* is now requested to nominate two War Correspondents for future operations, and it is extremely desirable that we should pick for these formidable tasks the best possible men. As I am sure you know, older men do not last long as war correspondents in these arduous times, and we are anxious to appoint young men who are steady, experienced and wise. I am having to bring a good man back from Burma in the first instance, but we know no one who seems better fitted for one of these two appointments than Philby.

I have talked the matter over with him, but being a very conscientious fellow, he seems diffident in the matter, and he feels that the decision should be taken by those in authority over him. I believe that, although he is on War Office establishment, the decision whether he might be released from his present work to resume his duties with *The Times* rests with the Foreign Office. With Philby's consent, therefore, I write to you to ask whether his release may be considered.

I am, of course, at your disposal should you wish to question me in this matter, which I hope may have your early consideration.

With kind regards,
Ralph Deakin.

This letter, incidentally, tends to confirm the thesis, advanced from memory by our informants, that Philby entered the secret world via Section D. It seems more likely that a Section D man could be on War Office establishment than someone who had entered direct into the main body of the SIS. Roberts, presumably, was one of the Foreign Office officials responsible for liaison with the SIS. (Our information is that around this time Patrick Reilly, later Sir Patrick and British Ambassador in Paris, was the principal Foreign Office Adviser to the SIS.) Roberts replied to Deakin expeditiously:

FOREIGN OFFICE, S.W. I.

Dear Deakin,

1st March, 1944

Thank you for your letter of the 23rd February about Philby.

Philby is not on the Foreign Office establishment and we have no direct say in the question whether or not he could be released from his present job. But his work is well-known to the Foreign Office and is of particular interest to us, and I am afraid that I must tell you that if ever we were consulted about the possibility of his being released, we should be bound to recommend most strongly against his removal from his present job. Please do not think that we do not appreciate the importance of the job to which you would like to appoint him, *but his present work is so important, and he performs it with such exceptional ability* [authors' italics] that I am afraid his departure would be a real loss to us.

Yours sincerely,
F. K. Roberts.

The Foreign Office were speaking for the "invisible men" of the SIS, the people who were determined not to lose Philby. It would, of course, have been difficult to release an important counter-espionage executive to work as a war correspondent where there would be a chance of the Germans capturing him. But it seems likely that the major reason for keeping Philby was the "important" work which he performed with "such exceptional ability." By this time, Philby had been given, or promised, a job in the SIS which more than made up for his failure to supplant Cowgill. This was his job as head of the SIS's new Soviet department. A contemporary colleague remembers that it was "late in 1944" that Philby left Section V's office in Ryder Street and moved to a room in the SIS head office in Broadway, nearly opposite St. James's Park Underground station.

Officially, the buildings were labelled as the Government Communications Bureau: Philby's office was on the seventh floor, just down the corridor from that of his old patron, Colonel Vivian. The Broadway offices were on the whole of the rather seedy civil service kind described by the realist school of espionage novelists, but they had more of the romantic trappings of espionage than either of the places Philby had worked in before. There were pigeons in a loft on the roof, maintained presumably against the possibility of some tremendous electrical failure in the capital. And outside the office on the fourth floor which "C" used there were two lamps, one red and one green. When people had appointments with "C," they waited outside until the red light went off and the green light came on, and then they went in. Security was taken very seriously at Broadway, and on the third floor of the building was a notice-board on which, weekly, a report on internal security was posted. Every member of the staff had to go past this board and note the rather school-masterly "reports" which were entered up on it. They made such complaints as: "Three addressed envelopes were found on a desk on the Fourth Floor last Tuesday"; or, "Secretaries on the Second Floor failed to destroy their waste paper again. This is the *last* warning." Conceivably Philby, as he walked past this notice-board, allowed himself some faint internal laughter.

There is some clash of evidence about the precise brief of the new department which Philby had been brought in to set up. At least one officer, himself connected with the *offensive* side of SIS work, says plainly: "It was certainly an offensive espionage operation. Philby was supposed to be setting up networks in East European countries for operations against the Russians." Another officer, who was connected with the counter-espionage side of SIS, says that when Philby began work in late 1944, he was engaged in counter-espionage—no matter what he did later. The fact that the new department was not, at least physically, part of the Section V set-up at Ryder Street, suggests that it was *not* started as counter-espionage. On the other hand, Philby was a counter-espionage expert, which supports the suggestion that the operation was *not* offensive. What is quite certain is that from the first Philby was exposing every vital detail of the rapidly growing department—by the end of the war he had 100 people working for him at Broadway—to the Russians. But the only outward sign of this was something which appeared to redound to his credit with his superiors: the fact that he always seemed to be working late at night.

One woman who worked at Broadway told us: "Sometimes I'd be back at the office until nine or ten o'clock, and on the way out I'd pass Kim's room. He'd be there sweating over papers. You always had the feeling that Kim was burning the midnight oil. I remember thinking to myself at the time, 'there's a young man who's going to go places.'" The reason why he should work so late is, of course, rather obvious now: even more obvious is the reason why Philby used to repeatedly countermand to his staff the strict SIS internal security rule that each worker should elaborately lock up his or her own desk at night. "Don't worry about that," Philby used to say. "I'll be working late tonight and I'll see to the locking-up." One of the secretaries recalls: "It used to worry me at the time. I didn't like leaving my desk open. But he was so charming I couldn't resist anything he asked."

Philby was clearly working genuinely very hard at this period of his life—for both the Russians and the West. In getting the job he possessed, he had pulled off one of the most remarkable technical feats of betrayal in the whole grubby canon of the espionage business. It must have been deeply satisfying ideologically, and perhaps even more satisfying professionally. The only strictly comparable case is presumably that of Colonel Redl, who before the First World War was simultaneously chief of the Austro-Hungarian counter-espionage system and the most important agent of the Russian (Tsarist) espionage system operating against the Austro-Hungarian empire. If it is true, as seems likely, that Philby had felt the need to emulate St. John Philby in doing something with his life on a large and spectacular scale, then he must have contemplated the approaching clash between the Eastern and Western power-blocs with some eagerness.

What was the rationale behind the setting-up and rapid enlargement of Philby's new section? (There had been, before his arrival, a section dealing nominally with Soviet affairs. But it consisted of one ageing officer.) There can be little doubt what the Russians, acting on Philby's information, must have made of it. Leaving aside for the moment the question of whether this was an espionage or a counter-espionage organisation—assuming that a strict and valid distinction always exists—it would have come to them as further confirmation of all their paranoia about the West. The most devastating point, to them, would have been that the British were beginning to construct their anti-Soviet espionage operation soon after the opening of the Second Front. It seems unlikely that in the three short years since the Anglo-Soviet alliance had been made against Germany, the Russians would have lost their fear and dislike of the British Secret Intelligence Service. (It would not, incidentally, have made any impression on the Russians at this time to point out that the very existence of the agent through whom they knew what the SIS was planning was due to the fact that they had themselves been conducting espionage against Britain at least since 1933. By the infinite regress of national self-justification which is common to all states, they would have defended *their* espionage as a response to aggression.) But there was perhaps a more prosaic, less ideological explanation of the initiative which the SIS took. It does not appear that they had anything else to do.

Although most sources place the *concept* of the new Soviet section *before* D-Day (June 6, 1944), its real expansion in terms of personnel and office space, seems to occur *after* D-Day. And this coincides with the period of marked humiliation when the major intelligence job of the war was taken away from the SIS. This job, naturally, was running the special intelligence operation for the invading armies in Europe: an offensive operation which one would have expected to fall under the control of "C's" department. But it did not. Instead, against what one participant described to us as "bitter" opposition from the SIS, a special intelligence organisation was set up called the Cabinet War Room. This was an extremely successful organisation, and it was controlled, *de facto,* by the star of MI 5, Dick White. It would be very difficult to think of anything which could have outraged the SIS more. Theoretically, an SIS man was joint head of the War Room: but White was the more formidable figure, and the practical effect. The undeniable fact was that MI 5, together with a gaggle of wartime "amateurs," was running perhaps the most exciting foreign-intelligence operation in British history.

No doubt the new energy of the SIS, furiously collecting information on every anti-Communist movement in Eastern Europe and making up long lists of potential agents, may have seemed very alarming in Moscow. But much of the activity which they probably took as evidence of inimical British intentions towards them seems likely in retrospect to have been the product of a humiliated department trying to construct a new and important role for itself. It is the very presence of Philby as director of the new section which argues that it could hardly have represented the most serious intentions of the British administration. Later, no doubt, the British were very serious about their anti-Soviet intelligence operations: but by then Philby was already built into the system. What seems hard to believe is that a calculated, if secret, act of British foreign policy could have been put in the hands of men who could in turn select, in 1944, a man with Philby's political past to undertake operations aimed against the Soviet Union.

There is no comparison with the events in 1941, when Philby was first taken into Section V to fight the Germans. Once again, the question arises of whether the leaders of the SIS simply knew nothing about Philby's past, or whether they knew about it and failed to investigate and take account of it. If they knew anything of it at all, and ignored it, this convicts them of political naiveté of an entirely fantastic order. For whatever might be the definition of an SIS Soviet section when it commenced operations at that time, it would clearly be only a question of time before the operations must become offensive by any definition of the word. (Indeed, as we show subsequently, Philby was to be involved in planning—and, of course, secretly betraying—subversive operations against Communist governments inside two years.) This is not a matter of right or wrong, and the question of who started the Cold War is not for the moment relevant. The simple fact is that a man of even residual Communist sympathies, once placed in Philby's position, would be bound to act in the way he did.

It is hard to believe that the SIS ever conducted any adequate examination of Philby's political history and attitudes. People knew about it, but did not take it seriously. "Ian" continued to be a close friend of Philby's, but he seems not to have bothered to take up the fact with anyone that Kim had been a Communist in Europe before the war. (The other SIS officer who knew about this period was no longer in contact with Philby by 1944, and did not know about the new Soviet section.)

Philby himself does not mention any re-examination by his superiors of his political attitudes. "My name was put forward," he says, "my suitability for the post was explained in flattering detail." Apart from any obvious question of loyalty, no sensible intelligence service would have asked a man with Philby's past—had they known it—to start work against the Soviet Union in 1944. At best, it would have been an unfair request. The only possible answer is that the chiefs of SIS decided that Kim's left-wing period was nothing more than a youthful fling; that is, they were either ignorant of the facts, or they knew the facts and were politically insensitive.

Either way, Philby must have felt that it was all too good to be true: he was, indeed, in a very odd mood when he visited Malcom Muggeridge in liberated Paris (where Muggeridge was stationed for the SIS). The two of them got very drunk, and Philby then insisted on going off to inspect the Soviet Embassy—the citadel in Paris of what was now more or less openly recognised as the "new enemy." Philby marched up and down outside the Embassy, shaking his fist wildly at the silent building. "How are we going to penetrate them?" He then took Muggeridge to see a flat where he had once stayed with his first wife, Litzi, and he told Muggeridge that she had been a Communist. Muggeridge, who was not aware of

Philby's new responsibilities, did not mention the incident to anybody in the SIS.

There has been some attempt, by apologists of the SIS, to pretend that Philby was in some way a wartime undesirable left accidentally behind in a contracted, peacetime SIS. This is, however, absurd. During 1946, he survived a major re-examination of the SIS, designed carefully to eliminate anyone of that description. Numerous officers were re-vetted, and some were asked to leave the Service. Philby was not one of these: he remained an important departmental executive. As the temperature of the Cold War dropped, Philby settled down in remarkable safety to his task of destroying the Western intelligence effort. People who knew him freely mentioned him as a potential Chief of the SIS: they did not know that he had just had an unpleasantly narrow escape from being exposed as the Soviet agent that he really was.

12. The Volkov Incident

"Ah, yes, Volkov. A nasty piece of work."
—KIM PHILBY. Moscow 1967

If there was one officer senior enough in the Russian intelligence hierarchy at the end of the war to know the work and whereabouts of Kim Philby *and* Guy Burgess *and* Donald Maclean, then he must have been an extremely contented man. With the world on the edge of the Cold War it is hard to conceive how any three Soviet agents could have been better placed: Philby at the head of the Soviet section of the SIS, Burgess dining Cabinet ministers and influential back-benchers, and Maclean in Washington at the centre of the Anglo-American atomic energy programme. From a Soviet point of view the outlook was extremely bright. That the Russians were prepared to go to any length to preserve this advantage is illustrated by a chilling incident in Istanbul in 1945.

With the war in Europe over and Japan about to surrender there was an atmosphere of lighthearted optimism which the growing breach with the Soviet Union had failed to dampen. The British embassy in Turkey, down from Ankara for the summer, was enjoying the long, hot days on the Bosphorus.

The pace in the Consulate, a solid stone building in the Beyoglu district, was leisurely and undemanding. Callers were few and boring, so when a short stocky man with a heavy Russian accent walked into the reception room one morning he attracted the enquiry officer's immediate attention. The man, obviously very nervous, demanded an immediate interview with a high-ranking British diplomat whom he asked for by name. (It was later established that the Russian mistakenly thought that the diplomat was the area SIS officer.)

The diplomat was found, the man was ushered into a quiet room and an interpreter summoned. No, the man said, no interpreter was needed. No one could be present at the interview except the British diplomat. When the two men were alone, the man explained the reason for his visit. His name, he said, was Konstantin Volkov. Ostensibly he was a newly appointed Russian consul in Istanbul. Actually, he said, he was the area head of Soviet Intelligence. He had arrived from Russia only five months earlier. In Moscow he had been attached to the NKVD (later the KGB, the Russian Secret Service) in an important position. He had a proposition to make. In return for £27,500 (an odd amount but possibly converted from another sum in roubles) plus a *laissez-passer* to Cyprus, Volkov was prepared to offer certain valuable counter-espionage information. Were the British interested?

The diplomat interviewing Volkov expressed cautious interest. This was not his field but there was a well established Foreign Office procedure for handling a situation like this: keep contact with the man until a specialist could take over. What exactly was for sale? Naturally, said Volkov, he was not prepared to give details until there was a deal. But—and here he handed over a batch of handwritten notes and sketches—this was an outline of what he had to sell. The British official read rapidly and with mounting excitement through the headings: addresses and descriptions of NKVD buildings in Moscow with details of burglar-alarm systems, key impressions and guard schedules; numbers of all NKVD cars; a list of

Soviet agents in Turkey together with their means of communication; and finally, almost as a throwaway, "names of Russian agents operating in Government departments in London." It was obvious that Volkov, before his appointment to Istanbul, had spent some time in Moscow acquiring material which could take him into the West with a golden one-way ticket.

It could, also, of course, be a one-way ticket to Siberia. For Volkov said that among the Soviet agents in Government departments in London were two Foreign Office diplomats and an officer of counter-intelligence—who was presumably Philby. Volkov was taking a huge risk: the risk that his offer would fall into the hands of one of the men he was offering to expose, which is exactly what happened. But he was presumably desperate, and no doubt assumed that the British would take the most careful precautions. (Incidentally, he was not the first Russian to offer such information.) Walter Krivitsky, a major Soviet intelligence officer fled to the West in 1940, and said that there was a Soviet agent in the Foreign Office. He was seen by Gladwyn Jebb, who asked him if he could furnish details. Krivitsky said yes: the agent was a man of good family![1]

The British official asked Volkov to wait a moment and went straight to his ambassador, Sir Maurice Peterson. Sir Maurice's reaction was one of sheer horror. He had for some time been trying to prevent what he regarded as an "invasion" of his embassy by SIS men under cover and he saw the Volkov business as a step in the same direction. "No one is going to turn my embassy into a nest of spies," he said. "If you must go ahead with this business do it through London." The official returned to the waiting Russian and told him that a decision would have to come from London and this would take time.

Volkov agreed to wait but he made three conditions: firstly, any outline of his documents must be handwritten by the man he was speaking to and not typed. There was a Russian agent operating in the British Embassy in Turkey, he said, so he could not risk anyone typing copies

---

[1] Krivitsky produced other minor details, such as that the young man wore a "cape" in the evenings: from his description of the cape it was thought later that he was referring to Maclean.

of his material: secondly, communication with London should not be by telegram because the Russians had broken a variety of British cyphers; thirdly, there must be a decision on his material within twenty-one days. If he had not heard by the evening of the twenty-first day he would assume that the deal was off. He departed after making complex arrangements to get in touch.

The British diplomat spent all night preparing a handwritten brief for the Foreign Office in London to pass on to SIS and it went away with the courier next day. After a week there had been no response and a cable was sent off from the embassy in Turkey pressing for a reply. Another week passed and there was still no answer. On the twentieth day the diplomat who had interviewed Volkov and realised the value of the material was almost frantic. Then at last, on the morning of the twenty-first day an agent arrived from London and announced that he had come to take personal charge of the Volkov affair. He was a calm, unhurried figure, wearing an old-fashioned cutaway collar with a flowing Byronesque cravat. It was Kim Philby.

The diplomat who had interviewed Volkov, with nerves understandably taut pointed out that the delay had probably ruined the whole deal and asked why the hell could not someone have come out sooner. Philby produced most casually an almost incredible excuse: "Sorry, old man," he said, "it would have interfered with leave arrangements."

The diplomat immediately tried to contact Volkov. The arrangement had been that he would telephone the Soviet Consulate-General and invite Volkov to come to his office to discuss some routine consular business, a perfectly normal practice. But when he got through, the conversation alarmed him. "I asked for Volkov and a man came on saying he was Volkov, but it wasn't. I knew Volkov's voice perfectly well and it definitely wasn't him." The diplomat waited a few hours and then tried again. This time the Russian telephone operator told him that Volkov was in Moscow. A man was sent to call at the Soviet Consulate. He returned to say that the Russians insisted that no one called Volkov had *ever* worked there.

Throughout the long afternoon, while the search for Volkov continued, the British diplomat tried to get some explanation from Philby as to what had gone wrong in London. Philby would not give him a direct answer, tried to change the subject and in general behaved in an evasive manner. "I finally made up my mind," the diplomat told friends later, "that either Philby was criminally incompetent or he was a Soviet agent himself." (Philby has since commented on this story in Moscow. It was, he says, the worst moment of his life when he heard about Volkov's offer.)

When it was clear that Volkov was not coming Philby returned to London and reported that Volkov's own insistence on courier communications had brought about his downfall. In the three weeks that had elapsed since his first approach, the Russians had had ample chance of getting to him. This theory appeared to be quickly confirmed. A Russian military aircraft made an unscheduled and quite irregular landing at Istanbul airport. While the control tower was still trying to think of something to do a car raced out to the plane. A heavily bandaged figure on a stretcher was lifted into the aircraft which immediately took off.

The news of what appeared an urgent Russian removal in the *bravura* style which was more common then was soon all around Istanbul. Someone at the British Consulate, remembering the Volkov affair, contacted the diplomat who had returned to Ankara and suggested that the heavily bandaged figure might have been the unfortunate Volkov and there is every reason to think that it was. The diplomat decided he could not leave the matter there and made a point of contacting an intelligence officer and passing on his doubts about Philby. But nothing seems to have happened. If there was an enquiry it was kept inside the SIS circle and in no way damaged Philby's immediate career. In good British bureaucratic tradition, however, the incident was on record and carefully filed.* It was to weigh heavily against Philby when he finally came under suspicion.

Philby's elimination of Volkov was a vital blow in the developing espionage battle between East and West. Even if Volkov had only succeeded in exposing Philby, it would

---

* We also have evidence that the incident went on file with the CIA and that it became one of the reasons why, later, the CIA insisted on Philby's removal from Washington.

have been a terrible setback for the Russians; for apart
from the specific operations Philby was able to betray
over the coming years, the presence of Philby at the heart
of the Western intelligence community enabled the Russians to plan their Cold War espionage as a logically
integrated operation. Apart from this, it seems likely
enough that the two agents in the Foreign Office whom
Volkov offered to betray were Burgess and Maclean. So,
for the first time, Philby came to the rescue of his Cambridge contemporary Donald Maclean.

In London Burgess (who presumably had never been
aware of his danger) was progressing without difficulty.
Harold Nicolson was one of several distinguished public
men who liked Guy and, when they could, helped him.
Nicolson and Burgess dined regularly together, usually at
the Reform Club, because Nicolson had a weakness for
the roast grouse there. Late in February 1945 during
one of these agreeable sessions, Burgess was able to give
Nicolson some interesting inside information on the Commission, consisting of Molotov and the British and American Ambassadors in Moscow, which was then settling
the composition of the new Polish Provisional Government. Burgess's sources were impeccable; he had brought
to the Club the cables Moscow and London had exchanged on the matter.

After so many years on the periphery of power Burgess
had managed to move close to the centre, albeit in a
humble capacity. In 1944 he had been offered a temporary job in the Foreign Office News Department and
accepted immediately. It gave him immediate access to a
good deal of diplomatic information, though not of the
highest grade. But more important, it offered a useful
back-door into the FO itself, which he had been regarding
hungrily ever since he came down from Cambridge.

His colleagues in the News Department were a lively
lot, including Osbert Lancaster and Richard Scott, later
Diplomatic Correspondent of *The Guardian,* and in the
nearby Ministry of Information, the irrepressible Earl of
Arran. Burgess, who liked to breakfast off brandy in the
Foreign Office canteen and had acquired the infuriating
habit of munching garlic like a fruit in his office, did not
allow his translation to Whitehall to inhibit his personal
behaviour. Lord Arran recalls one evening after a dinner-
party when Burgess insisted on stopping their cab outside

Buckingham Palace and urinating against the statue, a symbolic act which amused the sentries but embarrassed the Earl. News briefings during Burgess's period in the department tended to be hilarious; Arran remembers one where Burgess insisted on passing round a photograph of a handsome boy sunbathing. It eventually reached the official spokesman who was interrupted in full spate.

"Who is this, Guy?" he wanted to know.

"My new boyfriend, Rags" (the spokesman's nickname).

"Put it away at once, Guy."

The Burgess approach was guaranteed to enliven the dreariest conference and he became a kind of licensed jester.

Amazingly, he was soon promoted. After an interview he succeeded in getting himself "established," a long-cherished ambition, and in 1946 his friend from the *Week in Westminster* days, Hector McNeil, decided to appoint him secretary and personal assistant. McNeil was now Minister of State in the Foreign Office, which gave him Cabinet rank and meant that when Bevin was absent abroad or ill he acted as Foreign Secretary. These occasions were so frequent that Bevin called him "my indentured apprentice."

Burgess's value to the Soviet espionage system has been consistently played down by British official sources. But there can be no doubt that if the Russians were sufficiently efficient to keep in regular contact with him—which, of course, they were—they must have obtained large quantities of useful material. What would *we* not have given for a contact as well-placed in the Soviet Foreign Ministry at that time? No, one suspects that the official British attitude owes much to the fact that Burgess was such a grotesquely obvious security risk that an admission that he could have been important would be too humiliating. He should have been easy to catch. He made no attempt to restrain his personal behaviour. A friend who visited his office at the period said, "It has the charm of being entirely untainted by industry, sobriety or decorum." After a powerful internal memorandum Burgess had reluctantly eschewed his garlic-munching in office hours; now he habitually kept a bottle of milk on his desk from which he would take periodic gulps as a remedy against hangovers. He was the proud possessor of an advanced copy of Kinsey's *Sexual Behaviour of the Human Male,* which he claimed to keep for safety in a disused safe in the Foreign Secretary's room. He spent a good deal of his time producing inky caricatures of FO dignitaries and one of Bevin, which appealed to the Foreign Secretary, was actually stamped "Top Secret," and circulated jokingly as a Cabinet paper. His relations with McNeil prospered and in 1947 he accompanied him when McNeil led a British delegation to Paris. The friendship between Burgess and McNeil, a burly fair-haired man with a strong Scottish accent and an interest in Presbyterian Church affairs, remains something of a mystery. McNeil was a hard-line anti-Communist, nearer to the Churchill of the Fulton "iron curtain" speech than the Bevin of the 1945 Blackpool Party Conference when he talked about "Left understanding Left." In 1949 McNeil was to launch a bitter attack on Gromyko at the UN, claiming that the Soviet Union was sabotaging peace. Later, when Attlee and other senior Labour leaders visited Moscow and Pekin, he denounced the visit as "irresponsible and ill-timed." McNeil and Burgess should have been chalk and cheese, yet later in 1947 Burgess was again chosen to accompany him on an important foreign mission, this time to Brussels. Here Burgess kept minutes of the meeting between McNeil and Spaak which led to the setting up of the Brussels Treaty Organisation. His job was confidential and he clearly had a degree of influence. McNeil was trying to have him transferred from the "B" or executive branch of the FO to the administrative "A" grade, which involved Burgess spending six months in a political department instead of working in McNeil's private office. And so, after attending the Council of Foreign Ministers in London at the end of 1947, he switched to the Far East Department.

Here he enjoyed himself pointing out that all his colleagues, with one exception, were Old Etonians. He was also, for once, broadly in agreement with the FO line; recognition of Communist China was one of the few policies at which he could level no objections. He was even supposed to have written a long paper picturesquely entitled: "How Red are Yellow Communists?" Despite the Etonian atmosphere Burgess was not an unqualified success socially. "Surely he can't be one of us," said a senior colleague agonizedly, after his first encounter with Bur-

gess and his notorious finger-nails. Burgess was able to re-
gain ground, on the other hand, by ostentatiously leaving
his signed copy of Churchill's *Arms and the Covenant*
open on his desk. In 1948 he was transferred temporarily
to a new "black propaganda" anti-Communist department, known as IRD, which was being set up by
Christopher Mayhew. After two months Mayhew had him
removed and gave his reasons succinctly: "Burgess," he
said, "is dirty, drunk and idle." At this period Burgess
also suffered a rather serious accident which worsened the
insomnia he had suffered from for years. A colleague
pushed him downstairs in a Chelsea restaurant. Burgess
suffered a severe concussion and went on holiday to recu-
perate.

Accompanied by his mother, Mrs. Bassett, Burgess set
off for Tangier and Gibraltar. The trip was as memorable
as their pre-war jaunt to Cannes though, with the years,
Burgess's alcoholic intake had risen appreciably. He seems
hardly to have drawn a sober breath all the time they
were away. It would all have been unexceptional enough
by Burgess's eccentric standards if he had not taken it on
himself to call on all the SIS representatives in the area
and let it be known that he felt their work was far from
satisfactory. The results were catastrophic.

Burgess met his old school friend David Herbert,
younger brother of the Earl of Pembroke, in Dean's Bar,
Tangier. According to Herbert his political views were un-
disguisedly Marxist and he was incredibly indiscreet. "For
God's sake shut up, Guy," he kept shouting across the
bar, but it did no good. In fact the trip went from bad to
worse. Burgess was drunk in the Café de Paris by noon
and he managed to insult respectable British tourists by
noisily improvising on an indecent song which began:

> *Little boys are cheap today*
> *Cheaper than yesterday. . . .*

When one of them complained Burgess haughtily remarked that there was no law to stop him singing the
Eton Boating Song if he felt like it.

Burgess left for Gibraltar one jump ahead of the local
residents gunning for him, and installed himself in the
Rock Hotel. He began his drunken, rollicking fortnight by
dining in the restaurant and loudly announcing that Brit-

ain was shortly going to recognise Communist China. He also pointed out the head of British security on the Rock, who was dining at an adjoining table and took the revelation badly. By now Burgess and a rather confused Mrs. Bassett had joined forces with Princess Dil de Rohan and an American friend, Mary Oliver, who were also holidaying at the Rock. Mary became a boon companion of Burgess's and for two weeks they hardly stopped talking. Their conversations continued into the small hours of the morning, with Mrs. Bassett pounding on the walls of her adjoining bedroom calling: "Guy, go to bed, go to bed." The Princess, who had had intelligence connections during the war, tried to quieten Burgess down but it was a losing battle. He was extremely drunk all the time despite his mother's remonstrations.

Eventually he returned to London, leaving Mary Oliver with a bill for £400, most of which he had run up in whisky and champagne. Princess de Rohan decided she should report Burgess's remarks and in December 1949 a curious meeting of local intelligence men, reinforced by a London MI 5 official, was held in Dean's Bar, Tangier, to try and work out precisely what Guy Burgess had done.

They reported back and Burgess was questioned in London. He wrote a long, rambling explanation which he showed to Goronwy Rees, who advised him it was an inadequate apology and suggested he would do better to defend himself in person. Burgess followed this suggestion and just avoided being sacked from the Foreign Office. But he was severely reprimanded and removed from the Far Eastern Department. His career looked as though it had come to a dead end, but once again McNeil intervened and Burgess staggered on, indomitably.

13. The Albanian Subversion

Sink down in the slime
Embrace the butcher
But change the world: it needs it
—BERTOLT BRECHT, *The Measures Taken*

With Volkov out of the way Philby's position was again secure and early in the summer of 1946 he relinquished his London department to take an important new post "in the field." He went to Turkey under diplomatic cover, ostensibly as temporary First Secretary with the British Embassy, stationed in Istanbul and in charge of passport control. His real work, of course, was still spying for the SIS. The Diplomatic Service, who appeared to be his employers, were in fact only his hosts.

Philby clearly did not lose any rank by going out to Turkey. His subsequent appointment to Washington, if nothing else, proves that. But the *nature* of his work did change sharply once he went out "into the field." He was then bound to come into working contact with the Soviet espionage networks—and thus be projected into a position where his real work as a Soviet spy was not in any external way distinguishable from his pretence of being a British spy. Whether Philby took the lead in persuading his British superiors to send him to Turkey we do not know—he says he did not. But if he did not do so, he should have done, because once he was in the field he was almost impregnable.

In this context, the British Government's terse admission, seventeen years later, that they knew the truth about Philby's loyalty makes interesting reading. In 1963 Edward Heath said that the British were "now aware" that Philby had "worked for the Soviet authorities *before* 1946." [Authors' italics.] In other words, the knowledge that Philby had worked for the Soviets after 1946 was not new—he was working for them to the extent that any field agent must do so in order to survive. What was new was that he had been working for them *all along.*

Istanbul had been an important neutral centre in the war against Germany. Now, the East-West confrontation gave it an even greater importance. It was at the centre of a cold war which seemed likely to go hot at the drop of an ultimatum. Turkey has a long border with the Soviet Union and another border with communist Bulgaria. In the 1940s Stalin was loudly claiming a slice of Eastern Turkey plus the right to put Russian bases on the Bosphorus and the Dardanelles. The Turks, in reply, were clamouring for Western military aid. A civil war was raging in nearby Greece which looked as though it could easily go Communist. Much Communist shipping passes through the Bosphorus, and Istanbul has flourishing communities of Armenians, Georgians, Bulgarians, and Albanians, with direct links to the homeland communities behind the Iron Curtain. A better place to make contact with spies would be hard to find.

Philby worked from the Consulate General, a vast stone building in a walled compound in Beyoglu, the new part of the city. He established Aileen and the four children in a large house at Beylerbeyi on the Asiatic side of the Bosphorus, a scenic middle-class suburb with connections to the centre of the city by ferry. It was not the sort of place many Europeans would choose to live, mainly because of the lack of facilities. Philby preferred it because it was out of the diplomatic round, which he found a bore. He wrote to a friend in London: "I wonder why they don't hire the same bus to take the same people to all the same parties. . . ." Philby was well enough liked by the other British and Western diplomats. He had what one of them called a "quiet, cat-like charm." He was, however, most at ease with children. "Any child loved Kim," says a journalist who met him at this time. Philby could relax with children: they were outside the dangerous game he was playing, and they could not threaten him. Few people guessed that he was in intelligence work, for he was careful to be quiet and unspectacular. Those who did know what his job was did not think he was taking it very seriously. He drank a lot, and smiled vaguely at parties. People thought he had become a voluptuary, coasting easily towards middle age. He drank particularly hard during Guy Burgess's occasional visits from London. Guy always livened things up—usually by diving into the Bosphorus from the upper floor of the Philby house and swimming drunkenly back to repeat the act. It was only years later that someone noticed an odd thing about Philby's drinking: that he could turn it off when he wished. (A journalist who was with him in Kuwait, a dry state, noticed that Philby was quite unconcerned by the absence of alcohol.)

The Turks, of course, knew fairly soon that Philby was an SIS man. Indeed, a man on the Istanbul newspaper *Cumhuriyet* once asked Philby if he would be interviewed for a feature-article on "The Spies of Istanbul." Kim discreetly refused. All that the Turkish security men noted was that Philby used to have meetings with "students" from Communist Balkan states—but as that was his job, who cared?

He did make one attempt to infiltrate agents into the Soviet Union. Two Georgians, both in their twenties and born in Paris, were recruited and trained and, with the co-operation of Turkish intelligence, sent across the border near the Soviet garrison town of Akhaltsikhe. Their mission was to explore the possibilities of conspiratorial existence in Georgia: could they establish safe houses, obtain legal identities, set up courier lines? The scheme was a failure. One agent was shot crossing the border. The other, last seen running for the cover of a wood on the Soviet side, was never heard of again.

In the middle of his Turkish period Philby was brought back to England to take a "James Bond" course at a spy school near Gosport, a regular thing for directors and one which was essentially the same as for operatives—the idea being that directors would understand better the difficulties of working in the field. One of Philby's fellow students recalls that Philby was surprisingly good at things like unarmed combat, night sabotage operations and shooting with a pistol at phosphorescent targets in darkened rooms. He is remembered, as usual, as "a pleasant, ordinary chap with no interest in politics."

In Turkey Philby spent a good deal of time travelling around the Lake Van district close to the Soviet border on "Operation Spyglass," his own idea for a long-range photographic reconnaisance of the Soviet frontier area. He kept an odd souvenir of the period which in later years he displayed in his apartment in Beirut: a large photograph of Mount Ararat which stands on the Turkish-Soviet border. Most people who recognised the double-humped shape of the mountain would puzzle over the picture, much to Philby's amusement. Some of the more technically-minded would believe that they had solved the puzzle: the print had been made with the negative reversed: the little hump was on the left instead of on the right. This would amuse Philby even more and he would point out that the little hump was only on the left when the mountain was viewed from the Turkish side. The view from the Russian side was, like the photograph, the other way around.

The picture seems to have been an apt symbol of Philby's enigmatic status. Clearly, throughout his Turkish period, he was closely in touch with the Soviet intelligence network and equally clearly his superiors in London knew this. The vital question is how far the superiors had given him permission to venture into this moral twilight. The authors have had confirmation that Philby had been given permission to play the full double game with the Russians —to pretend to them that he was a British agent willing to work for them: which, unknown to London, was exactly what he was. This is the only way to explain the passionate defence of Philby by his colleagues of the SIS when the security officers of MI 5 were convinced that he was a traitor. It was to be some time yet before things did go wrong for Philby but when the day came the SIS stood by him with an extraordinary, apparently inexplicable determination.

In the meantime his star was still high and his biggest coup was still to come: in 1949 he was sent to Washington, with the rank of First Secretary, to be the SIS liaison man with the fledgeling Central Intelligence Agency. It is difficult to exaggerate the importance of this posting. The Central Intelligence Agency had been set up in 1947 and although beginning to feel its strength still tended to regard the SIS with some awe. Between the two existed what CIA officers describe as "a very special relationship," and with it, "an amazingly free exchange of information" took place. Philby was right in the heart of this. His contacts ranged from the director, a tough ex-Army man, General Bedell Smith, down through the ranks. He was privy to CIA planning; he told the CIA what the SIS was doing; he was often briefed by Bedell Smith himself on top policy and, above all, he knew what the CIA knew about Soviet operations.

This, by itself, would have more than satisfied Philby's Russian controller, but he was able to improve on it. Like most agencies of its type the CIA is compartmentalised as a protection against penetration—no one department knows the whole story. But an agent is prey to a normal man's need to talk to someone about his job and the only person he can talk safely to is another agent. In the CIA that other agent was often Philby. Because he was cleared to speak with Bedell Smith, Philby was cleared right through every department and merely by drinking around he could have learned more about the agency and its operations than any man except the director and perhaps one or two of his assistants. A high-ranking CIA officer, now retired, told us: "How much did Philby know? The sky was the limit. He would have known as much as he wanted to find out."

This explains the reason for the silence that has surrounded Philby's period with the CIA. If an intelligence agency has one or two men whose careers are going well, and these men—through no fault of their own—are "blown," the agency immediately retires them. This may appear ruthless but is obviously essential. What happens —as it did with the CIA and Philby—when the entire agency is "blown"? There is no choice but to cover up, reorganise, and keep going. When the extent of Philby's treachery was finally realised the CIA had no choice (short of disbanding the whole organisation) but to smile bravely and carry on.

The only positive result of the whole affair was that once it was known that Philby was a traitor there was suddenly an explanation for all the anti-Soviet operations that had mysteriously gone sour. The most important of these was the "Albanian massacre," an operation originally started by the SIS in 1946 and which became a joint SIS-CIA affair in 1949. Philby was associated with it from the beginning and at its bloodiest was co-director. It cost the lives of at least 300 men and for many years has remained one of the most carefully-concealed secrets of the Cold War. It has suited both sides to leave it that way. For the West, the Albanian affair was a humiliating operational disaster. For the Russians, it was an operational triumph, but not one to shout about. Spreading throughout the uneasy Soviet empire the news of Western willingness to back subversion movements in Eastern Europe might give all sorts of people the wrong idea.

The theory behind the operation was simple. The communist régime in Albania was not firmly established. The Germans had been driven out on November 29, 1944, but in 1946 the communists were still struggling with their reconstruction programme. In an area of central Albania known as the Mati, a part of the country traditionally loyal to the King, there was a small core of royalists ready to be the basis of a resistance movement. The original plan was that, if Britain could parachute enough well-trained agents into the Mati, they could organise a maquis-style operation which the British would then supply by air drops. If the movement showed strength the people would join it. In time a full-scale civil war could be provoked. The trouble that this would cause the Russians would alone be sufficient justification for the operation. But what if the anti-communist revolt in Albania sparked off others throughout the Balkans? The whole basis of the Russian satellite empire could be shattered by an uprising that had had its birth in one small guerilla operation.

The project appeared so attractive that SIS had no hesitation in putting it into operation. It came under Philby's control, but was run in detail by an agent who had come into SIS from SOE. Philosophically, of course, the operation grew out of the British-backed subversion campaigns of the war years, run by SOE. This time, the Communists were enemies instead of allies. There was no scarcity of suitable guerilla recruits—the Displaced Persons camps in Greece and Italy were full of anti-communist Albanians—and as a pilot project twelve were recruited and taken to Malta for training. The SIS instructed them in the use of weapons, codes and radio, the techniques of sabotage and subversion, and finally how to make a parachute jump. They were dropped into the mountains of the Mati throughout 1947. Results were disappointing. The inhabitants, a tough clannish community of Roman Catholics called the Malesori, were unimpressed by the arrival of a handful of agents offering to lead them in revolt. Although independent and warlike they had a peasant's faith in numbers and the type of warfare the agents tried to teach them—hit-and-run attacks on police posts, sabotage and terrorism—struck them as unmanly.

The operation dragged on in an inconclusive manner

until 1949. There were sabotage attempts on the Kucova oilfields and the copper mines of Rubik but no real success in raising a revolt. Then the Americans, weighing up the political situation, decided to lend a hand. The Balkans were by now the weakest sector of the Russian front: the communist rebels in Greece were on the point of collapse, Yugoslavia had broken with Russia and Soviet "technicians" and "advisers" had been forced to take over the running of Albania. A joint CIA-SIS operation could step up Albanian subversion to a point where the Russians would be forced either to withdraw or to suppress the revolt with a ruthlessness that would disenchant every Iron Curtain country.

Britain's Foreign Secretary, Ernest Bevin, was adamantly opposed to the idea. But the Foreign Office contained a vocal militant faction in favour of establishing resistance movements in virtually every country in Eastern Europe and which, in turn, was enthusiastically supported by SIS, particularly the old SOE operators who firmly believed the dictum that "diplomacy is war carried on by other means"—or as it might be, the same means. The issue was swung by the hawks in the American State Department who saw this as a chance to remould the face of Europe in a more sympathetic image. Bevin was persuaded to sanction another pilot operation. The Americans appointed one of their best CIA agents to act as joint controller of the operation, a man who now calls himself Christopher Felix. The British representative was their CIA liaison man, Kim Philby.

This time a better class of Albanian agent was wanted, so an approach was made to King Zog in exile in Cairo to recommend men for the job. Zog had no hesitation in offering his entire Royal Guard. Some declined the opportunity but most accepted, including Captain Zenel Shehu, leader of the operation, Captain Nalil Sufa, and Hamit Matjani, an agent who had been into Albania seven times since 1946. Matjani (known as "the tiger") had been one of the leaders of the anti-Nazi resistance and his courage and ferocity were legendary. Shehu and Sufa had followed Zog into exile and had sworn they would see him restored to his throne.

These three gradually gathered together a small army, mainly by setting up a "Committee of Free Albanians" in Italy, Egypt and Greece as a front for a recruiting agency.

The British provided Malta as a training ground and forward base for operations. They also found and crewed the small boats required for infiltrating the seaborne agents. The Americans put up the money and the use of Wheelus Field, in Libya, as a rear base and supply depot. It took some time to co-ordinate everything, and the first of the guerilla groups did not drop into Albania until the spring of 1950.

The first of the Albanian agents to land in his harsh homeland was a tough, taciturn peasant, now living in the West. He still feels bitter about the operation. "I parachuted into the Mati in 1950, and soon after Ihsan Toptani, of the King's bodyguard, joined me. Others came to join us. Some across the frontier and some by sea. But the ones who came by sea never found us. They landed and the police were *always* there."

For two years after the first landings, small groups left regularly from training camps in Cyprus, Malta and Germany, either for the parachute drop into the Albanian mountains, to filter across the Greek-Albanian border, or to cross from Corfu by boat. The whole operation was a series of disasters. *The Russians just seemed to know the guerillas were coming.* Month after month survivors struggled back into Greece with stories of the swift and bloody fate that had befallen their comrades.

Occasionally the Albanian Government itself announced details of its operations against the guerillas. In January 1951, the Ministry of the Interior reported a large and unsuccessful infiltration in the north. The report said forty-three émigré Albanians, who had entered Albania by submarine and parachute, had been defeated by the police in a gun battle lasting several days. Twenty-nine guerillas had been killed and fourteen captured. In October the survivors were tried in Tirana. Two were shot and the others gaoled for from seven years to life. The Ministry of Information claimed the operation was jointly organised by the U.S., British, Italian, Greek and Yugoslav intelligence services.

The last operation took place a few weeks before Easter 1952. (This is a significant date. Burgess and Maclean had already defected and Philby should have been under deep suspicion. Yet neither the SIS nor the CIA saw fit to stop the Albanian operation. Or perhaps, by now, it had gone too far to stop.) In a desperate effort to discover what was going wrong, Captain Shehu himself parachuted into the Mati with Captain Sufa and a radio operator. The Albanian militia was waiting for them at their rendezvous point, a house owned by Shehu's cousin; a man known to be loyal to the King. The militia forced Shehu's operator to broadcast an all clear signal to his base in Cyprus. The operator had been schooled to deal with a situation like this. There was a fail-safe drill which involved transmitting the signal in a way that warned it was being sent under duress and therefore should be disregarded. But *the militia knew the drill*. The all-clear went out and twelve more top agents, including Matjani, parachuted into an ambush at Saint Gjergji, near the town of Elbasan in northern Albania. The Albanian army was waiting in a big circle and the guerillas landed in the middle of it. No one surrendered. They were all shot.

Shehu, Sufa and five others were put on trial in Tirana, found guilty of crimes against the Albanian people and shot at Easter. The whole Albanian network was crushed and all the agents shot or gaoled. Toptani, who had been captured earlier, was gaoled for twenty-four years. Many of the local inhabitants who were suspected of having helped the guerillas were forcibly resettled elsewhere in Albania.

Those guerillas who survived have no doubt that they were betrayed: "Police were always waiting when a boat carrying agents came to the shore. How could they know where the boats would come in unless a traitor told them? Also, people who had been our friends when we left Albania were often no longer our friends when we went back."

Those guerillas who escaped to Greece were hurried out as an embarrassment to the Greek Government. The SIS bullied the Home Office into allowing them to come to Britain (where a "Welcome Home" party was held for them at Caxton Hall, London). It is unclear whether the Home Office was told the truth about these refugees. They were, according to one account, described as "good friends of ours from Greece." The Ministry of Labour found work for them with the Forestry Commission and at an ordnance factory but eventually most of them emigrated to Australia, Canada or to the United States.

The post-mortem on the debacle was prolonged. The Americans were uneasily convinced of treachery, but what few indications there were seemed to point to the former joint controller, Kim Philby—an impossible charge to make with such weak evidence. But, like the Volkov Affair it all went on file (mostly with the CIA) and in good time would all be put to use.

The effect of the failure of the operation was totally to discredit in British eyes the policy of "positive intervention" in Communist Europe, to weaken it for some years in America, and to make the Albanians lastingly suspicious of Western policy. The whole bloody mess lives on in Albania in a modern folksong. This version was recorded by A. L. Lloyd, a British song collector, in 1965.

> *Ej, on Monday evening near the muezzin's call*
> *A great tragedy indeed over toward Gojani!*
> *There was the sound of aeroplanes, aeroplanes of*
> *various colours*
> *carrying young men from America; from America*
> *and from England.*
> *Oho do they mean to drop criminals on us?*
> *Oho, the parachutes fall like birds, they fall like*
> *birds in parachutes.*
> *Quickly the news reached Püke, quickly to the*
> *police post at Püke.*
> *The order was given, the warning siren quickly*
> *sounded.*
> *Ej, Zenel Kadrija led us, Zenel himself led us.*
> *When we had climbed the forest-clad mountain, we*
> *met with the criminals.*
> *Zenel speaks, He calls in loud voice, "Will you*
> *surrender or do you choose death?"*
> *Nobody answers.*
> *A rifle cracks.*
> *While snow falls, while rain falls, while rifles crack,. .*
> *a pistol takes aim.*
> *Oh Zenel Kadrija! He died for Albania.*

Albania was by no means the only communist country in which Western intelligence services took an active interest after the war. An area closer to the Soviet heartland offered an even more glittering prize: the Ukraine. Physically the Ukraine is part of the Soviet Union. A revolt there would have had important repercussions. If communism was not secure in Russia itself, then nowhere in

Eastern Europe was safe from revolt. And in the 1940s it was just feasible.

There already existed in and out of the Ukraine an extremely strong and well-organised nationalist movement —the Organisation of Ukrainian Nationalists, OUN. With its fighting arm and parent, Ukrayinska Viyskova Orhaniztsiya—UVO—this movement had been a headache to the Russian authorities for more than twenty years. The movement had started after the unsuccessful war of 1918–20 against Russia. When the Ukrainian forces had been defeated and most of the leaders imprisoned, Eyhen Konovalets, an officer in a rifle brigade, fled the country and took the nationalist struggle underground. His organisation, UVO, was recruited from Ukrainian émigrés, many of whom had been soldiers. UVO soon began to infiltrate men back into the Ukraine to set up an internal resistance organisation. Most went to the western part of the country, which was occupied by Poland and which offered the best opportunity for subversion and sabotage. Konovalets got his resistance organisation working, and there was a spate of armed attack, political murder and subversion. Then he returned to Western Europe to carry on his work among the émigrés, recruiting, training and indoctrinating them. At that time four million Ukrainians lived outside their homeland, many in the United States and Canada. Through them, Konovalets received considerable financial backing, an important factor in running a resistance movement and one which enabled UVO to remain free from non-Ukrainian influence, except for a brief, disastrous period which now seems certain was due to betrayal by Kim Philby.

UVO had continued its subversion with varying success and the occasional setback (in 1926 one of its leaders, Symon Petlura, was shot seven times in a Paris street) until 1927 when it merged with other nationalist groups to become the OUN. Konovalets remained at its head. Then, in the late 1930s, Moscow cracked down hard on the insurgents. In 1937 and 1938 purges at Vinnytsia weakened the organisation, and in May 1938 it lost its leader when a Soviet agent who had penetrated OUN handed Konovalets a fast-ticking time bomb in a Rotterdam cafe. At that time a young Ukrainian called Stepan Bandera was serving a life sentence at Lvov for his part in the murder of the Polish Minister of the Interior,

Pieracki. When Germany invaded Poland, Bandera escaped and was elected leader of the OUN. His programme was that the OUN should help the Germans drive the Russians out of the Ukraine, after which he would set up an independent government. The Germans quickly killed any idea of independence by arresting Bandera and sending him to a concentration camp at Sachsenhausen. He was released in 1944 after promising to collaborate and was responsible for the deaths of many Russians.

In the Ukraine, units of OUN continued to fight both the Russians and the Germans. When Germany surrendered, and troops of the Soviet Union reoccupied the country, the partisans drew breath and then returned full-time to their major occupation—fighting Russians. When news of this revolt leaked to the West, British and American intelligence agencies fell over each other to offer help. The difficulty, the Western intelligence agencies found, was that, unlike Albania, there was little aid the West could offer. OUN already had clear and relatively swift lines of communication from Germany and Austria, through Czechoslovakia, to the Western part of the Ukraine around Lvov, and they had good supplies and resourceful men. So, hopefully, the Western agencies offered small arms, radio sets, codes, and, in isolated cases, forged documents. The Ukrainians accepted, and liaison between OUN and the CIA and SIS began. Almost immediately the operation that had been so tight and efficient began to go wrong.

It had been customary for OUN couriers and saboteurs to slip singly along the underground route to the Ukraine. Much of their work was the carrying of news and propaganda into the Ukraine and the smuggling out of works by Ukrainian writers, so the one-man team operation was both adequate and efficient. The first thing the CIA and SIS decided was that the infiltration patterns should be changed to provide for self-supporting groups of from three to eight men, equipped and trained to live for long periods without having to depend on any assistance from the local population.

The new system did not work. As in the Albanian operation, the Ukraine authorities seemed to know when the OUN teams were coming. In 1950 the movement suffered a severe loss when a high-ranking leader, Roman Shukhevych, was killed when his team ran into an ambush. He was replaced by Colonel Vasel Koval, an experienced and cautious soldier, but who failed to report on schedule. After several months' silence another senior OUN officer, M.V. Matvieyko, was instructed to enter the Ukraine and try to find out what had happened to Koval. Matvieyko was then in his late thirties. He was a reliable officer, married and devoted to his wife. He got into the Ukraine without difficulty and reported back on his secret radio wave-length on schedule. He was in contact with Koval's network, he said, and all was in order. He had not yet seen Koval but would be doing so soon. Matvieyko reported twice more. It was proving more difficult to contact Koval than he had expected but there was no cause for alarm. The delay was due to security reasons. Matvieyko went silent and nothing further was heard from him or of him for ten years.

Then, in 1961, an open letter, signed by Matvieyko and addressed to Ukrainian émigrés, was published in a pro-communist Ukrainian newspaper. In it Matvieyko confessed everything. He said he had been infiltrated into the Ukraine to work with the resistance by British and American intelligence agencies. But when he arrived, he wrote, things were not as he had been told. The resistance movement did not exist because there was no need for it. Conditions in the country were good and getting better. The government was benevolent and life in general was so attractive that he had decided to settle down.

Several of his countrymen in the West reconstructed what they believe happened to Matvieyko. A large part of the resistance in the Ukraine had been blown, they reasoned, about the time that Shukhevych had been shot. Matvieyko had contacted a totally penetrated section of the movement which had strung him along for a few weeks, hoping he would reveal other agents. His early messages had been sent in good faith. Then, when it had become obvious that Matvieyko was not going to implicate anyone else, he was arrested and shot. They do not believe that he would have written the letter attributed to him, even under pressure.

Two more couriers disappeared. Again, after a long silence, letters from them appeared in the Ukrainian press. The letters followed a pattern: émigré Ukrainians were fascist extremists who wished to crush socialist government and substitute capitalist control. They were being helped by Western intelligence agencies which had established training bases in Italy, Austria, West Germany and Scotland.

The debacle continued. In 1954 a large team of infiltrators was ambushed and wiped out in an isolated region in the Carpathian mountains. They were walking into the Ukraine and had stopped to rest when they were surrounded by border police and shot down. This was enough for Bandera. He decided to cut off what was left of the OUN internal structure and start all over again without any help from the CIA or SIS. His decision split the émigré movement. A splinter group continued to use the old network, but it soon became obvious that the material coming out through the established sources was merely propaganda. Bandera went ahead with his rebuilding programme. Contacts, routes, method of entry and codes were all changed. Slowly the new organisation began to function. Then, in October 1959, as Bandera tried to open the door of his Munich flat, a basket of groceries in one hand, his key in the other, a young Ukrainian stepped out of the shadows and aimed a tightly rolled newspaper at Bandera. Before Bandera could get his hands free, a fine spray of gas enveloped his head and he died in the doorway. Ukrainian émigrés believe that the murderer was a KGB officer who had penetrated OUN under the name of Bogdan Stashynsky and that the motive was revenge for Bandera's "war crimes" against Russians. Philby, on the other hand, says that the CIA killed Bandera because he was anti-American.

In the Ukraine, KGB officers began to arrest key OUN members, and by the mid-1960s the internal organisation was completely crippled. Slowly and laboriously, the émigrés are rebuilding yet again. No one will talk in detail of their activities, but it is apparent that some organisation is operating in the Ukraine. For example, Ukrainian literature protesting Soviet repression continues to reach the West, and in June 1968 three young British students were arrested and expelled from Russia when they tried to distribute leaflets in Red Square, protesting the detention of a number of Ukrainian writers.

How does Philby fit into all this? The first contacts between OUN and SIS and the CIA, principally between Bandera and SIS, were started just before the war. They were resumed in 1945. The department in SIS

under whose jurisdiction the Ukraine falls is the anti-
Soviet section. As we know, Kim Philby became head of
this department just before the war ended and remained
there during the vital period of liaison with Bandera. It
could be claimed that this is insufficient to blame Philby
for the entire betrayal of OUN, but Philby agrees that he
was involved in both the Albanian subversion and in the
SIS–CIA scheme to support the Ukrainian venture. It is
difficult to believe, therefore, that he had no hand in its
subsequent failure. While the Albanian operation was
at its worst, Philby, in Washington and remote from the
killing, was at the peak of his career. He had only one
nagging little worry: London had asked him to assist in an
enquiry into a leakage to the Russians of certain atomic
energy information. A British diplomat who had served
in Washington before Philby was a prime suspect. The
Foreign Office security representative and the MI 5 liaison man were helping build a case and, as one of them
said later, "Although no one had ever told us who the
suspect was, we all knew." It was Donald Maclean. Philby
could not foresee it but the Maclean affair—by an almost
freakish chain of events—was to drag him down as well.
Two years before Philby reached Washington, Maclean
had become deeply involved in the struggle between East
and West for nuclear advantage.

14. The Priceless Secrets

Knowledge is power.
          —THOMAS HOBBES, *Leviathan*

The Americans exploded their first atom bomb in the desert of New Mexico on July 16, 1945. The awe it inspired
in observers was best caught by Sir Winston Churchill
who was with President Truman in Potsdam when American officials broke the news. Waving his cigar to emphasise the point, Churchill said: "What was gunpowder?
Trivial. What was electricity? Meaningless. This atomic
bomb is the Second Coming in Wrath."
The Japanese certainly believed it to be so and with its

use on Hiroshima and Nagasaki a new era in warfare that warned of Doomsday began. If the first clumsy, hastily-contrived atomic weapon could wipe out two cities and 120,000 people, what would the highly-sophisticated weapons of the future destroy? In those early spine-chilling days of the nuclear age one fact was patently clear —no nation which wanted to remain a world power could afford a future without atomic weapons. Stalin received the news of "a new American weapon" at Potsdam. (Truman told him.) He took it with a Georgian poker face but he made certain on his return to Moscow that all the resources of Soviet science were concentrated on speeding up Russia's own efforts to get the bomb.

How far were the Russians behind? At the beginning of the war they were as knowledgeable as anyone else about the physical theories on which the bomb was based: not only had all the major discoveries been published but the Russians also had excellent physicists of their own. Given the time, they could certainly have produced an atom bomb—without any of the bonuses that atomic spies like Fuchs, the Rosenbergs, Gold, and Nunn May brought them.

What *was* important about the information the Russians obtained from their spies was that it enabled them to save time and valuable materials, to dispose in the best manner their limited resources. By short-circuiting the elaborate but essential technological processes necessary to learn if a certain theory works in practice the Russians were able to get the bomb years before the West expected. All along the sort of information they hungered for was not only the scientific details of American atomic experiments but things like: Can a bomb plant be built a long way from heavy industry? Have the Americans found a cheap and easy way of refining uranium? Does the gaseous diffusion process work? The Smyth report published in the United States after the war gave them a lot of valuable information on a platter, but there were still fields in which they would, had it not been for Maclean, have remained very weak.

Donald Maclean was not a scientist. It is likely that he did not even comprehend the scientific theory on which the atom bomb is based. But from February 1947 until he left Washington in 1948 he was in a position to filter the Russians information about American atomic energy projects, the British atomic energy programme, and the political differences arising between the two countries out of atomic energy matters. This is not a hasty or hysterical assessment. (It is shared by the American State Department, among others.) Maclean defected many years ago and there is no useful point in pretending at this distance of time that he was not a spy of major importance. Enough pretending has already been done. The British Government White Paper on Burgess and Maclean, issued in September 1955, carefully glosses over Maclean's period in Washington ("he served in Paris, at Washington and in Cairo") and refers inadequately to Maclean's espionage activities—"In January 1949 the security authorities received a report that certain Foreign Office information had leaked to the Soviet authorities some years earlier. . . . By the beginning of May [1951] Maclean had come to be regarded as the principal suspect." In the debate in the House of Commons on November 7, 1955, again the portion of Maclean's career when he was in Washington was glossed over. The facts of the matter are that Maclean's espionage achievements made it difficult for Britain to admit the damage he had done without giving comfort to the Russians and destroying the already shaky relationship between British and American intelligence organisations.

Maclean's period in Washington, the years of strain that were to wreck his marriage and disturb his mind began in the spring of 1944. Maclean crossed the Atlantic in the *Queen Mary* (later to figure in Burgess's life) and rented a small house at 2710 35th Place NW, near the British Embassy. He slipped easily into the pace and atmosphere of his new job and his colleagues quickly got the impression that Donald was, as one said, "the Golden Boy of the F.O." on his way to an eventual ambassador's posting somewhere like Rome or Bonn. He wrote clear concise memos on long and involved subjects, got on well with his ambassadors, particularly Sir Archibald Clark Kerr ("Archie thought Donald was a sweetie"), went in for a few pink gins and a game of tennis after work on Saturdays and cultivated a neat and insect-free rose garden.

He did not do so well on the social side, rather odd for someone well up the diplomatic ladder. He and Melinda rarely gave more than the occasional buffet dinner and at other people's parties tended to stand alone in a corner holding hands in a very un-Foreign Office manner. Melinda was happy to be back in the United States, happy with her house, and going through one of her periods of being deeply in love with Donald.

Then in 1947 this all changed. Maclean was designated by the Foreign Office to act as the United Kingdom's secretary on the Combined Policy Committee, a body concerned with atomic energy matters and composed of representatives of the United States, the United Kingdom and Canada. The CPC was set up under the secret Quebec Agreement of 1943 and made recommendations to Britain and the United States on the division of programmes in the atomic energy field and the assignment of British scientists to various U.S. laboratories and facilities. Because the Quebec Agreement was so secret, not even the Congressmen who drafted the MacMahon Act of July 1946 knew anything about it. The MacMahon Act set up the Atomic Energy Commission and made various provisions for the safeguarding of atomic secrets. Its effect was to deny nuclear information to Britain. The situation now bordered on the ludicrous. The Quebec Agreement, reinforced by an undertaking signed between Roosevelt and Churchill at Roosevelt's home, Hyde Park, in September 1944, and a secret Truman-Attlee agreement in 1945, made free exchange of atomic matter obligatory. The MacMahon Act made such exchanges illegal. The embarrassment that this caused the United States and the resentment it aroused in Britain gave a notable bonus to Maclean's blossoming career as a Russian agent—he was able to report a blow-by-blow description of the fight to iron out these serious political differences between two formerly unquestioning allies.

By the time he took over his post with the CPC the MacMahon Act had been in force for six months. It had slammed like an iron gate on the general exchange of atomic information, to the distress of many scientists and politicians on both sides of the Atlantic. But, inexplicably, there were chinks in the gate. The Act did not cover declassification arrangements, raw materials used for atomic energy programmes, and patents. So there was still a wealth of information available to Maclean.

What *did* Maclean have access to? This investigation brought to light the only known documentary assessment of the matter made by either the British or American Governments: a letter written by the State Department to Senator James O. Eastland, chairman of the Senate Internal Security sub-Committee which was then proposing to hold its own investigation into the damage done to the United States by Burgess and Maclean. It was dated February 21, 1956, and some of it is worth quoting in full, together with Senator Eastland's delightfully direct marginal notes. Eastland asked: "From 1944 to 1948 Maclean was Head of Chancery here and in that post was alleged to be fully acquainted with all the secrets of relations between the United States and Britain and with information regarding atomic policy. True or false?"

The State Department replied: "In February 1947, Maclean was designated by his government to act as the United Kingdom's secretary on the Combined Policy Committee which was concerned with atomic energy matters and composed of representatives of the U.S., UK and Canada. In this position he had an opportunity to have access to information shared by the three participating countries in the fields of patents, declassification matters and research and development relating to the programme of procurement of raw material from foreign sources by the Combined Development Agency, including estimates of supplies and requirements. During the course of negotiations which resulted in the *modus vivendi* concerning atomic energy matters followed by the three governments after January 1948 Maclean in his official capacity had access to information relating to the estimates made at that time of ore supply available to the three governments, requirements of uranium for the atomic energy programmes of the three governments for the period from 1948 to 1952, and the definition of scientific areas in which the three governments deemed technical cooperation could be accomplished with mutual benefit."

The references to ore supplies gloss over information which would have been a valuable guide for the Russian atomic energy programme. The Combined Development Agency was a creature of the CPC. Its essential task was the pre-emptive purchase (mostly from the Belgian Congo) of uranium ahead of the Russians—and everyone else. It is obvious that the Russians would have valued anything Maclean could tell them about where the West was buying its uranium, in what quantities and at what price—especially as in those years the world supply of uranium was thought to be limited. It was especially valuable for the Russians to know in 1948 exactly how much uranium Britain and America thought they would need *during the next four years*. For, given these figures any Russian scientist worth his roubles could calculate with reasonable accuracy how many bombs the West planned to make.

Maclean was also a party to details of extensive metallurgical research aimed at extracting large quantities of low grade uranium from Witwatersrand gold ore, the potentialities of which were first recognised by the American geologist G. W. Bain and the British geologist Professor C. F. Davidson in September 1945. The first pilot plant came into operation at Blyvooruitzicht in South Africa in October 1949 and full technical information on the process was not taken off the secret list until 1957. Maclean was in a position to tell the Russians in 1947, *ten years earlier*, that the research was under way, that it was jointly financed and fully co-ordinated, and that the West thought its chances of success sufficiently high to invest a considerable amount of money in it.

Maclean's work here was a classic example of the role espionage has played in enabling the Russians to "ride on the back" of the West's much superior economic power and altogether more massive technological resources. Without this kind of detailed knowledge of the fruits of the Western research and development programmes, the Russians would never have been able to capitalise on their theoretical scientific knowledge with the remarkable speed they in fact displayed.

(The only shadow on Maclean's career as a spy is a doubt that the Russians appreciated the value of all of the information he was sending them—that he was the victim of a Russian Colonel Dansey. This seems the only way to explain why they did not make more political capital out of some of Maclean's material. Why, for instance, knowing that Belgium had allowed Britain and America to carve up the world's richest source of uranium—the Belgian Congo—did not Russia use the then powerful Communist party to make more trouble for the premier, Paul-Henri Spaak?)

The Eastland document continues with an account of Maclean's period as head of the American Department of

the Foreign Office, an appointment that immediately preceded his defection. (This does not concern his Washington activities but since it is part of the one official document on the subject it is worth considering here.)

Senator Eastland had asked whether there was any
State Department information to indicate any possible
leaks from Britain or British nationals to the Chinese
Communists during the Korean War. The State Department replied: ". . . numerous decisions had been taken
which represented a general effort on the part of the
United States to localise the conflict in Korea. Those decisions reflected a basic judgement on our part, and the
conviction of other governments associated with us in the
Korean action, that an all-out war on the mainland of
China involving air, naval and ground forces was undesirable. On the other hand the Department found no indications that any directions were given the UN command
as to what action should be taken in the event of Chinese
communist intervention other than that the UN command
should seek approval from the Unified Command in
Washington before undertaking military counter action
beyond that required for the immediate security of the
UN command military forces. [Here Senator Eastland
had written in the margin "How helpful!"] Attempts on
the part of the United States Government to localise the
conflict in Korea were known to the British and to our
other allies and were in fact the subject of considerable
comment and speculation in the press. It is probable that
Maclean knew of this general policy [Eastland: "It was
specific"]. The Department does not know whether he
may have adduced the opinion that the United States
would not cross the Yalu river in case of invasion of Korea
by Chinese communist troops. It is possible that he may
have passed such beliefs as he may have had in this regard to the communists although we have no information
to the effect that he did so."

Both General MacArthur, the commander-in-chief of
the UN forces, and his chief of intelligence, General
Charles Willoughby, were certain that this information
had been passed to the communists. Just before he died
MacArthur complained that the Chinese not only knew of
this policy decision but of "all our strategic troop movements."

Eastland was at his caustic best when the State Depart-

ment, setting out what it believed to be the duties of the
American Department of the Foreign Office, quoted the
former Foreign Secretary, Mr. Harold Macmillan (during
the 1955 Burgess and Maclean debate): "This department in the Foreign Office deals principally with Latin-
American affairs. The United States questions which are
dealt with by the American Department are largely routine—welfare of forces, visitors and the like." Eastland
comments succinctly: "Nuts!"

So Maclean, through committee posts he held in Washington, was able to pass important information to the Russians. But his activities stretched beyond the committees
on which he acted and into the Atomic Energy Commission building itself. This has been disclosed by Admiral
Lewis Strauss, the former AEC chairman. Admiral
Strauss has described how he "learned that an alien was
the holder of a permanent pass to the Commission's headquarters, a pass, moreover, which was of a character
which did not require him to be accompanied within the
building." The holder of this pass was Donald Maclean.
Maclean was able to get his pass because there remained
in the AEC some Americans who considered Britain had
been badly treated and who favoured keeping some form
of co-operation alive. They were outnumbered by those
who wanted to stick strictly to the MacMahon Act.

Those who wanted to see the MacMahon Act reinforced to the letter were able to point to what they considered rather alarming lapses from elementary security
and there seems little doubt things were fairly relaxed in
the early years of the American programme. For example,
Mark Bonham Carter, a member of the distinguished Asquith family, was in the United States in 1947 and wanted
to go to Los Alamos. He was staying with some people
who knew a Los Alamos scientist. The scientist "wrote
out the required bit of paper" and Mr. Bonham Carter
walked right in.

The General Manager of the AEC in 1947 was Carroll
L. Wilson, now Professor of Industrial Management at the
Massachusetts Institute of Technology. Wilson favoured
maintaining at least some form of co-operation with the
British so when Maclean's immediate boss, the British
representative on the CDA, Sir Gordon Munro, approached Wilson for a pass for Maclean, Wilson took
what must be considered a courageous decision and

granted it. In the course of our investigation Professor Wilson admitted quite freely: "I gave the order for a pass to be issued to Donald Maclean. We had the CDA operating from an office in the AEC building. It was staffed by a full-time British secretary. Sir Gordon often had occasion to call on this secretary and he had a pass to allow him to do so. One day Sir Gordon asked me for a pass for his assistant, Donald Maclean. I knew Maclean and I saw no reason why I should not extend to him the same facility as had been extended to Sir Gordon. I had the authority to do so and I did it. If I had had any suspicion about Maclean then naturally I would not have given him a pass. But I thought Maclean to be safe. Strauss later revoked the pass. He had always been against telling the British anything." What Professor Wilson did not mention were his feelings when Maclean betrayed him.

Strauss heard of the pass from Rear-Admiral John Gingrich, who was in charge of AEC security. Gingrich had received a report from the building security officer, Brian La Plante, that Maclean was using his pass after office hours, several times a week and over a period of months. Strauss says he was stunned by this because non-escort passes were extremely rare (General Groves, head of the American atomic programme, did not at that time have one) and its use in this manner was highly unauthorised. He personally ordered the pass cancelled and this brought bitter protests from the British. "In view of the flak I had to absorb over this," Admiral Strauss says, "it was no little satisfaction for me to find out later how right I had been."

When security access to a building is tightly controlled, security inside can sometimes be limited. It is clear from the evidence of former employees that despite safes and security drill, there could have been material for Maclean in the AEC building even if only out of the files from his own CDA office. No one, except Maclean and his Soviet masters, knows what information he did get during his nocturnal visits but to any argument that he could not have found *anything*, there remains, in reply, this question: If Maclean was getting nothing out of the AEC building then why did he return there again and again,

How did Maclean's position look at this particular point in his secret career? Secretary of the CPC, on the CDA, a pass to the AEC, briefed by members of all three on policy, politics and development; fully informed from London on Britain's atomic energy programme, *plus* what could be picked up on the Washington cocktail circuit— this surely amounts to a formidable intelligence operation by any agent.

As could be expected, the strain of this sort of operation soon showed in Maclean's personal life. He began to drink more. His relations with Melinda began to deteriorate. He started to display an anti-American attitude. His "accelerated promotion" to counsellor in Cairo in September 1948 probably came just in time.

Maclean's first period of espionage on a grand scale was over. Summed up, how important was it? There are two clues, one public but overlooked, the other until now highly secret. The secret one was a decision taken by the CIA in 1956 to look at the possibility of snatching Maclean out of Russia. It went as far as examining aerial photographs of Moscow, locating and identifying Maclean's house, measuring the ground and the fence. In the end the scheme came to nothing but obviously the CIA would not have gone to these lengths for a spy of little importance.

The second clue is contained in a speech made by the Secretary of the Army, Wilber M. Brucker, on February 17, 1956, which was cleared by the White House and was the first public assessment of the diplomats by a U.S. official. It will certainly be the view of history. "Burgess and Maclean," Brucker said, "had secrets of priceless value to the communist conspiracy."

DOWNFALL

15. Crack-up

Maclean was guilty of serious misconduct.
　　　—WHITE PAPER on the disappearance of
　　　　　Burgess and Maclean, 1955

Maclean was a successful spy of the "nuts-and-bolts" description: he was able to pass huge quantities of valuable and hard-to-get facts across to his Soviet masters. His output would have been limited more by his nerve and the efficiency of the network that was serving him than by any limitation on the quantity of material available. (Philby's role was often different: the moulding of policy, the study of aims and methods, and the destruction of individual operations.) But Maclean paid a high price for his success.

His personality would no doubt have disintegrated, at some time in his life, under its own inbuilt stresses. But the nature of his occupation did no more than accelerate the crack-up. The Washington social circuit of Georgetown cocktail parties has broken many men with more native resilience than Donald Maclean. Both he and Melinda were relieved when his posting came to an end and he was transferred to Cairo. His anger against America and his deep distaste for American life had certain public expressions—he tended to dissociate himself from Americans and, increasingly, he was drinking too much. Nevertheless, when the Ambassador, Sir Archibald Clark Kerr (the late Lord Inverchapel , posed on occasion for photographs of the Embassy in action he usually invited Maclean, looking benevolent and judicious, to lend his profile. He was on these occasions so much the model of a rising young diplomat that it verged on self-caricature.

Inverchapel was no mean eccentric himself. He had arrived in Washington from Moscow, his previous posting, with an unusual parting present from Stalin in his entourage. As a special favour, the Soviet leader had arranged for the ambassador's valet, a Russian who spoke no English, to leave the Soviet Union with his master. It was not the kind of gesture which made the FBI sanguine about British security procedures.

Evgeni Yost, a 24-year-old originating from the Volga steppes, also doubled as the ambassador's masseur. When Inverchapel retired to Scotland and his Argyllshire estate in 1948, Evgeni accompanied him again. In 1981 he was still in Scotland, father of nine children and successful owner of a fish and chip shop.

Probably only Melinda realised how agonising were the tensions that Maclean buried beneath his urbane exterior; he had now got into the habit of treating her consistently badly, even while she was having her second child in 1946. All in all his posting to America had not been a great success and yet, in the autumn of 1948, his Egyptian transfer carried with it what in Foreign Office jargon is called "an accelerated promotion." Although his age and experience should have dictated a posting as First Secretary he was promoted to Counsellor and Head of Chancery—a considerable jump. The Ambassador in Cairo was an old friend: Sir Ronald Campbell, who had been Minister in Paris when Maclean was Third Secretary. Campbell remembered Donald, whom he respected and liked. Later, when the Cairo posting was to prove even more of a strain on Maclean than Washington, Campbell remained loyal to Donald, even though Maclean had committed a series of sins that would seem unforgivable. He did not simply misbehave; he misbehaved publicly.

But all this was far in the future when, in October 1948, the Macleans, with their two children, arrived in the lush Cairo suburb of Gezira. Melinda was delighted to be away from Washington and optimistic that their scarred marriage might be healed in the new atmosphere. Their house was enormous; it had a garden overflowing with scarlet and gold flowers, there were tall trees and tables and chairs for drinks parties in the cool of evening. She had two children to look after but there were also four Egyptian servants and an English governess. More important for Melinda, who had always been something of a snob, Cairo preserved, as if in aspic, many elements of the old British Raj as St. John had known it. Many of the British officials in Cairo had originally been in Indian postings. Now, transferred to a new country, they had brought their pretensions—and extremely generous for-

eign allowances—with them. Social life was as intense as
in Washington but more gracious; Melinda wrote ecstatic
letters to her family describing the *dolce vita* which she
had always felt should be the prerogative of a diplomat's
wife, though she had never previously experienced it.
Also, as wife of the Head of Chancery, she had taken a
step up the diplomatic social hierarchy.

But her husband was providing more cause for concern.
In Washington his anti-Americanism had aroused little
comment; it was anyway shared by many of his Embassy
colleagues who tended to dislike Americans for snobbish,
not ideological, reasons and also felt a certain resentment
at the way the USA had displaced Britain as the leader
of the democratic world. When Maclean, after too many
drinks, had criticised the States indiscreetly they had all
assumed that his objections stemmed from the same kind
of motivations as their own; it had certainly never occurred to anyone that his distaste was the result of pro-
Communist views.

But in Cairo his "Bolshie" views were more obvious,
and much less sympathetic to his new colleagues. Maclean
found the corrupt Farouk régime nauseous and made no
secret of the fact. He was also entirely out of sympathy
with Britain's time-hallowed policy of playing internal political groups off against each other and exerting no pressure on the King to initiate reform of any kind. Late at
night Maclean was now inclined to make virulent and
highly uncomfortable comparisons between the extreme
ease of the life the diplomatic colony shared with the
hangers-on of Farouk's court and the miserable fate of
ninety percent of the indigenous population. This was regarded as bad form.

So was drinking. He no longer got drunk like a gentleman but embarked on a series of epic, Dylanesque binges
which involved the Egyptian police and members of the
diplomatic colony. He was arrested by the Egyptians,
dead drunk and without shoes—they refused to believe he
had any connection with the British Embassy. His hangovers now reached such proportions that he was often absent from the office, a fact not known to the Ambassador,
who still found Maclean's work satisfactory.

But though the Ambassador was not told what was happening the Embassy security officer was.

Major "Sammy" Sansom, the incumbent of this post,

remarked in the course of the investigations for this book, "I was the most hated man in the Embassy." Sansom, a blunt bull-like man who rose from the ranks, said this with evident satisfaction. He believed that a security chief doing the job properly must inevitably be an unpopular figure, a questionable thesis, and accordingly he was exceedingly tough with any secretaries who were having indiscreet affairs with local gigolos. He had succeeded in having several sent home for comparatively minor misbehaviour, which nonetheless prejudiced Embassy security and he now wasted no time in reporting Maclean. "I thought him a brilliant chap but highly unreliable," Sansom recalls. "I reported his drinking direct via the diplomatic bag."

Despite the clarity of his reports Sansom, to his irritation, found that his recommendations about a transfer for Maclean were ignored. He became even more sceptical about Maclean's worth when the Head of Chancery brusquely turned down a suggestion he made that members of the Embassy staff should be subjected to spot checks to ensure that they were not illegally taking secret papers out of the building. The men had another row when the fifth copy of a top secret telegram from London was lost; Sansom thought Maclean was responsible for this carelessness. As Cairo was a "Grade A" Embassy, they were on the top level distribution list for policy and information cables from the Foreign Office and other important embassies, including Washington, Moscow and Paris. The Head of Chancery, who is a kind of works manager of an Embassy, has access to all communications —he passes them to the Ambassador—and therefore he is invariably the best-informed man in the place. Sansom, with perfect justification, felt that it would have been hard to find a man less fitted for such a responsible position.

Certainly, by spring 1949, Maclean's drinking had assumed formidable proportions. One Embassy wife of the period told a story which provides a fascinating vignette of the Head of Chancery in action. When Maclean stopped at her house on the way back from the Embassy in the evenings, he got into the habit of announcing his presence in a novel way. Instead of ringing the bell he liked to clamber over the garden wall and bark like a dog outside, pawing at the window to attract attention. The servants, children and visitors gradually became accus-

tomed to this. "Every time we heard a barking noise we
would say—'Don't worry, it must be Donald again.'"

Early in March the Macleans hired a wide-sailed barge
and set off up the Nile to have dinner with friends at
Helouan, fifteen miles from Cairo. Harriet, Melinda's sister, was with them on holiday; their idea was to spend a
picturesque couple of hours having a kind of floating
cocktail party before dinner. It was Melinda's idea; she
thought Harriet would be amused. But everything went
drastically, disastrously wrong. The wind dropped and the
voyage took nearly eight hours. There was plenty of drink
on board but no food. Everyone was bored, frustrated and
rather drunk by the time they arrived at 2 A.M. Everyone,
that is, except Donald who was as drunk as anyone had
ever seen him—lurching, mumbling and incoherent with
rage, most of it directed against Melinda.

She was the first casualty. Maclean's hostility towards
her could not be restrained any longer—he seemed to
have it in his head that she was responsible for the slow-
ness of the felucca. He pushed her up against the mast
and tried to throttle her; eventually the rest of the party
hauled him off and he went into a sulk, sitting on the deck
breathing heavily through his nose and snorting to himself
from time to time. The second casualty came as soon as
they arrived. An American in the party, who had also got
rather drunk, fell over and cracked his skull.

There was a tremendous furore and an old Egyptian
watchman, puzzled by the row, came down to the shore
and challenged the party with his ancient rifle. Maclean
lost his temper and jumped on the man, disarming him.
Then he started to swing the rifle round his head and it
looked as though they would soon have someone else with
a cracked skull. Lees Mayall, an Embassy colleague who
was as tall as Maclean, grabbed him from behind in an
attempt to remove the weapon. Maclean lurched over
backwards on top of Mayall, who fell awkwardly on the
shore. He discovered that he could not get up and that he
had broken his leg.

While this pantomime was taking place other members
of the expedition were ringing their host's door bell. The
house was blacked out, and everyone had gone to bed. It
took them a long time to persuade the host to let them in
at all. Eventually they were able to carry the injured
American upstairs to a bedroom and here once more the

evening descended into low farce. The bedroom they chose turned out to be occupied by a lady who was sprawled across the bed wearing only a pair of slacks, so they were forced to make a hurried exit. Maclean remained downstairs where he was bullying the Egyptian servant into opening the drinks cabinet, which the host had locked before allowing any of them in. Armed with a bottle of gin he returned to Mayall, still lying by the Nile, and offered him some as an anaesthetic. Maclean was maudlin and contrite and rambled on while they waited for the dawn and transport. When a taxi finally arrived he refused to get into it, insisting that the driver was an abortionist. The battle-stained party did not arrive back in Cairo until late the next morning. They were in considerable disarray.

Miraculously, the incident was hushed up and for a short time Maclean avoided mixing whisky and zebib, the Egyptian version of arak, a combination which invariably led to disaster. The Macleans had now moved to a house on the island suburb of Zamalek and were in dispute with the British owner of their previous house at Gezira. Inspecting his property after their departure he was amazed to find it looking as though an occupying army had been through it; electrical fittings had been wrenched out, windows smashed and furniture broken. He made a claim against Maclean to make good the damage, which appeared to have been caused in a fight, or a series of them.

It was becoming common knowledge among the Embassy staff that Maclean was in the midst of a serious alcoholic crack-up but, apart from occasional absences caused by hangovers, his work stood up remarkably well. Philip Toynbee has described in an *Observer* article how one morning Maclean woke up with a villainous hangover, "groaning, holding his eyes, and vomiting." But once he had arrived at the Embassy, with the sentry coming to attention and beginning his salute, "Donald's whole face and bearing changed. His body regained its lost dignity; his face became wise, benevolent and responsible." Maclean was still able to keep his separate personalities in compartments but the strain was evidently becoming intolerable. Soon he was to reach a point where the Foreign Office act, the "Sir Donald" persona he sometimes used to make wry jokes about, was completely submerged by the wild alcoholic bohemian.

Claude Lewin, the civil air attaché, was one of Maclean's most objective colleagues. "Skip," as Lewin was known, often used to lend Melinda his chauffeur-driven car to get home after parties where Maclean was drinking heavily, and on one occasion he recalls Maclean pushing his foot off the clutch when they were on the way back and threatening to throw him into the Nile. But it was the only time he saw him really drunk. For the most part he was a conscientious, meticulous worker, a great student of files, which he worked on late into the night, and an official whose diplomatic gifts expressed themselves in a careful regard for the Egyptians' *amour-propre*. When Maclean arrived a civil aviation agreement was being drafted, but in its first stages the documents contained no provision for the normal air practice by which an incoming flight requests permission to land. "Skip" thought that British planes should make this request as a matter of courtesy, even though it was understood that permission would always be granted automatically. Maclean emphatically agreed: "A good deal too much is taken for granted here already," he remarked. But his utility as a diplomat was nearing its end.

In later years wild rumours circulated about Maclean's Cairo peccadilloes. The Foreign Office security men, who formerly would never have heard a word against him, now appeared to be ready to consider the most preposterous canards. A senior diplomat was even asked to confirm that he had attended a party at Maclean's house in Zamalek where the Head of Chancery was said to have entertained guests assembled in the garden by posing in front of a lighted window, through which it could be seen that he was making love to an Arab boy. This story was a myth; such a party never took place, and there is no evidence of overt homosexuality at this stage. The truth, though less picturesque, was quite lurid enough.

The arrival of Philip Toynbee, himself recovering from the strain of a divorce, seems to have been the decisive factor in Maclean's ultimate Cairo crack-up. The two old friends consoled each other over long nights drinking zebib and, unfortunately, Melinda departed with her sister for a holiday, leaving them in the house unshackled. She might have had a premonition of what was coming. Maclean and Toynbee attended a party for Princess Fawzia,

King Farouk's sister, both very much the worse for wear. Seated on either side of her on a sofa they collapsed into an indistinguishable alcoholic huddle when she rose to her feet, doubtless deciding that their conversation had taken an undiplomatic turn. Toynbee recalls an incident at a dinner party where Maclean started a violent attack on a young Copt whom he thought, wrongly as it turned out, had decided to betray a set of former Communist friends at Cairo University. Again on this occasion Princess Fawzia was involved when Maclean appealed to her to back him up. She was an odd choice of ally and Maclean's sentiments must have sounded even odder coming from the Head of Chancery at the British Embassy. Toynbee, like many friends of Maclean, constantly had the impression that he was finally going to come out with whatever was worrying him. But Maclean, though he was anything but discreet, stopped short at a final confession.

His last week in Egypt was a spectacular one. On May 10, 1950, a British journalist, Miss Margaret Pope, who worked for an Egyptian paper called *Al Misri* and had unusually good official sources, received a police tip-off that a high-ranking British diplomat was being held in an Alexandrian jail. The British Embassy fiercely denied that any of their men were missing but, in the same breath, declined to issue an official statement to the same effect. Miss Pope rightly suspected that they were dissembling and tried another phone call twenty-four hours later. This time the press officer said he was prepared to meet her but specified with suspicious insistence that she should go to the Chancery, and not the headquarters of the British Middle East Office where their meetings normally took place. Again Miss Pope's journalist reflexes worked accurately; she agreed, but set off immediately for the BMEO, where she arrived in time to see a remarkable incident. Two Embassy security men were helping a lanky, unshaven figure down the steps and having considerable trouble, as he was tottering. They poured him into a waiting car and drove to Farouk Field airport, pursued by the indefatigable Miss Pope. She saw the same man helped on to a plane and went back to town for an explanation. The Embassy confirmed that the man was Donald Maclean and that he was returning home "suffering from a nervous breakdown." From other sources over the next week she pieced together the full story. Maclean had been arrested in Alexandria and confined in a special jail for drunken sailors. For two days his condition had been so bad that no-one had managed to extract any sense from him. The police, certain he must be a sailor, were inquiring among ships' captains to see who had lost a man, but without success. Eventually the prisoner had sobered up enough to insist that he was a British diplomat and the local consul had identified him. He was returned to the Cairo Embassy, in deplorable shape, and it was now clear that he was too hot to hold. The Egyptian press had got on to the affair and it was decided to ship him home before the publicity got out of hand.

The last week in Cairo had been an uproarious series of picaresque incidents worthy of Guy Burgess. In the course of a forty-eight-hour drunk he had forced his way into the flat of one of the secretaries attached to the U.S. Embassy, gone through her wardrobes, and dumped a lot of her clothes in the lavatory. As climax to the evening he had smashed a table, chopped up some of the furniture and smashed her bath with a marble shelf. Maclean had found the whole performance hysterically amusing; apart from the joy of destruction, he was delighted because "the bloody girl's an American." The sentiment would have appealed to Guy Burgess, who was as anti-American as Maclean. Burgess was shortly to have foreign service problems of his own. In August 1950, while Maclean was recuperating in England from his Egyptian excesses, Burgess was posted to Washington.

Burgess's posting to the U.S.A. with the rank of First Secretary has never been fully explained. By any standards it was a most curious appointment. It would be hard to think of anyone less well suited for such a job at such a period—the Korean War had begun in June 1950. The only explanation is that Burgess somehow convinced Hector McNeil that he should use his influence to get him the posting; but there is evidence that McNeil, Sir George Middleton—head of Personnel in the Foreign Office—and even Burgess himself, all had considerable reservations, and even forebodings, about what was to come.

Before he left for Washington, George Middleton gave Burgess some advice about how he should conduct himself. Burgess had pointed out that, given the political situation, he felt certain misapprehensions about his future job, particularly as his area was to be the Far East, and his role to explain Britain's policy there to the State Department. Middleton, according to Burgess, advised him to soft-pedal on his socialist views; it turned out that there had been an incident involving another politically-committed young man on the Washington strength, who had been overheard by an FBI informer talking like a Red at a private cocktail party. McNeil was even more specific. The week before Burgess left he gave a large party in the Bond Street flat which, by Burgess's standards at least, was restrained and respectable. McNeil, leaving, delivered a valedictory admonition: "For God's sake, Guy," he said, "remember three things when you get to the States. Don't be too aggressively left-wing. Don't get involved in race relations; and, above all, make sure there aren't any homosexual incidents which might cause trouble." A friend who was collecting his hat and umbrella in the hall was privileged to hear Burgess's response to this excellent counsel. "I understand, Hector," said Guy, looking his most mischievous. "What you mean is I mustn't make a pass at Paul Robeson." It was an inauspicious prelude to a spell in Washington which was to be little short of disastrous.

Within weeks of his arrival Burgess had clashed with his superior, Sir Hubert Graves, who was Counsellor at the Embassy; Graves had him removed from the Far Eastern Department and Burgess repaid him later in conversation with Tom Driberg by remarking: "Graves was the wrong type of ex-consul." Burgess was inflamed by what he regarded as the dictatorial approach of the State Department and the failure of the British Embassy to project their own government's policy with either confidence or conviction. He was particularly irritated by the role of General MacArthur, the friend of Chiang Kai-shek. Guy habitually referred to Chiang as "The mad satrap." It was clear that Burgess's days in Washington were numbered.

The Washington period would not have been of any particular importance had it not been for the fact that when Burgess arrived Philby offered to put him up at the family house, a comfortable diplomatic residence in tree-lined Nebraska Avenue. Philby told his Embassy colleagues that Burgess had been having a hard time in London and that he intended to straighten him out. Philby's decision, apparently a quixotic gesture, turned out to be fatal for his long-preserved cover. But he has since told people in Moscow that his Soviet superiors approved his plan to help Guy.

As a house guest Burgess had certain disadvantages and Aileen found him frankly a strain; he drank enormously, came home at all hours, and left empty bottles about the house. The Philby children, Josephine, John, and Tommy, remember "Uncle Guy" as a generous but slightly alarming figure smelling strongly of alcohol and tobacco. His thick fingers with heavily bitten nails were yellow with nicotine and constantly employed in making repairs to John Philby's "O" gauge electric train set which occupied a place of honour, covering most of Burgess's room in the basement. Burgess, who was always bringing presents home for the children, including a large wigwam, was fascinated by the trains and spent hours playing with them. He had time on his hands because it was soon clear that the Embassy regarded him as unsuitable for any responsible job.

Apart from his political opinions, he was too drunk. Squadron-Leader "Tommy" Thompson, the Embassy security officer, whose relations with Burgess were curiously similar to those of his Cairo colleague, Major Sansom, with Donald Maclean, reckoned that Burgess was at the office in an alcholic stupor several days each week. When Burgess arrived Thompson thought he was so obviously unsuitable that it could only be a deep-laid plot of MI 5. Burgess seemed to delight in baiting Thompson over security matters. Not only did he leave classified documents on his desk, instead of returning them to the safe at the end of the day, he also infuriated the Security Officer by losing the special pink slips which he was supposed to fill in explaining and apologising for these misdemeanours. In Cairo, Sansom had been tantalised beyond endurance by Maclean's supercilious disregard for his recommendation as security officer; Thompson now found himself identically placed. Both security officers were hampered by the Foreign Office's unspoken conception that the only people who might be disloyal were typists, chauffeurs and other minor operatives recruited from the lower-middle class. It was the job of security officers to pursue these people, and not to mess about with the diplomats. Burgess had a cavalier way with those he regarded as his social inferiors and Thompson, like Sansom, soon reached the conclusion that there was nothing to be done except get rid of Burgess. He did not have long to wait.

In February 1951, Burgess was stopped three times in one day for speeding by Virginia state policemen. His only comment afterwards was irritation that they had charged him with travelling at eighty mph: "I was doing at least a hundred," he said. More important from the point of view of Embassy security was the fact that he was accompanied by a U.S. citizen with a record for homosexual offences. The FBI report on the matter, a copy of which reached the Ambassador, pointed this out and Sir Oliver Franks decided the time had come to get rid of his recalcitrant junior.

It was not as if Burgess were even usefully employed. In order to keep him quietly out of the way he had been given the undesirable job of sorting letters, thousands of them, which listeners to a radio network had sent after a commentator had appealed to all those who thought Britain was dragging her heels over Korea to write to the British Embassy saying so. For weeks Burgess sat in the library studying this voluminous correspondence and replying to the less lunatic contributions. It was not a task calculated to endear the great American public to Guy Burgess.

In December 1950 Joseph Alsop, the distinguished American pundit and columnist, gave a party for Michael Berry, proprietor of the *Daily Telegraph*, and his wife, Lady Pamela. Burgess, who had known Berry at Eton, arrived uninvited and drunk; he was also conspicuous, as usual, because of his dishevelled appearance—the party was formal and all the other men were in dinner jackets. Burgess had a noisy argument, with Alsop eventually turning him out of the house. Burgess claimed later that during this party Michael Berry, hearing Burgess's by now standard condemnation of the Foreign Office, offered him a job on the *Telegraph*. The Berrys insist there was no such offer; and the incident was to assume a certain importance later on.

It was only a matter of time before Burgess was suspended but there was one more crucial incident before he left. Philby had insisted Burgess should get an apartment of his own but in February 1951 he spent a weekend with the Philbys. Aileen was busy with the new baby, Harry, and after lunch on Sunday, Philby and Burgess went for a walk in the garden. According to the story Philby told afterwards he then took Burgess into his confidence and gave him certain information that had come to him in his capacity as liaison man between the SIS and the CIA. This was that an MI 5 investigation of a security leakage first discovered in 1949 had eliminated seven hundred Foreign Office employees and isolated four suspects. Of these Donald Maclean was regarded as the most likely.

Philby was to claim publicly that he gave Burgess this information in all innocence, simply because he knew Burgess had been a friend of Maclean's at Cambridge. It was a thin story at the time but, as events proved, perfectly serviceable given the protective reflexes of SIS and their gentlemanly lack of scepticism. In Beirut, just before he defected, Philby stuck to approximately the same story, confirming that he had warned Burgess but admitting this time his intention was to get a message to Maclean. It is still a strange story.

Why was Philby, who could hardly have had any mock-modest doubts about his own importance as an agent, prepared to risk his cover for the sake of another agent whose best work was done? On the face of it, such a step is opposed to every canon of espionage. But there is one point which we should make briefly here—although it is spelt out more fully in later chapters. *Had Burgess not fled at the same time as Maclean, Philby would not have been suspected.* It is therefore highly possible that some other factor entered the situation after Philby had taken the first step.

There is a further point. Throughout this story, there is another silent, unseen actor: the many-headed Soviet network which serviced Maclean and Philby. Maclean, had he been successfully interrogated, would certainly have "cracked." And he might well have divulged information which would do massive damage to the Soviet organisation in the West. Had he been charged and proved guilty, the event would have reacted on Western concepts of security in a way that his mere disappearance could not do, and apart from anything else, the backgrounds of major Soviet assets like Kim Philby would have been remorselessly inquired into. The belief that Maclean had valuable information to give to the West is supported by the seriousness with which the CIA, at least, regarded the disaster of his escape.

Philby's choice of Burgess as the intermediary remains slightly mysterious. The two men were close to each other and almost certainly knew each other's role though there is little evidence that Burgess had been spying during his Washington period.

Burgess, of course, was indiscreet, drunken, and unreliable. But now and again investigation turns up traces of that curiously hard substratum in his character. He was never late for appointments. He always managed to do things he really wanted to do, and somewhere tucked away inside him was a powerful, if distorted, will. One is reminded of his remark years before when Hewit mentioned the apparent paradox of Philby working on the Franco side. "Kim would not have gone to Franco unless he had a very good reason," Burgess had commented. Never since that time had he said anything indiscreet about Philby, although he must have had at least some idea of what was going on. Now, perhaps for the first time, he learnt exactly what Philby was. Two months later he left on the *Queen Mary* for London.

16. Getaway

Back on Monday.
—GUY BURGESS to a sailor on Southampton
docks, Friday, May 25, 1951

Donald Maclean was waiting at 1 P.M. on the Foreign Office steps, a tall imposing figure in his grey suit and bow tie. He was in an excellent mood, as his friend Lady Mary Campbell observed as soon as she arrived to collect him, driving her jeep. Over the previous year the two of them had devised a code for indicating Maclean's mood, based on the black felt hat he invariably wore. If the brim were turned up all round it meant he was happy; if down, as she recalls, "Donald was feeling shaky and had to be treated with kid-gloves." On this occasion she was particularly pleased to see that Maclean's brim was contentedly up for the date was May 25, 1951, his thirty-eighth birthday. The two of them were joining her husband, Robin Campbell, who had been with Donald at Turquet's, the crammer's, seventeen years before. They had planned a celebration lunch.

For Maclean the year since his return from Cairo in such inauspicious circumstances had been a difficult one; yet in some ways he had been remarkably lucky. The Foreign Office had behaved generously. Sir George Middleton, head of personnel and a friend from Washington, had been understanding, and the FO consultant psychiatrist had recommended that he should have a six months' break to recover from "overwork." He also suggested that Maclean should go into a clinic, a sensible idea. Maclean pleaded to be allowed to consult a woman psychiatrist instead of having full-time treatment and unfortunately this suggestion was accepted. It was a self-destructive decision; the effects were probably worse than they would have been had Maclean continued to do a job in the Foreign Office. At least he would have had less time to brood —and to drink. As it was he spent several months doing little else, and his psychological state was adversely affected by his prodigious alcoholic intake.

His letters to Melinda were beset with fears and self-doubts, extravagant expressions of love, and heavy with a sense of guilt that was becoming one of Maclean's overriding characteristics. Although her mother arrived to help, he had left Melinda with bills to pay and the children to look after. In the course of the first three months she leant heavily on a wealthy Egyptian prince, who had been pursuing her for so long that it had become a joke among the Cairo diplomatic colony. Finally he seemed to have caught her and they went off on an extended holiday to Spain and North Africa.

Maclean, in London, Oxford and the country, did not allow this to disturb him. He told friends that he could not bear the sight of Melinda, and also that he felt miserably guilty at his own hostility towards her. All in all, he was in a sorry mess. Cyril Connolly, who had known him since the days of "Lady Maclean," when the weekend guests had put a female figure-head in his bed, came across him in London, and described the decline with his usual precision. "His appearance was frightening: he had lost his serenity, his hands would tremble, his face was usually a livid yellow and he looked as if he had spent the night sitting up in a tunnel. One evening a man leaving a night-club got into an empty taxi and found him asleep on the rug. . . . In conversation a kind of shutter would fall as if he had returned to some basic and incommunicable anxiety."

His friends thought this anxiety was to do with his sex-life, a subject he was now discussing with all the long-winded self-questioning and qualification of a subject under analysis. His analyst was an Austrian lady whom he called "Dr. Rosie." She had a reputation as a Jungian but judging from her advice, as relayed by Maclean to friends during many late-night soul-searching sessions, she must also have had more than a passing interest in her fellow-countryman Freud. She fastened, for example, on the more or less suppressed homosexual aspect of his character, which had been noticeable since his schooldays. She seems to have suggested that he was drinking to anaesthetise his guilt and release his inhibitions sufficiently for him to embark on homosexual adventures—most of which apparently took place when he was more or less drunk. Her advice was for him to face this element in himself frankly and live without fear. He seems to have taken it only too literally, with results that were more farcical than therapeutic. For several months he claimed, rather absurdly, to be passionately in love with a Negro porter who worked at a nightclub called the Moonglow in Percy Street. Maclean's suit did not prosper; instead on at least one occasion the porter beat him up quite severely. Maclean solemnly recounted the details of his chequered love-life to at least two experienced and sensible women of his own age or older. During the summer of 1950, with Melinda still away, he seemed to have re-created the pre-Melinda period in Paris, when he had leant on two older women to advise him. Now he had taken the process a stage further and acquired a woman psychiatrist as well.

Maclean's personality differed so radically according to his sobriety, or lack of it, that Philip Toynbee in Cairo had half-jokingly suggested he should christen his *alter ego* "Gordon," after the tusky red boar that appears on the label of an export gin. Toynbee had in the same spirit given himself a second name, "Charlie Parsley," so that whenever Toynbee got drunk it was "Charlie" who had misbehaved, not Toynbee. Now Maclean's friends started saying: "My God, Gordon was pretty bloody last night, wasn't he?" These people who kept Maclean going, many of whom had been through a few *louche* exploits of their own over the years, were kind, loyal and uncensorious. Cyril Connolly has described their assessment of Maclean's mental state in 1950 better than anyone else:

"It was not just over-work, but over-strain; the effort of being 'Sir Donald,' the whole paraphernalia of 'OHMS,' had been too much for him and he had reverted to his adolescence or his ideal of Paris days, the free and solitary young sculptor working all night in his attic. . . . 'Gordon' had given 'Sir Donald' the sack. The enraged junior partner would no longer put up with him."

This was all true, as far as it went, but what no one realised—how could they have done?—was that Maclean's passionate distaste for the Foreign Office was really philosophical in nature. Certainly he was heartily sick of diplomatic parties and official restraints, all the exigencies that the Service brings to bear on its budding "Sir Donalds." But this was the summer of the Korean war, and during his Egyptian tour of duty he had been responsible for projecting and carrying out Government policies which he regarded, with some justification, as despicable. To his friends, Maclean's conflicts all looked like personal ones; they did not understand that there was an enormous ideological content. The same was true of Burgess in Washington.

Maclean never as much as mentioned politics to his *confidantes*—they were not political people—but with men friends like Robin Campbell he hinted at his underlying problems with mounting indiscretion. When drunk now, lurching round the room and breathing noisily through his nose, he lapsed into long silences, as if battling with the violent impulses which invariably surfaced before the night was out.

Robin Campbell recalls one evening in the country when Maclean talked of his longing "for a leap of faith that would convince him that Communism was right." Campbell was not surprised by this; all Maclean's friends were aware that he was an extremist who had a strong, quasi-religious streak in his makeup. As Campbell remarked afterwards, "He talked on several occasions about Communism in the same way that a potential Catholic aware that he lacked the gift of faith might discuss religion." At the time it was a sensitive and sensible diagno-

sis. With hindsight Campbell might have modified it
slightly. Maclean was really talking like an already established member of the Church suffering from an invasion
of doubt and a crisis of faith.

There were also worse symptoms of despair; it was
clear that Maclean was desperately frightened. In August
1950 he stayed for a period at a friend's house in Oxford,
and wrote an abject letter. He was living, he said, "on a
diet of sedatives and pints of bitter." The precise, inhibited writing that had appeared on thousands of FO internal memoranda marked "Secret," now lurched chaotically
from left to right down the page as he continued: "There
are two men in a car waiting outside. They've been there
for four hours. Are they after me?" Then, with the obsessive and boring self-questioning of a man who was spending hours a week with an analyst, he went on to wonder
whether the strangers in the car really existed. Perhaps,
he thought, they might be a projection of guilt, the habitual Maclean guilt about drink and violence.

His friends assured him it was all paranoic nonsense,
and so did his analyst. Naturally they did not know his
main worry was that the "men in the car" might be the
stolid, bowler-hatted stalwarts of MI 5—that perhaps they
had finally got on to him. The "Eumenides with blood on
their paws," as he once called them in a literary moment,
were closing in to avenge the treachery in Washington. It
is highly unlikely that the men from MI 5, who by 1951
were following him with clumsy conscientiousness, were
on duty as early as the autumn of 1950. His fears were
therefore irrational in one sense; in another they were all
too firmly based on a logical foundation.

The *doppelgänger* Gordon was now thoroughly in command of "Sir Donald"; there were few people on the Soho
drinking club circuit who did not meet him fighting drunk
(the fights were usually unsuccessful despite his size and
physical strength). Boris Watson, proprietor of the Man-
drake Club off Dean Street, recalls: "He was always coming in, usually drunk. I must have thrown him out a dozen
times. I told him he could only use the place if he paid a
subscription, and he always said: 'I'm not going to join
this bloody place,' so I would throw him out. I made a
rule that he could come in with a member but not otherwise. Frankly, he was a damn nuisance."

The fighting was now a regular feature of his behav-

iour. One night during a skirmish in the neighbouring
Gargoyle Club he bit the painter Rodrigo Moynihan in
the knee. On another occasion he pushed Philip Toynbee
into the bandstand in the same club after an argument
about Chambers and Hiss. He was now given another
very appropriate nick-name—"The Lurcher," and he
would sway from bar to bar mumbling resentfully to himself, and at anyone unwise enough to cross his path. He
had also progressed beyond the oblique confused hints he
had previously let fall in front of Robin Campbell. One
night, red-faced and staggering in the Gargoyle, he ac-
costed several patrons with the words: "Buy me a drink.
I am the English Hiss."

And after a long dinner party in Chelsea he embarked
on a provocative conversation with Mark Culme-
Seymour. "What would you do if I told you I was working for Uncle Joe?"

"I suppose I would be very embarrassed."

"Well, wouldn't you report me?"

"I don't know. Who to?"

"Well, I am. . . . Go on, report me."

Culme-Seymour was embarrassed and confused. There
was a silence. Then Maclean launched into a long attack
on State Department policy over Korea, doubtless very
like the diatribes against MacArthur which Burgess was
delivering to Joseph Alsop and others in Washington at
much the same period. The next day Culme-Seymour felt
worried about the conversation and confided in Cyril Connolly. They decided that Maclean had probably been in-
dulging in a foolish and highly alcoholic loyalty test. He
had wanted Mark to prove what a good friend he was.
Anyway, if there was any truth in what he had said, MI 5
would doubtless know about it already.

By the time of this conversation there had been two
important changes in Maclean's life. Firstly, his psychiatrist had rather surprisingly decided that he had improved
sufficiently for him to return to work. This he did on November 1, 1950, as Head of the American Department in
London—he had told his superiors that he wished to remain in England for a spell. Secondly, his relations with
Melinda, after the usual ups and downs, had been partly
stabilised, temporarily at least. They were now re-united.

But it had been a close-run thing. During the summer
Melinda, in Spain with her family and the Egyptian

prince, had received a letter in which Donald more or less said that the marriage was over; he despaired of ever becoming an adequate husband. Melinda had reacted by appearing in London and telling Maclean that if only he could be sexually more active they might yet salvage the marriage. According to friends he then promised he would be more attentive, but after the first weekend ignored her again. She then returned to the Egyptian but only for a very short time. The prince found out that her brief encounter with her husband had led to another pregnancy, and his *amour-propre* (machismo) was outraged. They parted, acrimoniously. Melinda, having little choice, returned to London.

Deliberately she and Donald now decided to live out of town in the hope that the train-journey would discourage him from passing his nights drinking in London. It seemed a forlorn hope. They eventually found an isolated, ugly house called Beaconshaw near the village of Tatsfield, in Kent. Maclean became a commuter and for a time it worked reasonably well.

He was pleased, despite himself, to be back at the centre of things, and in some ways his new post was actually a promotion. In later years various attempts were made to play down the importance of his position, notably by Harold Macmillan, who claimed in the 1955 Commons debate that the American Department was mainly concerned with Latin-American affairs. "The U.S. questions which are dealt with . . . are largely routine, welfare of forces, visitors and the like."

This was correct in so far as the Department's executive powers were concerned. But the best comment on this typically airy and superior example of Macmillan's question answering technique was undoubtedly Senator Eastland's marginal comment on the State Department report, citing Macmillan, to which we referred in Chapter 13. "Nuts!" Eastland wrote.

Power of action is one thing, access to information quite another. In the Foreign Office, individual status is partly defined in terms of information access (as Head of Chancery in Cairo, a "Grade A" embassy, Maclean would have seen infinitely more important material than his counterpart in, say, Bogota or Prague). Now, as a Department head, he was on top "distribution lists" for other departmental material. This was the real importance of his job.

During his "Uncle Joe" conversation he had told Culme-Seymour that everything he did in the Department was designed to assist Communism. Culme-Seymour naturally did not understand the significance of this remark.

Between November 1950, when he began his American Department job, and May 25, 1951, when he very abruptly discontinued it, Maclean had good spells and bad. For days, sometimes weeks at a time, he would decorously join the shoals of commuters on the 5:19 from Charing Cross to Sevenoaks. He looked on these occasions rather more distinguished than the average commuter but just as dim and contented. But on other nights he would stay on in London drinking, periodically glancing at his wristwatch as if gauging whether or not he would make the last train to Sevenoaks. Often he failed to leave in time and the next morning, arriving in Whitehall with a crippling hangover, he would need to drink from the bottle of whisky he kept in his desk before he was up to shuffling through the latest memoranda.

Were the Russians still contacting him at this time? There seems nothing to have stopped them doing so, and the drunken, mysterious evenings in London might well have provided suitable occasions. Philby, the Russians' "man in Washington," was part of the investigation tracking down the leakage which had been discovered in 1949, and they could rely on him to tip them off if a suspect was about to be isolated—and watched. And the fact that there was vital information for the Russians to get from Maclean is highlighted by the Eastland document. The reference to Maclean's knowledge of the decision to limit the Korean conflict is particularly important: for President Truman's instruction only went to General MacArthur in November 1950, just after Maclean began his new job. The American Department of the FO was a mine of information on the question of the effect the Korean war was having on the Anglo-American alliance. One paper worked on, for instance, was detailing strains that were allegedly being caused to the British economy by America's purchases of raw materials for strategic stockpiling.

In April and May of 1951 Maclean seemed for a time to be deteriorating rapidly. Melinda's sister, Harriet, came to Beaconshaw for a visit and was shocked at her brother-in-law's condition. He was taut, irritable, and given to periods of brooding silence punctuated by sudden vehe-

ment irruptions of anger, invariably directed against the
British and American governments. Melinda, though she
never really understood very much about politics, had
been listening to similar outbursts for so long that some of
the opinions had rubbed off. She had always borrowed her
opinions and information from others; now she seemed
as repetitively anti-American as her husband. Maclean
talked to Harriet about politics and the boredom of com-
muting. He was obviously in sympathy with the Soviet
Union; equally obviously, he was worried and frightened.

He had good reason to be. Since Kim Philby's disclo-
sures to Burgess in the Nebraska Avenue garden, MI 5,
working with the FO security department, had grown increasingly certain that Maclean was their man. Accordingly they had him followed. They also took steps to
decrease some of the risks inherent in the situation and
Maclean must have noticed in April and May that though
he was still formally on the same distribution list many
secret documents of the kind that would previously have
found their way to his in-tray, were now diverted *en route*.
By now he knew, without any possible doubt, that the
men in the car outside were waiting for him.

Guy Burgess arrived back in England on May 7, right
in the middle of Maclean's bad period. Some commenta-
tors have tried to cast Burgess in the role of a kind of Soviet Galahad, returning home to organise a rescue
operation, but such an interpretation barely squares with
the facts. In the first place his return was highly leisurely;
had he felt there was a sense of urgency he could have
flown to London, and also left the States earlier. Instead
he came on the *Queen Mary* after a short holiday in New
York where he met, among others, Gladwyn Jebb, Britain's UN representative, and Alan Maclean, Donald's
younger brother, who was now working for Gladwyn Jebb
as his private secretary in the United States. There are
several apocryphal stories in existence about Burgess on
the boat, the most popular being that he was under the
surveillance of a CIA agent, whom he promptly spotted
and seduced. It is a good story, and certainly in character
with Burgess, but there is no evidence at all that he was
under any kind of suspicion at this time. He was, however, highly unpopular with the Foreign Office; Burgess's
main worry was finding himself a job.

It was clear that his diplomatic career was virtually finished. There was to be another disciplinary board and
though, thanks to Hector McNeil's influence, he had survived the board that had followed his Tangier trip, it was
highly unlikely the FO would be lenient a second time.
Burgess went to his old friend, Sir Harold Nicolson, for
advice and was asked whether he had any private money.
When he said he had Nicolson was firm: "Resign before
they sack you and find something else." Burgess said he
would think about it.

In the meantime he started looking for a job. He
sounded Michael Berry out again about working for *The
Daily Telegraph;* according to Berry, his response was discouraging but Burgess still went round London announcing that the job was virtually his. A week after he got
back he attended the Apostles' annual dinner, where he
told the wife of one of its leading members that he hoped
to work for *The Spectator* as motoring correspondent.
When the members returned to her house for drinks after
dinner Burgess made a determined effort to seduce a new
member which she interrupted. "I thought the poor boy
was a bit young for an old rogue like Guy. He disappeared
around midnight in a very bad mood and when I got up
he was on the doorstep in the hope that the young man
had stayed overnight. He was also looking for breakfast.
He told me he had driven to Shrewsbury and back—he
always liked driving fast at night." (One of the minor
mysteries of Burgess's life is that he always seemed to be
driving around in large cars without actually owning
them.)

In the course of the following week Burgess telephoned
Lady Maclean, Donald's mother, and asked for his private
address. It was a curious thing to do because he knew
perfectly well that Maclean was available from ten thirty
to five in Whitehall every day. The only explanation is
that he assumed Maclean's office phone was insecure. It
remains slightly mysterious because if it was then his
home line would almost certainly have been tapped as
well, and possibly his mother's. Perhaps Burgess drove
down to Tatsfield to deliver the warning face to face.
Whatever the truth about this it is known that in the week
of May 18 the two men met in the RAC club for lunch;
they had evidently chosen their meeting place with care.
They were unlikely to meet any colleagues, as they would

at the Travellers or the Reform. Burgess's later account of the meeting, which suggested they had chosen this unlikely rendezvous because the dining-room at the Reform was full, is as unconvincing as the rest of his version of the last ten days in England.

According to him the two had originally met at the FO because Burgess wished to show Donald a long paper he had produced on the dangers inherent in the U.S. approach to the Far East situation, for which he had been seeking FO support. During this meeting Maclean suggested the RAC club lunch. While they were on the way Maclean had burst out: "I'm in frightful trouble. I'm being followed by the dicks." He then pointed out two men "jingling their coins in a policeman-like manner and looking embarrassed at having to follow a member of the upper classes." He also added that the surveillance had been conducted so clumsily that a few days earlier the MI 5 car had run into the back of his taxi.

In the course of this lunch and two subsequent meetings Burgess claimed they found that they agreed warmly with each other's political views; both of them were obsessed by the "appalling situation"—the possibility of the U.S.A. extending the Korean conflict and provoking a world war. Finally Maclean had suggested that they should clear out to the Soviet Union and asked Burgess to assist him because his constant surveillance meant he could not as much as buy a ticket without MI 5 knowing.

Burgess replied: "Well, I'm leaving the Foreign Office anyhow, and I probably couldn't stick the job at *The Daily Telegraph*—and I think you're right. I don't see why I shouldn't come too."

And so the great defection was arranged. The advantage of this version according to Guy Burgess, is that it suggests the Soviet Union was in no way involved; and that neither was Philby. The truth was rather different.

It was also a good deal less vague. Philby had known from August 1950 onwards that MI 5 and Foreign Office Security were closing in on a spy of major importance. The London requests for files and documents made this perfectly certain though for a while it was impossible to deduce who the suspect was. But by the end of the year the requests they were receiving made it clear beyond doubt that Donald Maclean was the man on the spot. Although Philby, and a handful of other senior men in MI 5 and SIS, the CIA and the FBI, all knew that it was Maclean, his name was never mentioned. Official confirmation that Maclean was number one suspect only got to Washington in the first week of May 1951. Even now, as a senior official recalls: "We never used his name to each other. It was just understood who it was."

The same official did ask Philby if he knew "him." "Yes, I think we must have met at Cambridge some time or another," Philby replied, with characteristic vagueness.

At this point Philby knew it was virtually certain that Donald Maclean must eventually undergo interrogation, probably at the hands of William Skardon, the crack MI 5 investigator who, with his usual deceptive gentleness, had extracted an enormous amount of information from Klaus Fuchs (to whom he always referred nostalgically as "dear old Klaus"). Philby was well aware that Maclean, in the nervous condition he was in, would not have survived twenty-four hours with Skardon before telling all.

Philby probably informed the Russians in August 1950 that investigation was in progress, with Maclean in the list of suspects. He would have kept them informed with fair regularity as the net closed on Maclean, and at the beginning of 1951 it must have been clear that Donald's days were numbered. There can be little doubt what the Russians' response would have been: to press Maclean more and more fiercely. They would have wanted to get the last out of this rich vein before the roof of the mine fell in. You do not replace agents as well-placed as Donald Maclean with any ease.

It would not have been a very pleasant operation, but so long as Philby remained among the West's top counter-espionage men, the Russians could "time" the final squeezing-dry of Maclean, or any other source. This may well explain Philby's remark to his third wife, Eleanor, in Moscow—when he said that he felt that Donald Maclean's psychological condition was partly his fault. Philby had been calling the shots for the men who used Maclean.

The Russians, of course, would also have organised an "escape route." This was not because of any sentimental attachment to Donald Maclean, though he had served them so well. But there was the pressing need to demonstrate to other agents that the Soviets looked after their own. They had to find a way of bailing Maclean out. It was simply a matter of encouraging all the other agents who were still "out in the cold" knowing that they were daily running the risk of being caught. The knowledge that once the American and British authorities started closing in on them they would be whisked off to safety was vital from the point of view of morale. The Soviets were therefore determined that Maclean must under no circumstances be caught.

At the same time they did not want to lose a perfectly good agent while there was still even the remotest chance that he could continue operating. Evidence against him was, after all, circumstantial and comparatively slight. MI 5 claims that they had narrowed down to him out of hundreds of possible suspects thanks to the excellence of their staff-work would have been treated with considerable scepticism by anyone who had actually seen this uninspired, unimaginative conglomeration of ex-police constables in action. MI 5 was staffed by men of poor quality; there was always a chance that they had made a mistake. There seemed to be a strong possibility that MI 5 was guessing; accordingly the Soviets delayed.

It was a dangerous, complex game being played on a worldwide board, and one in which Donald Maclean could only be a terrified pawn. Perhaps the Russians misjudged the last steps: they could easily have lost contact with Maclean before they could tell him that it was all over, and he was going to be brought out. After all, once the "Eumenides" were following Maclean closely, it might have seemed too dangerous to maintain contact with him via a regular network. (The KGB could hardly have guessed—or believed—that Maclean was only being followed in office hours, that the detectives left him alone in the evenings and weekends.) This is where Guy Burgess could have come in: as a long-term Communist agent, but not an active network-member. He was in touch with Philby, and he could get through to Maclean. He could have passed the message to Maclean: do not despair. Hang on and stay cool. Everything is under control.

Considering the danger he was in, it seems remarkable that Maclean could have had his hat-brim turned jauntily up on May 25, when he met Lady Mary Campbell. Only days before, he had been through one of his worst-ever patches. On May 15, he attended a dinner-party and went afterwards to the house Cyril Connolly then owned near Regent's Park. Connolly wrote later: "Past midnight, there was a battering on the door and I let him in, sober-drunk, the first time I had seen him in this legendary state. He began to wander round the room . . . and then went out to lie down to sleep in the hall, stretched out on the stone floor under his overcoat . . . The departing guests had to make their way over him, and I noticed that, although in an apparent coma, he would raise his long stiff leg like a drawbridge when one of them was try-ing to pass. I put him to bed in an absent friend's flat and gave him an Alka-Seltzer breakfast. Hardly a word was spoken."

But on May 25, it all seemed different. Had Guy's mes-sage worked a cure? Maclean and the Campbells had de-cided to start their celebration of his thirty-eighth birthday at Wheeler's red-plush fish restaurant in Old Compton Street, Soho. They ate oysters and drank champagne. Maclean, though since Melinda's pregnancy and the mort-gage on the new house at Beaconshaw he had started being careful about money, insisted on paying the bill him-self. He was left with only a few shillings. After this they decided to stroll up to Schmidt's in Charlotte Street to eat some more solid food.

On the way they ran into Cyril Connolly, himself on the way to lunch in the Etoile. He thought Maclean was look-ing "rather creased and yellow, casual but diffident." At the same time he seemed calm and genial; not at all like a man who was within hours of the most fateful and irrevo-cable decision of his life.

During their luncheon at Schmidt's the Campbells found Maclean mellow and confident; significantly his main interest seemed to be planning for the future. He told them he was thinking of asking for a transfer to a more interesting department and asked if he could come and stay at their house, Stokke Manor in Hampshire, over the weekend of June 8. Melinda was going into hospital for her baby on June 6. He also told Lady Mary Campbell that he had finally got through his slightly ridiculous in-fatuation for the porter at the Moonglow; he seemed quite confident that his marriage with Melinda was now going at least moderately well, and that they had a future to-gether.

After luncheon Maclean went to the Travellers, cashed

a cheque for five pounds—a small sum for a man considering a journey—and after a couple of large scotches at the comfortable downstairs bar at the back of the building returned to his desk in the American Department. At 5:19, as usual on his good days, he boarded the train from Charing Cross to Sevenoaks. The MI 5 contingent followed him conscientiously as far as the barrier, and there they stopped. They had no orders to continue beyond this point. For some reason MI 5 had assumed that he could not come to any harm in the pastoral suburban scene of Tatsfield.

But the trap was about to snap shut. On the morning of that same Friday, May 25, Maclean's birthday and last day in England, there had been a brief, vital and secret meeting in the Foreign Office. About an hour after Maclean reached his desk at 9:30 A.M., the head of Foreign Office Security and a high official of MI 5 were ushered into the spacious elegance of the Foreign Secretary's room. It was a brief meeting: Foreign Secretary Herbert Morrison gave his authority for the interrogation of Maclean.

That high-level approval was the outcome of long and anxious discussion at lower levels on the day before, Thursday, May 24. Two officials each from SIS, MI 5 and the FO were at Thursday's meeting, trying to decide whether the time was ripe to confront Maclean. Both the SIS and MI 5 representatives argued for giving Maclean a little more time. They wanted the pressure of being followed, of being under suspicion, to soften him up further. And maybe they hoped against hope that time might provide a little more evidence. For they had *nothing* on Maclean except circumstantial evidence. He had had access to more of the right material at the right time than anyone else. But it would have been all too easy for Maclean to deny everything. If he did there was no chance that charges would stick: on the contrary, a convincing denial would have cleared him.

The FO men argued that it was time to bring the matter to a head. Maclean was jumpy and nervous: he would break now if he ever would. It would not have been unnatural if the Foreign Office people had hoped, subconsciously, that Donald might come through. The consequences of his guilt would be horrible for the Department.

In the end, their view prevailed. The decision was taken; Maclean would be confronted.

But the fact that May 25 was a Friday meant that the interrogation would not begin until the following Monday. Through an extraordinary oversight, entirely characteristic of both MI 5 and the Foreign Office, everyone blithely assumed that a delay of forty-eight hours was unimportant *because it straddled the English weekend,* a sacrosanct period during which it was thought, all normal life was in suspension. This assumption saved Donald Maclean and allowed Kim Philby to continue as a spy for very nearly fourteen years more.

On the morning of May 25 Guy Burgess surfaced in his New Bond Street flat around 9 A.M.—he had never been an early riser and anyway at this period, suspended from the Foreign Office and still without another job, there was no pressure for him to begin the day at dawn. Burgess began a leisurely perusal of *The Times*. His friend Jack Hewit made a cup of tea and delivered it to Guy who was still sprawled comfortably across the enormous double-bed which had provided strictly temporary hospitality for so many dubious characters.

There was no evidence that Burgess had a care in the world—rather the reverse for he was about to go away for a brief holiday. His companion was to be a young American, the proprietor of a progressive "off-Broadway" theatre, whom he had met on board the *Queen Mary* on the way over.

Burgess drank his tea and was smoking a cigarette when Hewit left for work shortly after nine. On the floor was his favourite brown bound edition of Jane Austen's complete works. On his dressing-table there was a large sum, nearly £300, in notes. This was in no way abnormal; for twenty-five years Burgess had been carrying large sums of money around with him. Hewit left this wholesome domestic scene just as Burgess was beginning to show signs of getting up. "Don't do anything I wouldn't," were his farewell words.

After Hewit left, Burgess shaved, dressed and made a few leisurely phone-calls, all of them purely social. But around ten o'clock something happened, either an incoming call, or a quick visit, that dissolved the comfortable pattern of his day. From then on he scarcely stopped moving.

It is possible to time the message fairly exactly because shortly before ten he was telephoning friends, among them Stephen Spender's wife, to ask whether they knew the address of W. H. Auden, the poet, who was on holiday somewhere in Italy (he was actually in Ischia though no one seems to have known where). At this time he seemed to have no worries except the exact itinerary of a holiday he was taking with the "progressive young man" he had met on the *Queen Mary*. But by ten-thirty when, punctual as usual, he kept an appointment with his American friend in the lobby of the Green Park Hotel, ten minutes' walk from his own flat, everything had changed completely.

Their original plans had been rather fluid but they had agreed firmly to take the midnight boat from Southampton to St. Malo. They were to travel on board the *Falaise*, which was returning via the Channel Islands, and Burgess had booked a two-berth cabin for that night two days previously at Victoria. They were therefore free if they wished to go by train to Paris from St. Malo or even to Italy. But from Burgess's future engagements it is much more likely they intended to return after a brief *tour d'horizon*, an hors d'oeuvre, as it were, before taking a longer and more ambitious trip.

Now, during a walk in Green Park, Burgess surprised his young friend by telling him, in a state of some agitation, that he might have to call the whole thing off—he would not know for certain until later but would tell him, one way or the other, by eight-thirty that night. (He never did.)

The young man afterwards remembered Burgess's precise words with perfect clarity: "A young friend of mine in the Foreign Office is in serious trouble. I am the only one who can help him." At almost precisely the same time that Herbert Morrison in the Foreign Office was signing the paper authorising Maclean to be wheeled up in front of Skardon; the first interrogation was scheduled for 11:00 A.M. the following Monday, May 28.

Nor does it seem likely that Maclean had learnt by lunchtime. Of the three he was certainly the least able actor; Philby never seems to have lost his poise and Burgess's personality was so many-sided and shifting that it was almost impossible for anyone to assess with any confidence what he was really up to at any given time. Maclean frequently lied, but whereas Philby was a cool master of duplicity, Maclean, a less finished dissembler invariably merely glossed the truth rather clumsily. When over lunch he enthusiastically accepted the Campbells' invitation to stay with them during the birth of Melinda's baby, scheduled to arrive within a fortnight, he was probably quite sincere.

But Burgess soon changed all that. He ordered a hire car, a cream Austin A70, and collected it from Wigmore Street shortly after two. He also bought a new suitcase and white macintosh from Gieves in Bond Street and packed it with clothes that suggested he did not know whether he was going to be in town or the country and wished to be prepared for either. He took, for example, both a tweed suit and a dinner jacket. In his black official briefcase he put the £300 from the dressing-table and a bundle of savings certificates. Burgess was leaving the flat with his luggage when Hewit returned from work. Hewit recalls that he seemed worried and in a hurry; they hardly exchanged a word at this meeting which was destined to be their last after a friendship that had lasted nearly fifteen years.

Burgess then drove to Tatsfield and it is unlikely he would have risked a call to the Foreign Office to give Maclean prior warning. They probably met at Sevenoaks station but there is no trace of this; all that is known for certain is that he dined with Maclean and Melinda at Beaconshaw, and that the two men arrived in the white Austin on the quayside at Southampton at eleven-forty-five. They rushed on board, leaving the car unlocked. A sailor noticed the car and shouted after the two last hurrying passengers. One of them called to him, "Back on Monday," and they were gone.

How should one assess this clumsy, slightly absurd yet, on the whole effective, episode which retrospectively attained a certain historical significance? Was it a sudden panic flight, a spur of the moment decision taken by the dominant Burgess, that connoisseur of hasty trips and eleventh hour departures? Or, on the contrary, should one rather look for evidence of an impertinently delayed Soviet *coup,* apparently casual yet meticulously devised and executed? Burgess, talking later to Tom Driberg in

Moscow, naturally inclined towards the first explanation, as if he and Maclean had been two diplomatic precursors of Kerouac, who suddenly made a wild, existential decision to take to the road, without knowing for certain where it would lead. That is hardly a convincing explanation.

The explanation which best fits the facts is that it was a mixture of careful Soviet planning and last-minute improvisation, largely by Burgess. We know that Edward Heath told the House of Commons that Philby had confessed to having "warned Maclean, through Burgess"—and in response to the direct question asking whether Philby was therefore the "third man" who had been so long sought, Heath said: "Yes, Sir." We know that it could hardly have been part of any thought-out Soviet plan that Burgess should have accompanied Maclean in his flight, because they would have understood its inevitable consequence, that suspicion would fall on Philby, their star agent. We have evidence that the actual flight from England was somewhat rushed, even amateurish. Yet once the two escapees were on the Continent, they vanished with great celerity and efficiency. We also know that the final decision to "take" Maclean came, at the insistence of the FO, *before either MI 5 or Philby's own SIS thought it right.*

There seems little point in doubting that Guy Burgess originally planned a genuine holiday that weekend, and a genuine return to England. In the last week, he made arrangements for May 28 and after, which make no sense, even as the most brilliant of double-bluffs. He had, for example, bullied Lady Pamela Berry into an arrangement by which he and his old friend Sir Anthony Blunt were to dine at her house on the Monday evening. ("Various people said afterwards that I invited Guy to dinner," she recalled afterwards. "That was untrue. As usual, he invited himself.") Had Burgess been looking for means to deceive MI 5 about his future movements, it would have been unnecessary to go to such lengths. And anyway, he himself was not under suspicion of any kind.

Everything points to Burgess having changed his plans, violently, in mid-morning on Friday, May 25. Could he have got the tip from Philby? He could have if *the decision that Maclean was to be interrogated was transmitted to the CIA liaison man in Washington.* Any questioner swiftly finds that this is a most sensitive area of inquiry, although one official who was closely connected with the affair at that time conceded that "it would have been usual form to send such a message." The reason to tell the CIA would have been fairly pressing in this case. It would have enabled the British to ask the Americans: "Can you think of anything more to throw at Maclean? Anything that might crack him?"

If a cable went to America that night, saying that Maclean was to be interrogated earlier than planned because of FO pressure, there would have been just time for Philby to contact his Soviet network. Presumably it would not have been impossible for the Russians to relay the message so that by Friday morning another agent could contact Burgess. (It would scarcely have been feasible to contact Maclean.) The message would have been: look, here is an emergency. They are going to hit Maclean on Monday. Can you get him out of Britain? Once he is out of Britain, we'll do the rest.

It would have been very much the situation to appeal to Guy Burgess—a situation made for "Brigadier Brilliant," the alter ego of his more self-regarding fantasies. And again it is worth emphasising that there *was* a core of will-power and ability buried somewhere under the drunken, flashy exterior.

And the emergency, of course, at this time imperilled Burgess as well. For if Maclean were to be taken and cracked, he would presumably say, among other things, that Burgess had given him a message earlier in the month. And that would lead back to Philby in a far more direct and obvious way than the mere fact of Burgess's disappearance along with Maclean would ever do.

This, at last, provides a rationale for Burgess's having gone along with Donald. For Maclean, even had he been in better psychological condition, would have had severe difficulty escaping from the country. He could not have booked steamer tickets on that Friday: he could not even have hired a car, as Guy Burgess did. He could only have set off from Tatsfield alone on Friday evening, with very little money, and hoped for the best.

No, the escape required the participation of "Brigadier Brilliant," and considering that he must have had to organise the getaway with very little briefing and very much on his own, he seems to have performed fairly creditably.

But he was, of course, an amateur, and he made a mistake. He should have come back to England. Had Burgess been a full professional, he could have planned for a return to England knowing that MI 5 could not, without quite fantastic luck, have "nailed" anything on him. And in that case, Kim Philby's cover might never have been broken.

Although Philby's own account of Burgess's disappearance, like everything else in *My Silent War*, needs to be examined with a highly sceptical eye, it makes sense when he says: "I was deeply dismayed." He claims to have heard the news from a Washington colleague.

" 'Kim,' he said in a half-whisper, 'the bird has flown.' I registered dawning horror (I hope)."

"What bird? Not Maclean?"

" 'Yes,' " he answered. " 'But there's worse than that . . . Guy Burgess has gone with him.' At that, my consternation was no pretence."

Philby does not, on the other hand, offer to explain why Burgess should have accompanied Maclean—even though he is at pains to build up Burgess as a major colleague in the Soviet secret service. The spur-of-the-moment hypothesis seems by far the most likely. If the Soviets were relying on Burgess for field operational plans, then theirs was a less formidable operation than the Western intelligence services generally insist.

Philby also offers another reason for the guilt he claims to feel about Maclean. He realised that Burgess, always a conspicuous figure, might easily have been seen with Maclean (as indeed he was). This track could very easily have led back to Philby himself. Accordingly, he decided to make an attempt to divert suspicion away from himself by giving those investigating the Washington embassy "leak" what he calls "a nudge in the right direction."

This stratagem was at least partially successful. Certainly it counted in his favour when, in due course, he came under investigation himself. For he was able to make capital out of the fact that he had written to his SIS chief, reminding him of the by now dusty and long-forgotten Krivitsky file, containing as it did a description of the Soviet Foreign Office spy.

The effect of this was the compilation of a short list of six men who came close to fitting Krivitsky's man. One of them was Maclean.

Insofar as anything can be learnt from Burgess's accounts in Moscow of the actual defection, it can be gathered that he hesitated. But it is easy enough to see why Burgess did not go back. He was uncertain how many traces he had left. Certainly, he had left a hostage to fortune when he told his American friend in Green Park that there was someone in the Foreign Office in trouble. If that had reached official ears—and Burgess could have had not the slightest doubt about the magnitude of the hue-and-cry that would erupt in Maclean's wake—why, then people would be looking into the question of the hire of the car, and the question of *who,* if not Guy's American, had been on the St. Malo boat with him? And there was Melinda: she knew Guy had spent the last evening with Donald, and she was bound to be grilled. Burgess had no way of knowing how reliable she might be. A professional might have avoided all those snags. But despite his hesitations, "Brigadier Brilliant" knew that he was an amateur, and that he was on a one-way road.

17. The Secret Trial

Mister, if you have to ask, you don't know.
—FATS WALLER, when asked to explain the meaning of "swing"

The row in Whitehall after the escape of the two diplomats was, naturally, a most horrible and ferocious one. The MI 5 investigators had been balked of an important prize, after a long hunt. The Government had been embarrassed in front of the Americans and the electorate. And the Foreign Office, which might have still hoped that the impact of Maclean's treachery could be minimised by a suitably discreet trial—with evidence in *camera*—found its reputation being dragged through the mud in the most public manner possible. Also naturally, everybody blamed everybody else, and long lists of suspects and alleged suspects were made.

As there had been three departments involved in the investigation—MI 5, Foreign Office Security and SIS —and as theoretically they were all possible sources of leaks, some intricate permutations of buck-passing evolved. But right from the start, one name inevitably ranked high on the list of possible suspects, and despite the fury of the SIS, the name was Kim Philby. He was inescapably suspect in the first place because he was virtually the only person who "linked" with both Burgess and Maclean: that is, he had been in contact with Burgess, and he knew about the net which was closing on Maclean.

It is this which has always been the most powerful evidence for the fact that Burgess's act in going with Maclean to Moscow was unpremeditated, and was a mistake. Had Maclean alone disappeared Philby would merely have been one of perhaps two dozen officers who were aware that the investigation was in progress, and there would hardly have been any reason why anyone would have started investigating suspects in Washington when there were so many to hand nearer home.

An interesting point is that it was not the "third man" incident in itself which convinced MI 5 that Philby must be a Soviet agent. The incident merely served to draw upon him a scrutiny which he might never otherwise have undergone. And it was the detailed examination of his record—including such failures as the Albanian subversion and Volkov's disappearance—which really stood against him. Philby may actually have been speaking the truth when Bunny Doble visited him in London not long after the defection. "I was in my office in Washington," he told her, "when my secretary came in and said that Guy Burgess had gone to Moscow. Imagine my shock!" He must have known that once Burgess had fled, he himself would come under suspicion. And, of course, he was summoned sharply back to London early in June.

To obey the summons, and not simply defect himself, must have taken a considerable degree of cool nerve—presumably, Philby went over his own record in his own mind with some anxiety, and decided that he had a good chance of getting away with it. All the same, he must have come into London, in the words of one of Len Deighton's spies, "with his flaps well down."

Already, he left one disaster behind him. His position with the Americans was shattered beyond repair. Their anger, at first, was not based on any specific claim that Philby was himself a Communist, or that he had tipped-off the much-wanted Maclean. They were merely outraged to discover that the immaculate Philby, ambassador of the much-admired SIS, to whom they had given a security-clearance astronomically beyond the reach of almost any American, had been so casual as to share his house with an obvious, unmistakable security-risk like Guy Burgess.

Miles Copeland, then a serving officer of the CIA, has told us that General Bedell Smith, Director of the CIA, sent an ultimatum of the greatest bluntness to the British. "Fire Philby," he said, "or we break off the intelligence relationship."

The energetic men of the FBI were also enraged, because their pursuit of the drunken, sodomite, leftist roadhog Burgess had been thwarted. There was a picturesque moment when a muscular, pistol-toting agent strode into the British Embassy and demanded to question Philby about the whereabouts of Burgess. It appears to have been after Philby's departure for England: anyway, Ambassador Oliver (later Lord) Franks and his staff made it clear that Philby was not available.

In England, there was a tense and prickly debate about how to deal with Philby. There was a hot-headed body of opinion among his SIS colleagues that there should not even be any question of "dealing" with him. It was inconceivable that he could be guilty of anything, and it was bad enough to have the McCarthyite Americans pillorying him because of his kindness to an old friend, without his own Service treating him in the same way. This view, however, could scarcely hope to prevail: the investigation of the defection was the responsibility of MI 5, and such a decision would hardly satisfy them. On the other hand, Philby was an important officer of a powerful Service which was—and still is—slightly above MI 5 in the Whitehall hierarchy, and which was responsible for its own security.

As in the case of Donald Maclean, which had to be conducted in co-operation with the Foreign Office Security Branch, MI 5 knew that they could not simply do as they pleased.

The first suggestion made by the SIS for dealing with the case was that General Sir Stewart Menzies, who had been chief of the Service throughout Philby's career, should spend a day talking things through with Philby, to see if anything had gone wrong with the man. This was, of course, rejected out of hand by MI 5 who had something altogether more testing in mind.

The trouble was that once MI 5 started to investigate an SIS officer like Philby, two radically different philosophies of security came into conflict. The SIS philosophy was based, plainly, on personal trust and the loyalty of officers towards each other. The MI 5 philosophy, on the other hand, was one of meticulous checking and cross-checking of files and records. The department was a group of spycatchers, trained in building up cases against suspects.

The SIS philosophy was not so impractical as it sounds. (It may have been applied sloppily, but that is another matter.) There is something to be said for the view that in espionage matters, it is often not possible to "prove" or "disprove" that a man is a loyal agent. There is a point at which the actions of an effective agent, however meticulously examined, are not objectively distinguishable from those of a traitor or potential traitor. One of the things the SIS men did understand was that in the last analysis a spy has no protection but the loyalty of his friends: his record, examined in cold blood at some arbitrary moment by an outsider knowing nothing of the conditions of his service, may give a fatally misleading impression. Certainly it is possible to see how the morale of an espionage service could collapse if its members became aware that their fates might be decided by the crude arithmetic of outsiders.

On the other hand, MI 5 obviously felt that by scrutinising a spy's record carefully, over a long enough period, some kind of profit-and-loss balance should emerge. Their philosophy, clearly, has prevailed—although some people now say that the men of the secret world have become altogether too careful and even bureaucratic.

The argument over Philby was not made any sweeter by the fact that since the wartime rivalry, relations between MI 5 and the SIS had not grown any better. The SIS was having a rough time trying to match up to the massive espionage effort of the Soviet KGB (it would have been rough enough, no doubt, even without Kim Philby's attentions) and at this time in 1951 still had not extracted any high-grade intelligence from Russia at all. ("We didn't get anything that really mattered until

Penkovsky," says one ex-desk man of the SIS.) Meanwhile MI 5, directed by Dick White under the command of the ex-policeman Sir Percy Sillitoe, had performed some creditable pieces of Cold War spycatching, notably the capture of Klaus Fuchs. The belief that an SIS "leak" had robbed them of another coup led to bitterness on an altogether new scale. The unpleasantness of the atmosphere can be gauged from a story about William Skardon, the man who had been cheated of his chance at Maclean. There is a Whitehall tradition by which the SIS men are known as "the Friends." At this time, and for some years afterwards, Skardon referred to them bleakly as "the Enemies."

Clearly, MI 5 would have liked to have given Philby the same treatment as they gave Fuchs: investigation followed by an exhaustive—almost literally exhaustive—series of interrogations by Skardon. This technique did not include any "third degree," but certainly in Fuchs' case it had produced, finally, a very curious psychological breakdown, after which he voluntarily confessed. Skardon's relentlessly polite questions, returning time and again to probe the tiniest weaknesses in his victim's story, might frighten some people more than physical brutality. The essentials of such interviewing are that the interrogator must never admit to lack of knowledge, and must return, hypnotically, to any tiny cracks in the smooth surface of his victim's denial. Skardon had had only one point against Fuchs: that a certain piece of information was *known* to have reached the Russians. "Everything's quite clear, really, Dr. Fuchs," he would say at intervals, "except for this bit." And of course, once the man does begin to talk—the interrogator must stay with him, yield to him, and follow him.

Whether such an attack, made wholeheartedly, would have broken through Philby's formidable defences is perhaps questionable. But fairly clearly the resistance on the part of SIS to having one of their best men grilled in such a fashion prevented the question being put properly to the test. But inevitably Philby had to be investigated, however the results of the investigation were to be deployed, and it is probable that Dick White's men set about the task with a certain relish. It was to take them a full year.

Meanwhile, Philby entered into the most shadowy period of his whole curious career. From mid-1951, when he left Washington, to late 1956, when he went to Beirut, his movements, employment and actions are the subject of numerous baffling and conflicting reports. Not the least baffling of these reports are the two utterances the British Government chose to make about his activities during the period: that is to say, Harold Macmillan's statement in Parliament in 1955,[1] and Edward Heath's in 1963—the second being made after Philby's defection to the Soviet Union. (Nothing, of course, was said about him during the immediate furore in 1951.) Both Macmillan and Heath said that Philby "resigned" in 1951.

But they both chose their words carefully: they said that Philby had resigned from his post in the *Foreign Service*. This was strictly true, but also strictly irrelevant, because Philby had never been in the Foreign Service except as the holder of a "cover job" as a temporary First Secretary. Neither Macmillan nor Heath mentioned Philby's real employment, which of course was as an officer of the Secret Intelligence Service. So although in each case the uninitiated would have gained the impression that Philby was dismissed from British Government employment in 1951, the words used did not in fact mean that. What really happened to Philby?

Suspicion against him emanated not only from MI 5: by autumn of 1951 he was clearly the Foreign Office's favourite candidate for the role of "third man." In October, Attlee's Labour administration was defeated at the polls, and when the Conservatives came into office it was naturally necessary to brief them on the facts behind the still-active public controversy. One of these Tory ministers has given us, in a confidential interview, an account of the brief the Foreign Office were offering. The essence of it was that Maclean had been warned that he was about to be interrogated by "the man who cracked Fuchs" (i.e. Skardon), and the prime suspect in FO eyes was "a man named Philby" in SIS. One of their reasons was that they did not care for his heady drinking, but a more

[1] Macmillan was answering Marcus Lipton's famous question which "named" Philby as the Third Man (see below). But the context was that as Foreign Secretary he was taking part in the debate on the White Paper produced by the Foreign Office, four years after the event, dealing with the defection of Burgess and Maclean.

damning one was that "there had been some trouble over a potential Russian defector in Turkey." (Clearly, the Volkov incident.) According to this minister's recollection, the FO claimed that the SIS were protecting Philby, and insisting that he could not be guilty. But the most interesting thing is that, as he recalls it, *Philby appeared to be still a member of the SIS,* although in what precise capacity our informant was unsure. Some time later, we obtained a cross-check on this when a diplomat who was Foreign Office Adviser[2] to the SIS admitted reluctantly that during his time (which was *before* Philby went to Beirut) Philby was being used as "a field agent."

Subsequently, further evidence emerged—largely from "sightings" of Philby by non-official sources—which supported the thesis that he was more or less continuously employed by SIS throughout the nineteen-fifties. (A part of this evidence is discussed more fully in the following chapter.) The SIS, it seems, took the view that they did not see why they should entirely lose the services of their best operator because of the prejudices of departments which did not understand the real mysteries of the Great Game.

The most amazing thing is that the Albanian operation —as we pointed out in Chapter 13—was not cancelled. This stands as much against the CIA as the SIS. Seemingly, the CIA felt that Philby was too insecure to work with them in Washington, but that it was all right to send men out on a dangerous mission in the planning of which the suspect Philby had been deeply involved. The only creditable explanation is that they did not suspect his true role even after the bloody Albanian debacle in 1952.

Although it may be difficult to understand what the Western intelligence organisations were up to at this time, Philby's intention seems obvious enough in retrospect. He was trying to work his way back into a position where he could again be of major service to the Russians. And indeed, had he not thought there was a reasonable chance of success, he would surely have defected to the Soviet Union more or less immediately. The Russians would

---

[2] The Foreign Office Adviser is a senior diplomat who acts as the day-to-day link between the FO and the SIS. It is necessary for the SIS to obtain his assent to projected operations.

have wanted him to "come home" if his hopes with the SIS had been definitely destroyed, as it would have been in their interest to debrief him before his accumulated knowledge of Western intelligence fell out of date.

What he had lost beyond recovery was his glittering executive role with the SIS, and with it his prospects of becoming Chief of the Service. How good had those prospects been? There has been some attempt to minimise them—General Sir Stewart Menzies, commenting on our original articles in *The Sunday Times,* declared that Philby was "never very important" in the SIS. But it is difficult to see this as more than a routine denial. For if Philby, successively director of the most important section of the SIS during the Cold War and link-man between the CIA and the SIS, was not important, then who was? What was the SIS doing sending an "unimportant" man to Washington to have, almost literally, free run of the CIA headquarters?

Mr. Donald McLachlan, a former editor of *The Sunday Telegraph,* and a wartime officer of Naval Intelligence, has argued that Philby could never have reached the top of the SIS, because this post is reserved for a man with an armed-Service background, which Philby did not possess. One can only point out that the man who had been running the SIS for more than ten years at the time Mr. McLachlan made this claim was Dick White,[3] who as has been explained elsewhere in these pages, is an intelligence officer of civilian background.

Claims like this need not be weighed too heavily against the assertions of numerous ex-officers of the SIS that Philby was manifestly "on the way to the top." A widely experienced diplomat and intelligence officer, who knew Philby well, made a more convincing moderation of Philby's chances when he said that Philby, on ability and past performance, would certainly have become one of the top three or four in the SIS, but was unlikely to have become "C" because he would probably have been considered insufficiently conventional in his personal behaviour to be appointed to such an important position in the hierarchy of Whitehall. It is, in fact, abundantly clear that Philby had excellent prospects (he once said himself that he was "on the way to a knighthood") and several ex-SIS

[3] He was knighted in 1960.

men declare that when he lost his executive post in 1951 he was given a "golden handshake" as compensation.

The MI 5 investigation of Philby matured roughly a year after the defection which first brought him under suspicion. And after some labyrinthine negotiations between the SIS and MI 5, a fascinating solution was chosen. It was decided to make Philby stand what amounted to a secret "trial," in which he would be cross-examined on all the evidence which had been found against him. It seems an extraordinary idea, but one or two ex-SIS officers to whom we have spoken claim to have heard of similar "trials" in the secret world.

The lawyers who were recruited to take part in the trial were all former members of the secret world themselves, and for the difficult role of prosecuting cross-examiner MI 5 turned to one of their bright young men of the wartime era. This was Helenus "Buster" Milmo, who since returning to the Bar from MI 5 had made great progress, and become a QC. (He was later a judge.) Milmo's brief was to find out by confrontation whether there was enough against Philby to sustain charges in the real courts. How much was MI 5 able to give Milmo?

They had, of course, the Volkov incident, and must have had some details of the misfortunes of the Albanian subversion campaign—and these were of course "bull points." But they had failed to get to the bottom of Philby's interlude in Spain, a period which was very vulnerable to close examination. When The Times had hired Philby as its correspondent, he was already in Spain, having gone out as a freelance correspondent (see Chapter 7). When MI 5 interrogated him about Spain, Philby says, they made the mistake of assuming that "The Times had sent me to Spain direct from a desk in Fleet Street." But if MI 5 had only looked at the Spanish immigration records (which we examined unofficially when researching this book), they would have learned that Philby had arrived in Spain in February 1937, three months before he entered The Times's employment.

Philby was worried that he might be interrogated about this. "The enterprise had been suggested to me, and financed by, the Soviet service . . . and a glance at my bank balance for the period would have shown that I had no means of gallivanting round Spain. Embedded in this episode was also the dangerous little fact that Burgess

had been used to replenish my funds." Philby had prepared a story in case he was asked to explain how he
had financed his Spanish trip—he had sold his record
collection. But all this, coupled with the fact that Krivitsky, the Soviet intelligence officer who defected to the West
in 1940, had told the British that Soviet intelligence had
sent a young English journalist to Spain during the Civil
War, would have weighed heavily against Philby. Did
MI 5 know the depth of Philby's Communist commitment
in Vienna in 1933–34? (For once one knows the full story
of that interlude, one sees at once that it was no passing
youthful brush with the Left, but was the real thing.) It
is a curious point that none of the people who knew the
details of Philby's Vienna period seem to have been questioned by any investigators in 1950–51, whereas in going
over most other areas of Philby's past one tends to find
traces of the MI 5 men fairly readily. If MI 5 did investigate the Viennese period, they did it in lighter boots than
most of the investigating they did elsewhere.

If they did not know enough to start looking, this is certainly evidence that the relationship between MI 5 and
SIS was strained beyond the breaking-point, because there
was still at least one officer in the SIS—Philby's school-
friend "Ian"—who knew that Philby had been a Communist in his European period. Relations between the
departments were quite possibly so bad that SIS men either were not officially informed of the MI 5 investigation
into Philby, or were perhaps not encouraged to go out of
their way to help it. Another explanation might derive
from the use to which the information was to be put: it
might have been felt that no matter how much was known
about the Vienna period, it would not help Milmo in his
task of cross-examining Philby in courtroom style with
criminal charges in view. If so, this was a pity, because it
would surely have made excellent psychological ammunition for one of William Skardon's lethally cosy interrogations.

The "trial," which took place in high summer, 1952,
was a dismal failure from everybody's viewpoint except
Philby's. Unfortunately for his opponents, Philby had
clearly worked out that if MI 5 were still asking him questions, they must still be in the dark. As Philby asks in his
own book, "What evidence . . . could be brought against
me?" He says that his early left-wing associations in Cam-

bridge were well-known, but he had never joined the
Communist Party in England, "and it would be difficult to
prove, eighteen years after the event, that I had worked
illegally in Austria, especially in view of the sickening fact
that most of my Vienna friends were undoubtedly dead."
This is a strange thing to say. It would have been very
easy to have proved this. Both Naomi Mitchison and Lilly
Jerusalem were aware that Philby was working for the
Communist underground at this time.

The fact is that MI 5 made no move to check on
Philby's Vienna period, so his oblique contempt for their
efficiency was justified. The main case against him turned
out to be, according to Philby, highly circumstantial. "Two
days after the Volkov information reached London there
had been a spectacular rise in the volume of NKVD wire-
less traffic between London and Moscow and Istanbul.
Furthermore, shortly after I had been officially briefed
about the Embassy leakage in Washington, there had
been a similar jump in NKVD traffic." Philby handled
this easily. He simply said that he was unable to account
for it.

Perhaps MI 5 might have got more if Philby had become flustered for a moment under the heat of a successful cross-examination—but he never allowed Milmo to get
into his stride. He answered every question in the most
elaborate and deliberate manner possible: advancing at
first a screen of minute details to give himself time to
think out all the possible angles to the question. And he
used his stammer mercilessly. Not only can a bad stammer be highly destructive of the rhythm and tension of an
essentially verbal performance like cross-examination, it
also engenders, however irrationally, a certain sympathy,
or at least involuntary queasiness, in even the most hostile
listeners. Behind the stammer, of course, Philby's mind
was working fast. An MI 5 man gave us a hypothetical
example of the kind of exchange that took place between
Milmo and Philby:

Q: "Was it a fine day?"

A: "Well . . . there w-w-was a t-t-temperature of about
f-f-fifty-eight degrees, I suppose. And there . . . was a
s-s-s-slight wind from the south. I suppose you could say
it was a fine d-day."

"Buster" Milmo, a beefy and determined Irishman, was
generally reckoned to be one of the best and most aggres-

sive cross-examiners at the Bar. But a few hours of
Philby's stonewalling would probably have destroyed the
technique of any cross-examiner who did not have one or
two really destructive things to throw at his opponent—
and Milmo did not. "It must have been maddening," said
another observer of the trial.[4] "Once you looked through
the case, you saw the whole pattern, and you *knew* that
Philby was working for the Russians. You even knew why,
if you knew anything about his father. It was that mad
idealism. But it was all circumstantial. There was nothing
hard."

Milmo tried on three successive days without shaking
Philby even slightly, and towards the end his questioning
began to grow angrier.

Philby even grew a little cocky. "It began to look like
the stupidest man in the world cross-examining the clev-
erest," said one of the attendant lawyers nastily. But it
was an unfair remark, for no one in Milmo's position
could have done more. The day after it was all over, he
was still fuming when an acquaintance bumped into him
in South Kensington. "I just couldn't get him," Milmo
kept muttering.

One of the central problems of the trial was the question of Philby's contacts with the Russians. There can
scarcely be any doubt that he had contact of some kind
with the Russians—his real masters—while he was in
Turkey, whether or not he crossed the Turkish-Armenian
border physically. How much did the British know about
this period? What had they told him to do?

Suppose the SIS believed he was deceiving the Russians, making them think he was ready to give them information, while still remaining loyal to the British?
There would be no way to prove, one way or the other,
what Philby was really doing, which side he was really on.
Suppose he could be shown to have passed information to
the Russians, personally or via a network of agents. It
could easily be shown, in return, that it was part of his
job to locate and contact the Russian networks, and by
testing their reaction to selected titbits of information, try
to work out what were the things that they were trying

[4] One of the very few among Philby's old SIS colleagues
who believed in his guilt at this time.

hardest to discover—or to work out how much they already possessed.

We asked two ex-officers, one of SIS and another of MI 5, who had been deeply concerned with the Philby investigation: were you in difficulty because Philby had a right to play a "double game" with Soviet Intelligence in Turkey? Both of them replied, guardedly, in almost the same words: "Yes, it was something like that." This, of course, is where one approaches the most involuted and inexplicable areas of the espionage business—but we believe the Philby controversy revolved around the fact that, like all other spies and agents, his loyalty, short of simple faith, could only be tested by making an elaborate profit and loss account of his operations. And most of the MI 5 officers believed that Britain was showing so bad a loss on Philby that he must be working for the other side.

The trial and investigation seems to have served one purpose. It made Dick White of MI 5 morally certain that Philby was a traitor. According to accounts given by several people close to White, the thing which made him so certain about Philby's guilt was the business of Volkov, the unlucky defector. Was this because the Volkov affair was in 1945, *before* Philby went into the field, and before he had any legitimate excuse for compromising with the Russians? One returns to that intriguing point about Edward Heath's statement to the Commons after Philby's defection. "We now know that Philby worked for the Soviet authorities *before* 1946." [Authors' italics.] In the bizarre conditions of the secret world, the fact that Philby worked for the Russians *after* 1946 was inadmissible evidence.

Although Dick White made up his mind about Philby, the quasi-judicial performance in 1952 appears otherwise to have been the reverse of useful. One reason was that any other form of interrogation was more or less preempted, because Philby now knew pretty thoroughly how much could be thrown at him, and knew that none of it was dangerous. This eliminated one of the most important psychological ingredients of a "quiet" interrogation: suspense. Skardon, of course, had wanted to have a try at Philby ("I would have worked on him for months," he told colleagues). And it would have been a truly fascinating battle if Skardon had been given a clear run.

He was allowed to interrogate Philby for some hours

after the trial. But it was without result, and in the circumstances Skardon probably did not have the heart to make much of it. Eventually, he was told to suspend his inquiries.

Before leaving the mock trial to examine traces of Philby in the field, it is worth mentioning one very understandable reason why so many people in the SIS, and for that matter a good many in the CIA, found it hard to admit to themselves that Philby was a real Soviet agent. To make the admission meant more than a setback. It meant, at one plain level, that a great many people had to face the fact that their careers which they had thought to be honourable and successful had been made entirely meaningless. It was almost literally unthinkable. It was probably one of the factors which gave the fanatically determined Philby the chance to fight another day.

18. A Field Agent?

Five Greeks for one Jew
Ten Jews for one Armenian
—ARMENIAN PROVERB

Although there are a few diplomats and ex-SIS officers who will admit that Philby was working for the SIS in *some* capacity in the years between 1951 and his departure to Beirut in 1956, none of them are willing to explain what the man was doing. A diplomatic contact went about as far as anyone would go when he said that Philby was "a very junior figure" working on Middle Eastern projects. This man stressed at some length that Philby no longer controlled any other agents.

To track Philby's movements through this period is a detective task of almost absurd complexity. A spy's career is by its nature difficult to investigate, founded as it is on deceit, and shrouded by both the spy and his employers in layers of secrecy and confusion. At least in other periods of Philby's life there are a few guideposts to work by: identifiable jobs in identifiable offices—even if they are cover-jobs—and identifiable tasks being performed, even if their nature can only be verified by tedious cross-checking amongst minor participants. (In the Albanian case, for instance, it becomes a matter of inquiry amongst Albanian émigré communities.)

But between Washington and Beirut, Philby's career passes through a baffling limbo: it is only possible to catch the most fleeting and mysterious glimpses of the "field agent" at work. The evidence tends to be confusing and contradictory, and there is no point looking to the SIS, the CIA or the KGB for reliable clarifications. Our most intriguing piece of evidence about the period is so curious and difficult to verify that little can be done with it except set it out, point out the difficulties which surround it, list the deductions which can be made from it if true—and leave the decision to the reader.

Briefly, this evidence suggests that Philby spent part of the early fifties working from a secret British establishment in Cyprus. His task would appear to have been to arrange for penetration of the Soviet Union via the Armenian communities of the Middle East: a task which would certainly have been feasible at some level, because expatriate Armenians, even at the height of the Cold War, maintained remarkably strong and regular links with their homeland behind the Iron Curtain in Soviet Armenia. We found *one* source who gave a detailed and circumstantial account of meetings with Philby in Cyprus from 1951 onwards. This source then produced a further detailed and circumstantial account of a meeting with Philby in 1952 in Turkey, only a few miles from the border with Soviet Armenia.

After making checks on the credibility of this story, we published it in outline in our series of articles on Philby in *The Sunday Times* in October 1967. Philby himself, who obviously read the *Sunday Times* articles, has since commented to Western visitors that they presented "a true bill on the whole"—with the exception of this story, which he denied. Apart, however, from the general consideration that any testimony of Philby's must be deeply suspect[1] for both professional and ideological reasons, there could well be particular reasons for him to deny or minimise

---

[1] As explained earlier, our practice with any information purporting to come from Philby himself has been to accept it only when it accords convincingly with independent evidence.

his connections with an Armenian "underground highway" crossing the Turkish-Soviet border. This is because there is some evidence that in 1963 Philby made his escape from the West via Eastern Turkey and Soviet Armenia. In other words, he might be protecting something.

Certainly there were, in the early fifties, some distinctly odd British establishments in Cyprus. Most of these came under the "British Middle East Office"—BMEO—which had recently moved to Cyprus from the Canal Zone of Egypt. The BMEO had been set up by Bevin to coordinate political and military thinking among the various Embassies and Army HQs which were running Middle Eastern countries when the Allies started to clean up the War. Its first chief was the Australian Richard Casey, later Lord Casey. By 1951, moved to Cyprus, it had become one of the more curious expressions of British power in the Middle East. It was not so much secret as mysterious: even its terms of reference seemed deliberately vague. They included spreading goodwill for Britain via technical, agricultural and forestry projects and coordinating political advice to the military from all the Middle Eastern embassies. By the time it was settled in Cyprus in a variegated sprawl of offices around the island, it had become, in the words of one Cyprus veteran, "a little Whitehall in the sun . . . an umbrella for the lot—all the odds and sods and funnies."

One of BMEO's mansions was a collection of huts in a little forest at Athalassa: the area was generally known as "the stud farm." Unlike most stud farms, however, it appears to have had radio masts, underground installations, and a heavy security guard. Nobody seems to have been quite sure what went on in this place. When we asked Sir Andrew Barkworth Wright, Governor of Cyprus from 1949 to 1954, about this little village at Athalassa, he said: "I visited there once. I never quite knew what they did. What did they do?" It sounds, of course, very much like a secret office.

Our informant maintains that Philby had an office at this place in 1951—which today consists merely of a few rusty huts difficult of access because of Greek roadblocks. Further, he told us that Philby spent a good deal of time drinking in the nearby towns of Kyrenia and Limassol at this time. This can be corroborated to some extent, in that it is fairly easy to find witnesses in both places who be-

lieve that **Philby** was there in the early fifties. The only
trouble is **that** he also visited the island later, between
1956 and 1963 when he was working in Beirut under
journalistic cover. It is impossible to be quite sure that
there has not been a confusion of date.

However, our informant said that what was really interesting about Philby at this period was not the time he
spent with the British community, but the time he spent
among the considerable Armenian community of Cyprus.
The Armenians are an old and cultured people whose
original home is to the north of the Caucasus range which
divides Turkey from the Soviet Union. The capital of the
Republic of Soviet Armenia, the town of Erivan, lies
within sight of the twin-humped outline of Mount Ararat
standing on the border. The Armenians have settled
throughout the Middle East, and indeed the world, but
unlike the Jewish people who were scattered by persecu-
tion, they have always maintained the Armenian homeland around Erivan. Although conquered by the Turks in
the sixteenth century, they succeeded in becoming the administrators of the Ottoman Empire, and so preserved
their cultural identity.

From time to time, the Ottomans, enraged by the stubborn individualism of the Armenians, fell upon them in
an obscene fury. The most recent massacre of the Armenians took place in the early 1920s at Samsun. Far from
destroying Armenian cultural unity, the massacres had
the effect of cementing the Armenians more solidly together. Wherever they settled, in Britain, France, the
United States or the Levant in general, they maintained
a dedicated programme designed to keep alive their own
culture. (Their language and script, and their poetry and
music, have unique cultural fingerprints instantly recog-
nisable even to an outsider exposed to them for a relatively short time.) Like all persecuted minorities, the
Armenians have long been accustomed to the idea of
secret and underground communication: and being an
exceptionally shrewd, determined and energetic minority,
they are exceptionally good at it. The Iron Curtain certainly did not cut off the inhabitants of Soviet Armenia
from their fellow-Armenians throughout the Middle East,
and there were several well-established channels of communication. One route, for instance, is said to have run
from Soviet Armenia across the border to Agralik on the

slopes of Ararat, via a short-haul bus to Dogubayazit, thence with a long-distance lorry-driver through Patnos, Van, Diyarbakr, Urfa and finally to Hakkari on the Syrian border. There a second-hand tyre dealer would insert letters in fresh envelopes and re-address them. During the fifties, it is said, a message from Soviet Armenia could reach the Armenian community of Cyprus within four or five days.

How difficult a barrier was the "Iron Curtain" at this time? Probably, it meant a good deal more to the civil servants of Washington, London and Moscow than to the mountain-folk of the Ararat area. The area between Erivan in the Soviet Union and Van in anti-Communist Turkey has been divided many times over the centuries by arbitrary and widely-differing borders. Once, the greater part of Eastern Turkey was part of the vast Kingdom of Armenia: at another time, it was under the control of Tsarist Russia. The one certain legacy this has left with the thinly-scattered population of Muslim goat-herds has been to co-operate overtly with occupying administrations, and to look after their own interests cautiously and in secret.

The border, or Curtain, existed physically as a line of barbed wire, with, on the Russian side, a watchtower at half-mile intervals with sentries, binoculars and high-powered rifles. (Behind these, at five-mile intervals, lay the Russian blockhouses.) But the people on each side of the wire look exactly alike: their women wear the same bright headdresses and gowns spangled with bright coins and beads. The harsh moon-landscape is the same on both sides of the wire, and the Russian soldiers even at the chilliest stages of the Cold War still exchanged amiably obscene insults with the apolitical goat-herders. The most obvious evidence of trans-Curtain trafficking was visible in the tumble-down tea-houses in the hamlets on the Turkish side of the border: stubs and cardboard holders from Russian cigarettes stamped into the floor. It could never have been a border like the one at Checkpoint Charlie, and it would certainly have been beyond the capacities of the Turkish Army and its eighteen-year-old conscripts to make it so. It could scarcely have been a formidable barrier to the letters carrying, variously, news of a new grandchild in Erivan—or details of the underground's dream of a Free Armenia.

This was territory Philby had certainly known during his days as "passport officer" based in Istanbul, when he had taken his famous picture of Ararat. It is the kind of border that the intelligence-services of both sides know that they cannot close, even if they want to: there are always places where information and agents can filter from one political system into another. Van, Ararat and the Armenians were known to Philby from 1948: our later informant says that when in Cyprus Philby used to make regular visits to the main centre of Armenian cultural exchange, the Melkonian Institute. The Institute is primarily a school for Armenian children, which gives an excellent education to university-entrance standard plus schooling in Armenian history and art, but in the evenings it is used for formal and informal gatherings to hear lectures on art, poetry and literature, and to hear music or watch dancing. To some of these gatherings non-Armenians are welcomed. The Institute, of course, has nothing to do with espionage in any form. But it would have been a useful place to meet Armenians if one was interested in using them for espionage.

Our informant (not an Armenian, but an Englishman who claims to have been living in Cyprus at the time) goes into some detail about Philby's visits to the Institute, describing Philby's enthusiasm for what he called the "set-my-people-free" songs performed by Armenian folk-groups. He also describes a friendship with a particular Armenian family, and an apparently Platonic relationship with a young Armenian girl whom Philby is alleged to have described—to her father's delight—as being "as straight as the letter Alef and as slim as the moon on its back in the seventh night of Ramazan." If, indeed, this is one of the plants and inventions which are the perpetual nightmare of any journalist investigating the espionage business, one can only record that it is rather more imaginatively carpentered than usual. It also has the advantage of not being in basic discord with ascertainable facts; for instance, Philby's friends and acquaintances in England during this period do recall that he made trips out of the country on occasion, apparently to the Middle East.

In trying to follow up the story of Philby's activities in Cyprus, we came across an even more curious episode. This was described to us by two informants: one who declined to give his name to us, and another who was willing to give his name, but only in confidence. Their story is that in the winter of 1952 a party of twelve British scientists were making a journey along the Turkish side of the Turkish-Soviet frontier. They were studying topography, agronomy, meteorology and the cultural, sociological and environmental condition of the mountain people.

Possibly there was a little more to the trip than pure science, because it appears that the scientists were "debriefed" by Foreign Office men after the trip. It is not surprising: this was, after all, a crucial strategic area. Equipped with permits from the Turkish authorities saying that they were on a cultural visit, the scientists set off from Ardahan in the north down the wintery trail towards Dogubayazit on the southern slopes of Ararat. Progress was slow and difficult along the snow-covered mountain roads. Occasionally, when close to the border, they could see parties of Russian soldiers in Soviet-built jeeps bouncing along to relieve the watchtower parties.

At Dogubayazit, they were to fill up with petrol for the long leg back west to Erzerum, "the last city of Turkey." When the six trucks rumbled into the petrol depot, they were immediately the centre of enormous interest, as any traveller is bound to be in so remote and rarely-visited a territory. And surprisingly, the villagers said, when they heard that the scientists were English, that there was *another Englishman visiting Dogubayazit*.

This, it seems, struck the party as very curious, because they had not heard in any of the villages they had come through that there was another "outlander" in the district. However, they trudged through the snow to the Dogubayzit tea-room: like every other tea-room near Ararat, a grass-and-branch roof held up by spindly poles, and faintly scented by the aroma of Russian cigarettes.

They pushed open the nail-studded wooden door, and found Kim Philby sitting lazily on a bench and exchanging a few words of Turkish with the locals. The encounter is described in some detail: one of the scientists knew Philby slightly, having met him in Cyprus. He is supposed to have asked: "What on earth are you doing here?" To which Philby, not at all unhorsed, replied coolly: "Collecting geological samples. I'm on holiday." Believing that Philby was involved in secret work, the scientist asked no more questions.

Philby is described as wearing a thick anorak, with

khaki trousers tucked into heavy woollen socks. At his feet, he had a rucksack and a battered briefcase. He was sipping tea, and smoking. He did not, however, have any geological specimens, and did not seem to be embarrassed by the lack. He allowed the scientists to assume that he was travelling on foot, despite the appalling conditions, and after swapping a few inconsequential remarks and some glasses of tea, he agreed to accept a lift to Erzerum.

How had Philby got there? The scientists were sure he could not have come from the north, the way they had come, or they would have heard about so strange a traveller. He could not have come from Van in the south, because the road was blocked by snow. The road from the east, and the Persian border, was also blocked by snow. Yet as they drove west to Erzerum, none of the Turkish officials and soldiers at the checkpoints recognised him as a man who had recently passed going the other way. Two of the scientists, we were told, came to the conclusion that Philby could only have got to Dogubayazit along the sixty-mile road around Ararat from Erivan.

Conceivably, there is a date-transfer here also: this meeting could have taken place during Philby's period based in Turkey from 1946 to 1948. But one of the informants, methodically, went to the trouble when cross-examined of producing detailed diaries and relating the event to entries. Again, if an invention, a good one—and for what purpose?

Assuming this story to be genuine, what would it mean? It would fit in with the role we know Philby to have played as a "field agent" for the SIS during this period, and it could be explained on the basis that the SIS were being either very naive, very sophisticated, or perhaps a bit of both.

There could be every reason for putting a man under some suspicion of working for the Russians into contact with them. If he *is* the Russians' man, they will be unhappy at his demotion from the superb position in Washington, and they may feed him some genuine information to help him restore his credit. If he is *not* their man, they may well think that he is, and act in exactly the same manner, anyway. In fact, in such a situation, the loyalty of the agent is more or less irrelevant to anyone except himself.

There is every reason to think that the SIS at this time

would have taken fairly desperate measures to contrive some penetration of the Soviet Union. This was still before Oleg Penkovsky began to work for the West, and until then it is thought that the West scarcely managed to get any worthwhile information from agents inside the Soviet Union. And nobody in the Service would have been better fitted than Kim Philby to approach the Russians.

Why Dogubayazit? It would have been, ninety-nine times out of a hundred, a safe way of making a quick exit from the Soviet Union. Philby could easily have entered via the Bosphorus and Black Sea shipping routes, for the Turks did not then examine northbound passengers very closely. Coming out that way, however, would have been harder, because naturally the Turks did check southbound ships rather closely. The border-jump at Ararat would have been more practicable.

Checking over the whole set of incidents in Cyprus and Ararat, one finds no direct corroboration which could not also have been invented or planted. One or two of the contacts mentioned by our original source denied all knowledge of Philby, but in each case there were obviously understandable reasons why they would. Certain other contacts who might have amplified and confirmed refuse, rather mysteriously, to discuss the question of whether Philby was in Cyprus and what connections he might have had with the Armenian community there. As to objective detail: the huts are there, and the right villages and roads certainly exist in the right places in Turkey. And, as we said before, it is possible to find witnesses in Kyrenia and Limassol who are almost sure—but not quite—that Philby was there in the early fifties.

19. Philby's Comeback

The trouble with the newspaper game is, you don't get the choice who you're making trouble for. It's . . . blind-man's buff played with straight razors.

—MURRAY SAYLE, *A Crooked Sixpence*

Philby's employment as a "field agent" in the early fifties was probably a matter of occasional, even erratic, assignments rather than steady work on the payroll. Of this period, Edward Heath said to the House of Commons in

1963: "He (Philby) had some employment, presumably arranged by himself," and this was not a very revealing remark. Quite clearly, people in official positions are less than happy to make even glancing references to Philby's connections with the SIS before 1951. About the post-1951 links, there is a determination not to reveal anything at all.

Philby during the early 1950s was, perhaps, comparable to a man who had been one of the major editorial executives on a big newspaper, who had been forced by some accident or scandal to become a "freelance." And there is some evidence that he found the situation discouraging: in Moscow he has told members of his family visiting him that he "nearly got out [i.e. defected to the Soviet Union] in 1955." The reason he gave was that "I began to think there wasn't anything more I could do." In this case, it seems not unreasonable to believe him.

He seems to have been hanging on in the hope that times would change—which they did. And this is supported by the fact that he clearly did not try really seriously to construct any other career for himself during these years, despite the fact that he had five children to support. He was helped to a remarkable extent by his friends, and as some of them were members or ex-members of the secret world, the possibility can hardly be dismissed that some of their subventions were in fact sums being channelled to him "under cover" from the SIS.

Philby had many interesting friends: among them the late Tomas Harris, an art dealer with Spanish connections, who had also been a friend of Guy Burgess. During 1954, Harris approached a partner in the firm of André Deutsch, the English publishers of this book. Harris suggested that Philby might be able to write a fascinating book about his career and exploits.

The most interesting thing about Harris is that during the war he had worked in MI 5, as a specialist in deception operations and control of double agents. So, apart from any other consideration, he knew exactly what Philby's career had been, and must have had a good idea of what his "exploits" had been. However, the projected book was apparently to be chiefly about the tragic way in which Philby had been removed from his "Foreign Office" post in Washington because of his fortuitous association with the defector Burgess. André Deutsch agreed to pay a considerable advance for the book.

Philby never wrote the book. But the advance was paid back by Harris. The explanation produced was that Philby had suffered a "writing block." Harris spent a good deal of time with the Philby family, who were now living in a large, somewhat dilapidated house at Crowborough in Sussex. He was godfather to Philby's third child, Dudley Thomas, and according to Ralph Izzard, a veteran journalist, who knew Philby well, Harris paid for the education of one, perhaps more, of the children. None of the children, by the way, were State-educated: they went to expensive, if not particularly distinguished schools.

Another friend who helped Philby—although with influence, rather than money—was Richard Brooman-White, his old SIS colleague from the Iberian sub-section of Section V. Brooman-White, after several abortive attempts to get a seat, had at last won Rutherglen, in Scotland, for the Tories, and so was in a position to speak up for Philby with some effect when his name came up in the continuing behind-the-scenes debate over the "third man" question. When he stood for Rutherglen, Brooman-White described himself as a "journalist," which was a polite fiction. He was an SIS operative. Perhaps the most remarkable thing about Brooman-White is that he performed one—unpaid—assignment for the SIS after he became an MP, which involved his visiting Turkey to prepare a paper on future war planning.

Brooman-White, a lean, energetic man who came of the same Eton generation as Guy Burgess, was a fascinating example of the SIS character. There is a ring of the old, spacious days of secret-service work about some of his exploits. He had a penchant for disguise: not only did he make himself up as a Portuguese, he is said to have worked in the Middle East disguised as an Arab. (Brooman-White was an attaché in Turkey between 1946 and 1947, when Philby was there. He presumably worked for Philby in some sort of intelligence connection. It is too much to believe that a wartime SIS colleague was there by accident.) He was a master horseman, and a fine shot with a pistol. Indeed, he frequently carried a pistol in Britain, let alone more dangerous places, and Lord Craigton, who once had a neighbouring constituency to Brooman-White in Scotland, tells a marvellous story about this weapon. One peaceful evening, he and Brooman-White were in a boat on a Scottish lake when a pheasant poked its head up over the bank several yards away. Brooman-White whipped out his pistol and blew the bird's head off with a single shot. "There we were," recalls Craigton, "two Tory MPs sitting in the middle of a lake with a dead pheasant and no idea what to do with it." Brooman-White was clearly well thought-of in the Service, because when he died in 1964 there was an excellent turn-out from the SIS for his funeral, led by Sir Stewart Menzies and Sir Dick White.

Philby did make one or two gestures resembling the activities of a man trying to earn a normal living. He went to Spain on a brief assignment for *The Observer* in 1952. He negotiated briefly for the post of Foreign Editor of *The Economist*. He had a short time with an import-export firm in the City, and his family remember a brief period when he was supposed to be a toothpaste salesman. But overall, he looked exactly like a man marking time, waiting for something to happen.

And of course what everybody was waiting for was the White Paper which was to be published on the Burgess-Maclean affair, and which had been promised ever since 1951. Once it came out, there would be a full-dress debate in Parliament, which might well settle the "third man" issue for good. But the White Paper was long in the womb. No doubt the Foreign Office, remembering the famous apology of La Bruyère for the length of a piece of writing which he had "not had time to make short," were ceaselessly re-polishing the document to make sure that when it emerged the public would not be bored by details which could be regarded in any way as otiose. When it arrived in September 1955 after four years' work, it ran to a terse four thousand words.

The White Paper was not exactly regarded as a charge of dynamite. In fact, it did not reveal a thing that was not already publicly known, and so the debate might well have been approached in a mood of anti-climax. But all that was changed, dramatically, when Lieutenant-Colonel Marcus Lipton, the Labour MP for Brixton, rose in the House of Commons to ask the Prime Minister, Sir Anthony Eden, whether he would "move to appoint a Select Committee to investigate the circumstances of the disappearance of Burgess and Maclean in particular, and of the efficiency of Civil Service security arrangements in general?"

To this, Eden replied: "No, Sir." But that did not matter, for Lipton's first question had merely been the necessary Parliamentary gambit to get the Prime Minister on his feet. He now came in with his "supplementary"—which was the real point of the exercise. "Has the Prime Minister," demanded Lipton, "made up his mind to cover up at all costs the dubious third man activities of Mr. Harold Philby, who was First Secretary at the Washington Embassy a little while ago; and is he determined to stifle all discussion on the very great matters which were evaded in the wretched White Paper, which is an insult to the intelligence of the country?"

It was tortuous wording, but at last the name "Philby" had been publicly linked with the magic phrase "third man." Something was out of the bag, even if it was hard to be sure whether it was the cat or some other kind of animal altogether. Not surprisingly, the Prime Minister replied that his answer was still: "No." But he said that the Government took the view that it was desirable to have a debate on the subject, and it was clear that the Government were committed to making a public commitment of some sort about Philby within a very few days. It seemed as though the guilty man was about to be exposed—but Philby has since claimed in Moscow [1] that it was the "happiest day of his life" when he heard that Lipton had named him. If he knew what the result would be—that the Government would have to clear him (and he may well have done so) then his delight is easily explicable.

How did Lipton's question come about? Even today, many of the people involved are unclear what happened. They merely share an uneasy—and, as it happens, justified—suspicion that they were pawns in some subtler gambit. Colonel Lipton himself seems to favour the idea that the American Central Intelligence Agency planted the information on him, presumably to embarrass the British Government into taking action against Philby. A more conspiratorial interpretation yet is that Philby's old friends arranged it, knowing that lack of proof would leave the Government no choice but to clear Philby.

In fact it was J. Edgar Hoover who engineered the

[1] *Daily Express* interview, published November 15, 1967.

whole affair. Motivated partly by his anti-Communist zeal
and partly by a sense of personal betrayal—he had been
a dinner guest in Philby's Washington home—Hoover had
been trying for some time to get Philby's name into the
open and then to force a full-scale investigation into his
activities. After the publication of the White Paper, Hoover stepped up his efforts. At 3:45 P.M. on September 29,
1955 (the Bureau was always meticulous about timing
and dating events), a reporter from the International
News Service called Hoover's office for a long, off-the-
record chat. Hoover recorded an account of the conversation:

"————[the INS man] stated that he had been contacted by an individual who claims to know the identity
of the third man involved in the Burgess–Maclean case
and to have the full story. This third party is a British
subject named Philby who was formerly connected with
the British Government in this country."

This, of course, was no news to Hoover. Ever since Burgess and Maclean had vanished, Philby's name had appeared high on the FBI's list of suspects simply because
Philby knew of the investigation into Maclean and was,
therefore, in a position to tip him off, and because of his
close association in Washington with Burgess. (The FBI
had a log, for example, of all the telephone calls Burgess
made when outside Washington; most of them were to
Philby.) But Hoover expressed surprise and then, with
apparent reluctance, went on to give the INS man all the
material needed for a story: Philby had been employed
by British intelligence in Washington, he was a heavy
drinker, he had access to classified information, he had
been recalled to London after the Burgess–Maclean disappearance, and a representative of British intelligence had
been sent to Washington to make sure that he did return.

Playing a deep game, Hoover told the INS man that he
was on the trail of "some very hot information." He went
on, "But I cautioned him that in the White Paper, which
had just been released by the British Government, there
was no mention of Philby's name, apparently because of
lack of direct proof against Philby and the fact that
Philby was in contact with lawyers and threatening heavy
libel suits if any paper prints his name in connection with
this matter." He concluded by suggesting where the INS
man might apply pressure: "I told————that his friend

in Europe might want to check with the British in this matter since the White Paper did not reveal the identity of the third man involved."

Whether the meeting with the INS man occurred fortuitously or whether Hoover set it up does not matter. Hoover seized the opportunity to implant in the INS man's mind the name of Philby as the third man. The seed matured quickly. Within a month, Jack Fishman, the resourceful editor of the *Empire News,* a British Sunday paper now defunct, was planting the vital question on Lipton. It was a textbook example of an ancient journalistic device to evade the laws of libel, which hinges upon the privilege that a newspaper has of reporting anything said in Parliament with impunity. The theory was that once Lipton had "named" Philby in his question, the *Empire News* would be able to write a story about Philby using the question as a peg. In the sense that the operation eventually did more good than harm to Philby, it might be said to have misfired. But of course the truth of the quotation at the head of this chapter—that journalism is "blind-man's buff played with straight razors"—was particularly stark and unavoidable in this case. The razors were very sharp, and the Administration, by its policy of evasion and double-talk about the case had ensured that the blindfolds were even more opaque than usual. It would be ridiculous to blame Fishman, Lipton and the *Empire News.*

From what source did the *Empire News* get its story? The first forthcoming witness we discovered was Mr. Henry Maule, London correspondent of the New York *Sunday News,* who worked part-time for the *Empire News.* The man who actually passed the information to Lipton, says Maule, was the late Johnny Hunt-Crowley, a staff man on the *Empire News* with a flair for crime reporting. Maule says that he understood that the source was "a man Johnny met on the train up from East Grinstead, where he lived." Seemingly, this man was a junior officer of MI 5, who had picked up Philby's name as a result of persistent INS enquiries and who resented the fact that Philby seemed likely to get off scotfree. As Maule recalls it, Hunt-Crowley brought the "man from East Grinstead" into the *Empire News* office on Saturday, October 15, ten days before Lipton's question in the Commons.

That day, Maule and Hunt-Crowley wrote a story for the *Empire News* which named Philby as the "third man." But at this stage, no Parliamentary question had been tabled: all that there had been time to do was pass the information which the *Empire News* had to a Labour MP. This was not Colonel Lipton, but another aggressive back-bench questioner, the late Norman Dodds. The paper's legal advisers, not surprisingly, felt that it would not be possible to name Philby without the gravest libel risks —and so the story finally said only that the identity of the "third man" was known, and that Dodds was demanding action.

The story, as published, began: "Prosecute the third man who tipped off Burgess and Maclean to escape to Russia, a Socialist MP is asking the Foreign Minister, 'or I will name him in the Commons!'" It went on, under Hunt-Crowley's byline: "Mr. Norman Dodds (Dartford) told me this yesterday: 'I have asked Mr. Macmillan to set the law in action to decide on the third man's guilt. It would be iniquitous if he were to remain hidden and absolved from public judgement. Out of courtesy I asked the Minister to reveal publicly what I know. But if he hesitates to do this it is my duty in the interests of public security to tell the House the name of this man.'"

The text of this ringing statement had been agreed between Dodds and the *Empire News* men. And indeed, Fishman makes no bones today about it. "We announced that Norman Dodds had received evidence establishing the existence of the third man, and he had—our evidence," Fishman told us. When we asked for more details of the origins of the evidence, Fishman said that Hunt-Crowley's "man from East Grinstead" was only a corroborative source. Fishman said that he himself received the first tip, from a contact in Germany, and worked on the story alone for several weeks.

During the week after their guarded story appeared, the *Empire News* men tried to bring the whole business into the open by arranging a Parliamentary question to name Philby. Dodds, however, declined to do so after all —on the advice of Mr. George Wigg,[2] doyen of Labour's back-bench inquisitors, and already thought to be quite an expert on defence and security matters. Wigg told

[2] Now Lord Wigg of the Borough of Dudley.

Dodds that he should first ask the Foreign Minister for
an inquiry. Undaunted, the *Empire News* got in touch
with Marcus Lipton, who agreed to put Philby's name into
a question. But it was obviously an enterprise to daunt
even the boldest of MPs, and shortly after his initial undertaking, Lipton began to waver. Fortunately, Henry
Maule's American connections saved the day. Maule had
the right to send to the *Sunday News* in New York any
story that was "spiked" by the *Empire News,* and with
Fishman's enthusiastic backing, he sent a story for their
issue of October 23 which actually named Philby, and
due to the more permissive nature of American libel laws,
was published. This strengthened Lipton's resolve enormously, and the appearance of the story in the U.S., although engineered by the *Empire News* men, appears to
have given Lipton his idea that the CIA were behind it.
Colonel Lipton still hankered after the idea when we interviewed him in 1967, although he confessed that his
final decision to "have a go" was turned by the fact that,
as a young Zionist, he had met the pro-Arab St. John
Philby in the Middle East during the twenties. "If the son
was half as barmy as his father, he was bound to have
done it," was Lipton's view—and not so far from the truth,
after all.

When Sir Anthony Eden gave his non-committal answer to Lipton, with only the delicate promise that more
would be said in the debate, a storm of publicity exploded around Philby's name. Hoover moved to capitalise
on it. On November 2, eight days after Lipton had named
Philby, Hoover cabled the head of the FBI in London
to tell him what to do. "Legal Attache, London England.
Donald Duart Maclean, Guy Francis de Moncy Burgess
stop Espionage stop Public identification of Philby as
individual who may have tipped off Burgess Maclean and
requests of Bureau from other government agencies for
information on Philby's role make it necessary that Bureau furnish information on Philby to certain high US
government officials stop Bureau plans to advise certain
high-level government officials of Philby's role.—Hoover."

It is not difficult to guess what Hoover had in mind.
FBI files made available to us under the Freedom of Information Act make it clear that American intelligence
officers suspected that Philby was being protected; not

only by his brother officers in SIS but possibly by senior Foreign Office officials. If the FBI gave its dossier on Philby to every high-ranking U.S. government official, up to and probably including the President, it would be harder for the British Government to resist American demands for a full-scale investigation. But Hoover had reckoned without several peculiarly British factors, which together, wrecked his scheme.

In the Commons on November 7, the Foreign Secretary, Harold Macmillan, was at his most urbanely authoritative when he came to discuss the question as to whether Burgess and Maclean had been tipped off.

"The possibility of a 'tip-off' had to be seriously considered," he said, "and searching and protracted investigations into this possibility have been undertaken, and are proceeding even at the present time.

"In this connection, the name of one man has been mentioned in the House of Commons, but not outside. I feel that all honourable Members would expect me to refer to him by name and to explain the position. He is Mr. H. A. R. Philby, who was a temporary First Secretary at the British Embassy in Washington from October 1949 to June 1951, and had been privy to much of the investigation. . . . Mr. Philby had been a friend of Burgess from the time when they were fellow undergraduates at Trinity College, Cambridge. Burgess had been accommodated with Philby and his family at the latter's home in Washington from August 1950 to April 1951; and of course it will be realised that at no time before he fled was Burgess under suspicion.

"It is now known that Mr. Philby had Communist associates during and after his university days. In view of the circumstances, he was asked in July 1951 to resign from the Foreign Service. Since that date his case has been the subject of close investigation. No evidence has been found to show that he was responsible for warning Burgess or Maclean. While in Government service he carried out his duties ably and conscientiously. I have no reason to conclude that Mr. Philby has at any time betrayed the interests of this country, or to identify him with the so-called 'third man,' if indeed, there was one."

The result, naturally, could only be a humiliating withdrawal for the unfortunate Lipton, who for some time had an unpleasant time with some of his fellow Labour MPs, who regarded him as tainted by McCarthyism. (Of course, in 1963 when Philby disappeared to Russia, the Colonel had a hugely enjoyable vindication.) But in 1955 it was Philby's day, and on November 10 he held a relaxed Press conference at his mother's flat in Drayton Gardens, South Kensington, and said that the last time he had spoken to a Communist "knowing he was a Communist" was in 1934. Philby's voice, so far as can be checked from television transcripts, was for once almost free of stutter, and in fact he handled the conference so brilliantly that next day at least one old SIS colleague rang him up to congratulate him. As another officer, who had served with Philby in Turkey, told us: "I think you will find that the question, and Kim's performance with the Press, changed a lot of people's feelings about him." The whole episode had been a wonderful boon for Philby. He had been hanging round the fringes of the secret world for several years, playing the part of the injured hero, the good-tempered martyr to security. He had many important friends and contacts: tacitly and skilfully, he was persuading them that he was a man who had been given an outrageously raw deal. The incident in Parliament, of course, fitted in perfectly with this campaign by Philby.

What lay behind Macmillan's clearing of Philby—an action, incidentally, which astounded and alarmed the members of the Central Intelligence Agency who had been concerned with the case? Part of the answer appears to lie in Macmillan's patrician attitude to the intelligence services. This was perfectly summed up in his famous aside: "I don't expect the gamekeeper to come and tell me every time he kills a fox." One of his close advisers at the time told us that Macmillan felt that the Philby affair was a squabble between the secret departments which they should have settled for themselves. Macmillan, in any case, is not one of those statesmen who is over-impressed by intelligence services, although he makes the right noises about them in public. As perhaps the most sophisticated political operator of his time, he certainly had a very low opinion of political intelligence: reserving what respect he did have for what he called "nuts-and-bolts information." By this he meant dimensions and capacities of weapons, details of the equipment of foreign armies, and the like. All in all, he was not disposed to be too much impressed by the denizens of the secret world.

The brief which he had received to accompany the White Paper was a general one, and did not particularly explore questions of Philby's having been the "third man." But when Lipton's question exploded in the Commons, it was necessary for another brief to be prepared. There is some dissension over just how this supplementary information was prepared, but most sources agree that the document was more notable for what it left out than what it said. "It was a bum brief" is the blunt comment of one of a few old SIS hands who thought Philby guilty. Macmillan, as Foreign Secretary, was getting the SIS view. MI 5, who took the view that Philby was suspect, would have given a very different brief. But Macmillan was not their Minister: MI 5 was not his department. He *could* have asked for MI 5 advice, but it would have meant "trespassing" outside his own ground, something Macmillan was always scrupulous in avoiding.

The brief contained only what could be proved against Philby: that is, his connection with Burgess in Washington, and rather faint traces of a Communist past. It did not catalogue all the ambivalent but suggestive incidents which had so thoroughly made up Sir Dick White's mind at the secret trial in 1952. It did not go into the Volkov incident or the Albanian disaster. The best explanation is that the leaders of the SIS had prevailed upon the Foreign Office that "mere suspicions" could not be adduced against a man in a brief to the Minister. This, of course, is by no means an improper attitude, and it would have chimed with Macmillan's own libertarian feelings.

What happened now to Hoover's campaign? He was forced to call off his G-men and, the FBI, too, officially cleared Philby. On December 29, 1955, an internal FBI memorandum noted:

SUBJECT: Donald Duart Maclean *et al.*

During a recent review of all references in Bufiles [FBI files] on Harold A. R. Philby, abstracts were made and placed on 3 x 5 [index] cards. Philby is suspected of tipping-off the subject that he was under investigation. From this review there does not appear any basis or justification for an investigation of Philby.

ACTION: Authority is requested to retain these abstracts for ready reference in the event of future enquiries from Bureau officials or other Government agencies concerning Philby.

So the Philby files were placed in cold storage, and Hoover for the rest of his life remained distrustful of British intelligence and the British in general.

There is evidence that Macmillan, too, became somewhat worried about the sweeping vote of confidence he had given Philby in Parliament. According to one of Macmillan's private *cabinet,* he later added a somewhat contradictory rider to his decision to clear Philby. Philby, he said, must not be used any more as an agent. In reply to criticisms that this contradicted his liberal stance in the House, Macmillan merely said: "I'm not having him shot. I'm only firing him from a situation where it's his job to be above suspicion. And I'm protecting his reputation." Obviously, in view of Philby's employment in Beirut, it was a decision which was either rescinded or ignored after Philby's polished showing with the Press next month. This argues, perhaps, a curious condition in the Secret Intelligence Service. But there is powerful evidence that the SIS was in an odd condition at this time, and its defects were about to promote a public debacle, precipitating, at last, major reform.

Early in 1953 Sir Stewart Menzies retired from the post of "C." He was succeeded by another soldier, Major-General Sir John Sinclair, who was known as "Sinbad" because he had served in the Navy (as a submarine officer) before changing to the Army. Sinclair had been Menzies' deputy for some years before taking over, but he was not so deeply-versed in the ways of Whitehall as Menzies had been. And almost certainly it was Menzies' extreme care in dealing with other departments, and with Government, which had protected the out-of-date SIS organisation for so long—rather than any excellence of its own. He had kept it out of trouble, in other words. Sinclair, it should be said, set about improving the SIS in many ways. In particular, he began to re-organise recruitment so that the entry-standard of officers should be more comparable to other branches of government service. He also began to formalise the conditions of employment for SIS officers, whose morale had suffered from the uncertain natures of the contracts of service and pensions.

However, he was unfortunate in that the existing organisation was becoming less and less capable of handling the complexities of modern intelligence work. Relations with the Foreign Office, MI 5 and the CIA worsened rapidly towards the mid-fifties.

Sinclair does not seem to have been blessed with the most fortunate of subordinates—and conceivably he was at a disadvantage in that he did not have Menzies' long-established authority. There seem to have been a number of officers in the SIS who believed that the most drastic and adventurous solutions should be applied to Britain's intelligence problems. The swashbucklers, whose attitude to world affairs seems to have been as light-hearted as that of the "Bolo Liquidation Club," seemed to be getting a little out of hand. At first, the situation was "held" by the appointment of a new Foreign Office Adviser, with considerably more authority than any previous FOA. Also, the Adviser in question, Sir George Clutton (later Ambassador to Poland), was, beneath a mannered exterior, one of the toughest and most able operators in the Diplomatic Service. The fact that all operations by the SIS had to be "passed" by Clutton certainly improved relationships with the Foreign Office, if not with MI 5.

Then, in early 1956, came the explosion. The powerful Russian cruiser *Ordzhonikidze* was due to arrive in Britain, carrying Bulganin and Khrushchev on their famous tour of Britain. The Prime Minister, Sir Anthony Eden, had pinned a large part of his reputation on his patient attempts to come to terms with the Russians, and moderate the Cold War. He regarded the visit of B & K as crucial.

Not long before the ship arrived, the idea was put up that the SIS might arrange to have a look at her bottom while she lay in Portsmouth Harbour. (The *Ordzhonikidze* was thought to have a number of unusual features which made her extremely fast.) Sinclair, about to go on leave, did not have time to discuss the matter, but pointed out that the project would have to be cleared. In a ghastly chain of events, the project *was* cleared: it appears that Clutton's successor was presented with it on the day his father died, and "initialled it off" while considerably distressed by that event. Sinclair's subordinates then went ahead and arranged for the frogman Lionel Crabb to go to Portsmouth and dive under the cruiser.

The organisational incompetence of the SIS *apparat* was displayed in the choice of Crabb. He was middle-aged, short-winded (he could not swim effectively without his flippers) and eccentric (he used to sleep in his frog-suit between rubber sheets). He was charming, but drunken and unstable. Far worse than selecting Crabb, though, was to go through with the operation at all: it indicated a total lack of political sensitivity in the SIS. It could scarcely have been possible to imagine that the hypothetical advantages of examining the *Ordzhonikidze*'s underside could be balanced against the international repercussions of failure and exposure. However, the officers in charge do not appear to have thought that the operation might have been approved mistakenly. The most charitable explanation is that the old "have-a-go" spirit got a little out of hand.

When Crabb failed to return, and the Russians began to make their delighted protests, uproar began in London. "There was a raspberry you could hear from one end of Whitehall to the other," one diplomat said. The Prime Minister took it as a personal affront, and the affair became all the worse when it exploded over the newspapers. (The prime cause of publicity was that the Portsmouth police rather publicly tore a page out of the register at the hotel in which Crabb had spent his last night on earth. An SIS officer has told us that MI 5 were asked to arrange for the disappearance of this incriminating piece of evidence. Perhaps MI 5 did not try too hard to be discreet on behalf of the sister-service.)

Sinclair was exonerated from blame by the inquiry which was held into the affair. Nevertheless, as his period of service was about to draw to an end, the occasion was bound to lead to a high-level reconsideration of the whole policy of SIS leadership. The name of Sinclair's successor was decided early enough, by Eden and Macmillan, in cabal with Sir Norman Brook,[3] Secretary to the Cabinet, and Sir Burke Trend,[4] deputy-secretary to the Cabinet. In the wake of the Philby troubles, and after this final *betise*, they decided that they could not rely on anyone from the SIS. They decided to appoint Dick White, the

[3] Subsequently Lord Normanbrook.
[4] Later Secretary to the Cabinet.

head of MI 5. "They felt," says an American to whom the decision was later explained, "that he was the only man they could rely on." It was, inevitably, a decision which the "old guard" of the SIS must have hated. It represented the final victory of MI 5 "bureaucracy" over the old, swashbuckling traditions of the secret service. In order to ensure that there was no trouble at the takeover, the decision was kept deadly secret for three months while White made ready to hand over MI 5 to his deputy, Roger Hollis. The secrecy was so deep that the Americans made it the first priority of the CIA man in London to find out who the new "C" was going to be. But he failed. (In the event, the Americans were delighted with the appointment of Dick White, a man who had been educated at two American universities as well as Oxford, and had numerous friends in Washington.) But in the long interregnum before White moved into the chair, an arrangement had been maturing within the SIS which was bound to displease him a good deal.

One of the first discoveries Sir Dick made when he arrived in July was that his old bogey, Kim Philby, was *still* on the books. He called Philby in for a long interview but Philby fenced and the result was inconclusive.

In April, Philby had begun negotiations to establish a new cover, as a correspondent in Beirut. A senior Foreign Office official (clearly acting for the SIS) had made an official approach to *The Observer* on Philby's behalf, and roughly simultaneously, Philby himself approached *The Economist* through a third party. It had always been a sore point with Donald Tyerman, then editor of *The Economist*, that, although he checked on Philby with Harold Caccia at the FO, he was never told either by the Office or by *The Observer* that Philby's initial *entrée* had been strictly an official one.

There is considerable evidence that the FO was interested specifically in placing Philby in Beirut. He had family qualifications, and the posting to an important espionage centre had special attractions for the FO and SIS.

By the time Sir Dick took over, the negotiations seem to have gone too far to be stopped. White is said to have been extremely angry. But Macmillan's response was cooler: he set so little store by political intelligence that he assumed Philby could do no harm in Beirut. The practical effect on Philby's career of the White take-over was that in his boss's eyes, anyway, he was totally and decisively labelled as a Soviet agent.

20. Endgame in Beirut

"When the cow stumbles, the butchers begin to run."

—LEBANESE PROVERB

The English-speaking community in Beirut used to be a little village, racked like all exile groups by feuds, quarrels and alcoholic remorse. Everyone knew everyone else and the event of a stranger tended to be celebrated like Thanksgiving or Christmas. Philby's arrival in September 1956 was treated, however, with a certain amount of reserve. It had not taken long for word to pass about his recent background and a slight taint of the Third Man debate still clung to him. The reserve soon melted. Philby was so obviously a man down on his luck, gamely trying to re-establish himself in the tough, competitive trade of a foreign correspondent after nearly seventeen years away from journalism; a man who had made mistakes (and admitted them), the worst, so his Beirut friends soon decided, being an ill-advised but not discreditable personal loyalty to the appalling Burgess.

What really established him was his old, reliable charm. The mature Philby was one of those rare men who appeal equally to men and women. Men found him straightforward, apparently totally lacking in guile, a genial drinking companion and reliable friend. Women were bowled over by his defenceless, vulnerable quality, accentuated by the pouches under his eyes, unkempt clothes and agonising stammer. And he was great for remembering birthdays and anniversaries. The extent to which he established himself can best be judged by the tolerance he was shown in his later alcoholic decline. He became a bottom-pincher (even an Ambassador's wife was not spared), a suspender snapper, and the face on the living room floor. After each new outrage his friends would say, "Well, Kim will never be invited there again." But he always was.

An early indication of this compulsive charm was the fact that although he had stolen Eleanor, wife of the American journalist Sam Pope Brewer, public sympathy seems to have been wholly on Philby's side. "Everyone liked Kim so much," a British friend said, "so there was no sign of the two factions which might normally develop in a case like that." Philby simply took over Eleanor's friends as well as his own and after a brief flurry of excitement, and some forced moralising, the English-speaking community settled back to its regular pattern of drink in the sun.

On the professional side, Philby began his cover job as a correspondent for *The Observer* and *The Economist* with certain advantages: although he only spoke "kitchen" Arabic, he seems to have arrived with a compendious knowledge of the Middle East, no doubt derived from his SIS years. We find him years later reeling off the names of Yemeni tribes with a savage delight in his store of such minutiae. And, of course, he was the son of the eminent Arabist St. John Philby whose fame gave Kim an impeccable parentage in Arab eyes.

He had left Aileen and the children in Britain and to begin with he took a room in an Arab fleapit, the Hotel Bassoul, an old haunt of his father's. (The Bassoul has since been demolished.) Mail is not usually delivered to private houses in Beirut, and to only a few hotels, so Philby had his letters addressed to the Hotel Normandy, on the seafront in Ras Beirut. The Normandy was then considered the second hotel in Beirut after the St. George. Many other luxury hotels have been built since, and the Normandy has now dropped down the scale. In 1956 it possessed a good deal of slightly tawdry glamour. The bar there speedily became Philby's headquarters. It was ideal for journalists (and presumably spies); it was quiet, drinks were considerably cheaper than they were at the St. George (Philby was short of money when he first arrived but his finances improved after an early visit to London, presumably to see his SIS chiefs). Arabs in any state of scruffiness were admitted, and there was a convenient side door which opened directly on to the street. A good place to meet anyone as discreetly as could be done in Beirut.

The Normandy was little used by journalists in later years. It seems that when Philby went there every day the improbable *pique-assiette,* Colonel Slade-Baker, a British journalist who sported a monocle, also showed up daily hoping to touch Philby for a drink or a story, and these two formed a small nucleus around which other journalists gathered. St. John sometimes called in when he was visiting Beirut. The regulars could tell when he was expected because Kim would smarten himself up and make an effort to remain sober. Philby was greatly missed at the Normandy.

Aileen was still in Britain and late in 1957 became seriously ill. Philby flew back to London but Aileen died on December 11 from congestive heart failure, myocardial degeneration, a respiratory infection and pulmonary tuberculosis. She was only forty-seven. In her last years she had become convinced of Philby's treachery but was unable to bring herself to do anything about it. She remains, perhaps, the most tragic figure in this narrative. After the funeral Philby went back to Beirut.

What one gets looking back on Philby's Beirut period is a glimpse of the two separate sides to his head and the effort he put into keeping them hidden from each other. As a husband (he married Eleanor after her Mexican divorce in 1958) and as a family man he appeared kind and considerate. Once his affair with Eleanor had started he moved to an apartment in a rather unfashionable part of Beirut between the downtown commercial district and the expensive Hambra section of Ras Beirut. It had an excellent view of the harbour and Philby ran an open house. Friends dropped by at all hours of the day and night.

He kept birds and a pet fox cub (a present from veteran correspondent, Ralph Izzard) and enjoyed taking the children for picnics to the Dog River in the mountains above Beirut where he would happily eat sandwiches under the olive trees. On their quieter evenings at home he and Eleanor would sit cross-legged on the floor, a bottle of whisky between them, and spend half the night listening to their extensive collection of records. He took Eleanor on a trip to the Empty Quarter of Arabia, fulfilling one of those pre-marital promises most men rarely keep. He took the family sailing in the harbour, remembered their birthdays, wrote affectionate letters to Eleanor when he was away (and often when he was not), and gradually built up a wide circle of friends, none of whom ever had the slightest suspicion that the Philby they knew was not the real one. Two of these friends were John H. Fistere, a former *Fortune* magazine writer and his equally American wife.

Kim and Eleanor used to share Thanksgiving turkey with the Fisteres—self-inflicted punishment, one would think, for someone as reportedly against the American way of life as Kim. They carried on an association at other times over the years, intimate enough for Fistere to describe Philby as one of his closest friends. After Philby defected, Fistere, like all those who had known Kim in Beirut, combed his recollection for clues which might have indicated that Philby was concealing strong left-wing political views. He could recall only two—very slight straws in the wind indeed. One night Fistere was arguing with a group of Arab nationalists on a well-worn theme: were the fundamental aims of American democracy and Russian Communism the same? Yes, said the Arabs. Of course not, said Fistere: the aim of Soviet Communism was to enslave free men. Fistere appealed to Philby, who managed to stammer out that he thought the fundamental aims were the same. "I always assumed Kim was for the Free World," Fistere recalled recently. "I could not understand how he could equate Communism and the American Way."

Another time a question of nationalities came up. "I was born in India, brought up in various parts of the Arab world, and I was at school in England," said Kim. "I don't feel that I have any nationality." This shook Fistere. "I just couldn't believe it. Kim seemed such a Britisher. It sounded as if he was denying his country."

Another couple, Yussuf and Rosemary Sayigh, used to talk Middle East politics with Philby for hours. After he had left they spent days trying to remember anything he had said which could have indicated a pro-Russian leaning. In four or five years of close friendship they could remember only that he had once said that the medical system in Russia was good. These tiny anecdotes, worn smooth by retelling among Philby's friends in the months after his disappearance, are remarkable only because of their meagreness: this is *all* that they can remember.

It is clear that Philby's stammer, seen in retrospect, was

a most valuable defence for a man successfully concealing his political views. He rarely initiated political discussions; it was too painful for his hearers to restrain themselves from helping him pronounce the words. He was, however, a great listener and conversational counterpuncher, specialised in the witty interjection and apt summary, all the more effective for being wrung out against (apparently) terrific internal resistance. The result was that Philby took part in innumerable political encounters (his business as a journalist was, after all, at least three-quarters politics) while managing to persuade people as different as Arab nationalists and American Rotarians that he was one of them.

On his professional front he was equally careful. He filed his first story for *The Observer* on September 30, 1956—"Western Oil Threat by Lebanon"—and continued to file, with occasional exceptions, balanced, impartial copy. The exceptions were his references to Nasser. He maintained close links with a group of Arab Nationalists, mostly Palestinian refugees, centering on Dr. Wahid Khalidi of the American University of Beirut. This group regarded Philby as easily the most pro-Arab foreign journalist stationed in the Lebanon and by pro-Arab they meant pro-Nasser—"He started writing favourably about Nasser, who was then getting a very bad press in Britain in the wake of Suez, from the beginning of his Beirut assignment. His attitudes to Arab problems seem to spring from conviction, not any attempt to get himself accepted."

In fact everyone accepted Philby for what they thought he was: a former British intelligence agent who had been badly treated by McCarthy-ite Americans. His past was such an open secret that some of his friends had no inhibitions about questioning him on it. On the beach in Beirut one day in 1958, Mrs. Douglas Stuart, wife of the then BBC correspondent in the Middle East, asked Philby point-blank: "Kim, tell us about the 'third man' business." Philby agreed. He said that he had known Burgess very well and had never suspected that Burgess was a Communist. When he went to Washington, Philby said, he was on the road to a knighthood. He was good at his job and the Americans liked him. At about this time there was a security leak high in the Foreign Office and it was he, Philby, who narrowed the suspects to Maclean. Philby said that in the meantime he met Burgess

who was on a last-chance appointment in Washington.
Philby invited Burgess to stay with him—"the sort of
gesture anyone would make to an old undergraduate acquaintance."

When Maclean defected he (Maclean) persuaded Burgess to go with him. After the flight Philby was recalled to
London. The Americans would not talk to him. They believed that he had tipped off Maclean. His own office was
convinced of his innocence, but MI 5 was not. He was
interrogated for three days by a man with a face of ce-
ment and steel. The interrogation decided nothing. Philby
resigned. It was almost impossible for him to get a job,
he said, until *The Observer* hired him.

The interest in this story is that it represents a Philby
melange of truth and lies, brilliant because it is so credi-
ble. It served to emphasise his role as the sympathetic
intelligence agent whose career had been ruined because
of his loyalty to a friend.

Philby travelled widely for his papers. He filed copy
from Amman, Riyadh, Damascus, Sharjah, Bahrein, Bagdad, Teheran and Cyprus. He travelled so widely, in fact,
that a former CIA agent, Miles Copeland, later compiled
a breakdown on the distance Philby had travelled and the
copy it produced. There was, Copeland decided, an un-
justifiable discrepancy: Philby had visited too many
places for two few journalistic results. What Copeland did
not know, although he might have suspected, was that
Philby was still with SIS. Cleared in the House of Commons, he was still trying to work his way back into SIS
and, at the same time, still keeping the interests of his
Russian masters uppermost. The SIS later claimed that
they knew by this time of Philby's duplicity and were using him; that they were feeding him twisted political information in the hope of passing it to the Russians. This
claim involves us in one of the endless permutations of
espionage, for did Philby also know that the SIS knew?
And in turn let them *think* that they were using him while
all the time *he* was using them? All that is certain is that
Philby was engaged in intelligence work while he was the
Observer-Economist correspondent in Beirut and that
when it suited him he made reports on his work to the
SIS. He visited Cyprus twenty times between 1956 and
1958 ostensibly to cover the *Enosis* (Union with Greece)
revolt and worked hard on his Armenian contacts. He

became friendly with an Indian lawyer called "Rusty" Rustomji, and they did some heavy drinking together. In Cyprus, Philby was vaguely anti-British and strongly anti-Greek. He thought the Turks were getting a bad deal in Government service and were being generally ill-treated by both the British and the Greeks. He attacked Rustomji for being a special constable and for being foolish enough to fight for Britain in the Second World War. Yet he showed a strong interest in all the places Rustomji had visited (mostly to defend British servicemen at courts martial) and asked questions like: What was the *real* attitude to Britain there? How did the police feel? How long would the Government last?

Most of these conversations took place over drinks at the Ledra Palace Hotel, the Nicosia Club, or at Armenian or Turkish nightclubs. They sometimes visited a nightclub called the Chanticleer which stayed open until the last man—usually Philby—had left.

In Beirut the years staggered by. As far as a journalist can have a routine, Philby had one. He rose around 10 A.M. as often as not with a hangover; drank a prairie oyster to his own recipe; and walked some five hundred yards downhill to the Normandy Bar. Here he checked his mail and had his first drink of the day. Most afternoons he held court at the Normandy, and many evenings he dined out with his wide circle of friends and contacts. His work for *The Observer* and *The Economist* remained solid and competent, leaning heavily and with meticulous accuracy on facts about the Arab world (an echo, perhaps of all those "damned wadis" of his father's).

He expanded his official contacts and seemed to spend more time than any other correspondents with people from the British and American embassies. He was a constant caller on the SIS area officer—an old friend—and friendly with the retired CIA agent, Miles Copeland. He was not accepted without reserve, however, and at least one of his Lebanese friends was once taken aside by a newly-arrived CIA agent and warned, "Be careful of that guy. Don't get too friendly with him."

The likeliest-looking concrete case in which Philby could have done a particular job for the SIS was during the events which led up to the United States Marines landing in the Lebanon in 1958. Nasserite groups in the Lebanon early in 1958 began to agitate against the plans of the Western-oriented President Chamoun, who intended to alter the constitution so that he could stand for a second term. Rioting broke out in May, and became uncontrollable. The Marines landed on July 19—at the request of the Government—to restore order.

Philby was extremely prescient about the arrival of the Marines. He told fellow-journalists three days before that the Marines were coming: and not in the usual manner of a journalist making a hopeful prediction. He spoke as a man who knew with certainty what would happen.

Now, the authors have been told that it was largely SIS information—passed to the CIA—on which the Americans were acting at this time. The SIS information came from the station chief in Beirut: Philby's old friend. Philby, of course, with his Nasserite contacts, would have been in a strong position to provide some, if not all, of the material on which the SIS based their reports. It looks very much like Philby deciding that it was worth the risk of losing a few Arab contacts in order to ingratiate himself with the SIS.

In his last year in Beirut Philby's friends began to notice a change in what had become a fairly regular pattern of life. Philby seemed to be undergoing some such collapse under strain as Maclean had suffered in Cairo more than a decade before. But this was happening to a man of considerably more self-discipline than Maclean ever possessed, a man who was a thorough professional in the difficult business of maintaining a long-term front. His periods of drunkenness became more frequent. On occasions two martinis sent him rolling into the gutter. His family life broke down and friends ceased to call as often, complaining they could not stand Philby's incoherence and Eleanor's constant complaints about money troubles. (Philby could still raise cash for a friend in trouble. He found £140 in a hurry for Ralph Izzard when Izzard, caught on a bank holiday, needed to rush to London to see his sick child.) He even became pompous—a characteristic not usually associated with Philby—over his pro-Arab beliefs. A young English girl was at one time telling a story in Beirut about how she had dined with a group of Arab sheikhs, and had caught one surreptitiously switching plates with her. She later learned that the sheikh was afraid of being poisoned. This story brought a laugh, but Kim was very disturbed and lectured everyone present about how this was a slight on fine Arab hospitality. They had trouble in getting him to end his lecture.

A mordant sense of humour which Philby had kept concealed now appeared, and an elderly ex-army officer was his first victim. The officer had conceived a passion for a girl Philby knew, but could make no progress. Philby invited them both to dinner and arranged that they should sit beside each other. He drew the officer aside over drinks and told him that the girl reciprocated his passion but was terribly shy. This was a case, Philby said, for the direct approach. Hands used freely under the table would not be unwelcome. Philby watched with drunken amusement a furious struggle which ended with the girl trying to pound the officer's head into his soup.

Philby's neighbours called the police at least four times because of noisy domestic rows or because Philby was throwing empty bottles over the balcony into the street. There was more trouble when the pet fox cub escaped and terrorised the building until Philby cornered it in the stairwell. The concierge later seized an opportunity to tip the fox over the balcony while Kim and Eleanor were away at a party, arousing in Philby a rare display of overt fury.

The drinking grew worse. His journalistic output dried to a trickle. Social evenings lasted only long enough to get Kim into a taxi. Public functions became a horror for Eleanor, worrying what outrage her husband would attempt next. His friends began to get used to him and often a party would continue over Philby's prostrate figure on the floor, staring glassy-eyed at the ceiling. When it was time to go, the men would carry him out. Eleanor told friends that Kim was having terrible nightmares and would wake up shouting: apparently for help.

Everyone imagined that some sort of domestic, emotional or financial trouble was behind Philby's collapse. The real reason they would never have believed—the SIS had finally learned beyond all doubt that Philby was a Russian agent and Philby knew they knew.

What had happened was the one mischance no agent can guard against: a defector, a second Volkov. Over Christmas 1961, the highest KGB officer ever to defect fled from the Russian embassy in Helsinki. His subsequent cover name has usually been Anatoli Golitsin. His revelations astounded the joint CIA-SIS team that interrogated him. He "blew" at least 200 KGB agents, among them the SIS man George Blake,[1] two spies at the top of West German intelligence, and a catastrophic leakage from America's codes and cyphers headquarters, the National Security Agency; and with no possibility of error, he pointed to Philby. When the first long interrogation of Golitsin was complete, an SIS man, a close friend of Philby's who had been in Beirut as area head of the SIS, arrived from London and began a battle of wills with Philby. The SIS man made no progress and was finally forced into a frank and embarrassing confrontation. He stated the charge bluntly: The SIS now knew that Philby had been working for the Russians and had been doing so for a long time. Philby took the accusation gracefully, admitted it, and then shrugged it off with a tantalising remark he has since repeated several times—"Knowing what I did, I could not have done anything else."

We can only speculate on what he meant. The phrase might have been clarified at Philby's trial. But there was, of course, no trial. When the SIS man returned to London and made his report Sir Dick White faced a delicate decision. Philby could be eliminated in Beirut—a messy, dangerous and perhaps impossible task. Sir Dick rejected this as abhorrent and impractical. The Lebanese security police could be taken at their word—"There is no reason why we should interfere with the removal of a wanted British subject to his homeland"—or the SIS could try to persuade Philby to return of his own will and face charges. The result of either of these courses could prove politically embarrassing. The first rumours of what became the Profumo Affair were already being whispered in Whitehall, and a spy trial, with the demands for an enquiry into the SIS which it would create, was the last thing the Government—and the SIS—wanted. Sir Dick settled for the fourth choice: an attempt could be made to "frighten Philby into defecting." For the sake of SIS morale Philby would be confronted and broken down—broken down in a way which could never be done in England—and then forced into exile.

---

[1] Blake was sentenced to 42 years jail but escaped from Wormwood Scrubs prison, London, on October 22, 1966, and is, at the time of writing, living in Russia.

At the end of 1962 another SIS agent "visited" Philby in Beirut. His methods were determined: the results apparently thorough. On the night of January 23, 1963, Philby, on his way to a dinner party at the house of Glen Balfour Paul, First Secretary at the British Embassy, suddenly stopped the taxi and got out "to send a cable from the Post Office." He never made the party. Since the arrival of the second SIS agent Philby had been in touch at three-hourly intervals with his Russian contact in Beirut, and when it looked as if the SIS man was about to move, Philby and the Russians put an emergency plan into operation.

Over the next few weeks an angry team of CIA men marched around Beirut. They had had their own instructions for dealing with Philby but he had left town before they were ready, and they were now convinced that he had been warned. Given Philby's contacts in Beirut, and his popularity, this is not unlikely.

Philby surfaced in Moscow six months later. (In between there had been a series of non-committal letters and telegrams to Eleanor.) His arrival created some stir in the West but the public was kept ignorant of the background. To the ordinary newspaper reader all that had occurred was that a journalist, suspected of being the Third Man in the Burgess-Maclean Affair but later cleared, had defected to the Russians. There was speculation that Philby had been some sort of British agent but no indication of how important he had been or the damage he had done.

How did Philby get to Moscow? We are able to reveal, for the first time, that Philby arrived on Russian soil four days after he left Beirut, i.e. on January 27, 1963. As to his exact route, it would appear that although the SIS and the CIA have theories—the best one is that he left on a Russian freighter—they have never been able to confirm them. Philby has never spoken about his flight, not because it could reveal any intelligence material but, we believe, to protect people (not involved in espionage) who helped him escape. The one clue is that Philby told one of his children that he arrived in Moscow with his feet heavily bruised from a long and difficult walk. The theory most likely to be correct goes as follows: Philby was driven to the Syrian border in a Turkish truck and crossed using forged papers identifying him as a Turkish

diplomatic courier. He made his way across Syria into
Turkey. From there on, using his knowledge of the country gained during his earlier periods there and his contacts with Armenians which he had built up in Cyprus
he walked into Soviet Armenia. Then, feeling safe for the
first time in thirty years, he "went home" to Moscow.

21. Through the Curtain

*We ended by appealing to the future, that en-
lightened and upright judge who always arrives,
alas! too late.*

    —ALEXIS DE TOCQUEVILLE, *Recollections*

In his latter years in Moscow, Guy Burgess—unlike Donald Maclean—spent a good deal of time with Western
newspapermen. Therefore, they besieged him, searching
for news, when it was learnt that Philby had vanished
from Beirut. Burgess passionately denied that Kim could
be in Moscow, saying: "I am the first person he would
contact if he were here." No doubt Burgess was right, except that Philby would have had pressing engagements to
keep before he could go round Moscow looking up old
friends. Probably, the espionage experts of the KGB
spent several months "debriefing" him: certainly, they
would have wanted to extract every piece of information
he had about the West before it became out of date.

Spring turned into summer without any sign of Philby.
And then Guy Burgess disappeared from his sixth-floor
apartment overlooking the Novaderchy Monastery. The
Western correspondents assumed that he had gone to
meet Philby, but in fact he had gone into the Bodkin
Hospital to die. He had lived at a furious rate, and now
a lifetime of dedicated drinking had caught up with even
his astounding constitution. He was suffering from liver
trouble and hardening of the arteries, and on August 19,
1963, he died.

Before his death, was he re-united briefly with Philby?
On July 3, *Isvestia* had announced tersely that by unan-
imous vote of the Praesidium, H. A. R. Philby had been
made a citizen of the Soviet Union. By a codicil to his

will, made shortly before he died, Burgess left Philby a third of his £6,200 estate, a sum of about £2,000, making a kindly capitalist gesture from one Marxist to another.

What sort of life was Philby coming to? His own predecessors had adapted to it very differently. Burgess was the less successful because, despite his Marxism, he was a quintessentially English figure, too much at home in London to be quite at home anywhere else. And he had, amid all the baffling and contradictory elements in his makeup, a streak of realism and clearsightedness which made it impossible for him to suppress his discontents by ritualistic attention to the holy texts of ideology. In the 1930s, when dewy-eyed visitors to the Soviet Union—not necessarily Communists—were speaking in terms of a heaven on earth, Burgess made blunt comments on the housing problems and the appalling confusion of urban Moscow. And in the 1960s, he could be equally blunt. Shortly after their arrival in the Soviet Union, he and Maclean were taken for detailed debriefing to Kubishev, an austere industrial town 550 miles southeast of Moscow. "Kubishev," Burgess said later, "is a vision of hell. Can you imagine Glasgow on a Saturday night in the nineteenth century?" And for a time, Burgess was troubled by the puritanical Russian attitude towards homosexuality. He remained, however, uncompromising in his defence of the Soviet position as a whole, in some ways going further than most Russians would do. The authors, for instance, have spoken to a young Russian (now living in Britain) who met Guy Burgess on a river-trip some years after the Twentieth Party Congress. As it was by then acceptable, even normal, to voice some criticisms of Stalin, they did so. To their surprise, Guy Burgess rounded on them angrily, declaring that Stalin's ruthlessness had been necessary, and in the long run beneficial.

Things improved for Guy after 1956. This was the year in which, due to the initiative of Richard Hughes of *The Sunday Times,* Burgess and Maclean were produced for the first time to the Western press. The improvement, however, seems to have been largely due to a particularly effective piece of political forecasting on Guy's part which impressed the Russians deeply. After the fall of Eden, the Soviet Ambassador in London, in common with most people everywhere, predicted that Rab Butler would become the new British prime minister. But Burgess, with his intimate knowledge of the thirties and Appeasement, knew that the Churchillian wing of the Tory Party would never tolerate Butler. He told the Russians that Macmillan would win. In the wake of this successful forecast, Burgess acquired a *dacha* outside Moscow and, for a while, a chauffeur-driven Volga.

He corresponded more freely with people in the West —his letters arriving with postmarks from Sussex, Bermondsey, Cheshire and other unlikely spots—and he began to receive visitors. To one of them he confided what seems an extraordinary problem, granting Brugess's sexual facility in the past. He had been unable to locate any boyfriends, and had therefore been living in a state of enforced chastity since arriving in Russia. Presumably, this could only have been due to a lack of familiarity with Russian language and customs, plus a certain concern about the possible censoriousness of the authorities. However, his visitor, who had swiftly identified the chief meeting-place of gay Moscow, passed the news on to Guy, who wasted no time in following-up the tip. He found the authorities were prepared to be tolerant, and was soon comfortably installed in an apartment on Boshaya Progovskaya with the last of his life-long succession of friends. This was a blond electrician named Tolya, who played the guitar. Later, Guy acquired an Alsatian dog, also called Tolya, and this led to some notable confusions. For example, in a letter to Tom Driberg, MP, there was a page which ended with the line: "The writing is unsteady because Tolya is nibbling at my arm." Driberg assumed this was a reference to the Alsatian Tolya until he turned the page and saw that the line continued: "He has now put on the Ninth Symphony."

His letters, in erratic blue scrawl, sought continually for news of gay London, particularly of people with whom he had conducted affairs. Although he would have liked to gossip about the present, he was reduced to delving into the past. When the obituaries of two notoriously homosexual British ambassadors appeared in *The Times* (naturally without any reference to this aspect of their careers) Burgess was moved to a flood of nostalgia, particularly about one of them known familiarly as "Rhoda." In another letter he wrote: "The difficulty is that I can have so little interesting to write—gossip about people you don't know or aren't interested in. I can only think of Genghis Khan and Tamburlaine . . ." (He had just been on a trip to Samarkand.)

Clearly Burgess dreamed of England. He still regarded himself as an Englishman, even a patriotic one. Like many of his former Establishment colleagues, he disliked the Americans because of their strength, their lack of ancient tradition, and their contempt for sophisticated English behaviour. English institutions—schools, clubs, even the Church—exercised a compulsive fascination for him. But in Moscow he was a snob out of water. He was not too welcome in such salon circles as existed: the Russians did not object to hard drinking, but did not care for his upper-class English manners. To them, the voice (he never troubled with learning Russian) and the Old Etonian tie meant nothing.

There were a number of unfortunate escapades: the most spectacular being at a cocktail party in the new Chinese Embassy in 1961. Burgess got roaring drunk, and perhaps inspired by memories of his desecration of Queen Victoria's statue in London, he insisted on urinating all over the fireplace. The Chinese, who were very proud of this ostentatious object, decorated with marble specially imported from the homeland, were furious. The incident led to a serious quarrel with Donald Maclean, whose diplomat's sense of decorum was outraged. (Coming from the hero of the Cairo escapades, this must have struck Guy as a bit rich: but Maclean was capable of being distinctly Janus-faced in such matters.) As he aged, Guy spent more and more time at home with the Tolyas, drinking, reading and lounging about the flat in blue silk pyjamas. Driberg and other friends had sent him modern furniture and numerous books: he had an extensive library including a rare *Decline and Fall of the Roman Empire*, several autographed first editions of Evelyn Waugh, and all the publications on the subject of his and Maclean's defection. These were heavily annotated in blue ink. One of them referred to him as being "suspected of homosexual activities," and Burgess had written in the margin: *"Suspected!"* On the news of his death, his acquaintances among the Western press visited his flat, hoping to glean something from these notes. But naturally, the KGB had been there first, and everything compromising had gone. Burgess was supposed to have written an "explosive" volume of memoirs, but there was no sign of the manuscript. There were, however, numerous memorabilia. There was the autographed copy of Churchill's *Arms and the Covenant*. There was a letter Anthony Eden had written to Burgess: simply a few words of thanks for a minor service Guy had done for the great man during a trip to America. In a cupboard hung the blue pyjamas and a set of wellmade suits with the name of Burgess's tailor (in High Street, Windsor, under the shadow of Eton College) on the inside pocket. And there was a drawer which contained nothing but Old Etonian bow ties, all rather the worse for wear.

Donald Maclean, applying the same careful industry which had advanced him in the British Foreign Office, made a much more serious business of coming to terms with Russia than did Guy. Apart from anything else, he learnt Russian, and went to work regularly in the Russian foreign ministry. Unlike Guy, he had the skills of a real diplomat to help him: he was accustomed to the business of settling down in strange environments. And in September 1953, he was joined by Melinda and the three children. This represented a considerable feat on the part of the girl from Chicago, who had contrived to fool most of her acquaintances in the West about her intentions.

She had then been living for some time in Switzerland: at least one agent of the Secret Intelligence Service was regularly in touch with her. Perhaps the SIS saw her go, and gained something from watching the operation. But this particular agent is so circumstantial in his detailed accounts of her obviously simulated mental condition ("she couldn't get a job in Geneva: it was desperation") that it seems likely Melinda deceived them to the last. In the course of an intimate and apparently entirely sincere conversation with a close woman friend Melinda had made it apparently clear that she no longer cared for Donald. "All I want," she said, "is a gentle husband who will look after me. I don't even care if he's fat." This conversation took place at the tiny ski resort of Saanenmoser during the very weekend Melinda must have been in touch with the Soviet contact man who was organising her journey. So sharp was the shock of her disappearance that people began to wonder whether she had been a Communist all along, and the idea was reinforced when

Mark Culme-Seymour, the old friend from Paris days, ran into the reunited Macleans a year later in Leningrad. Culme-Seymour was then working as a sales representative for a British engineering group. Maclean, he thought, looked terrible: he was drinking unhappily and had lost a good many teeth somewhere along the line. They spent an awkward weekend together. Maclean had no doubt changed, but there was a more remarkable change in Melinda. She told Culme-Seymour that she had known she was going to Russia right from the beginning, even before Donald himself had defected. And when Donald said anything which implied even the faintest criticism of their new life, or of the Soviet Union, she jumped down his throat. Perhaps it is true that Melinda all along was a deeply dedicated Communist: if so, she was the most remarkable dissembler of them all. All in all, she bears more the appearance of a woman who found it worthwhile to adopt the mores of the people amongst whom her interest lay.

Her relationship with Philby did not last, and there remains some doubt as to whether they actually married. In 1974 they separated. Soon afterward Philby went out for dinner with his fellow KGB man, George Blake. Blake came with two Russian girls, translators at Moscow's Scientific Institute, one of whom was called Nina. Philby married her soon afterward. She is at least twenty years younger than he is, but their relationship appears warm and stable.

Clearly, the two of them are well-enough off materially. They have a large apartment in Moscow, and they are amongst the Soviet élite who have no problem in obtaining whatever clothes, cameras, records or other consumer durables they desire. So far as can be ascertained, Philby himself has never been deeply interested in material possessions, and so should not find it hard to adjust to such unavoidable austerities as Moscow imposes. If his father is anything to go by, he will not suffer any particular discomfort through spending the last years of his life among a people of alien culture. He once pointed out to somebody in Beirut that there was no reason why he, Philby, should feel particularly English—having been born in India, brought up largely in the Middle East, and having lived so much of his life outside England.

Of the three men we have written about, Philby clearly was the least obviously alienated. He was not an eccentric like Burgess, or a man crippled by inner stress like Donald Maclean. He almost submerged in drink during one period in Beirut, but now he appears to have gone back to his normal habit, that of a heavy, but reasonably controlled drinker. He is the one who makes it clear that one cannot dismiss the "Cambridge defectors" as mere degenerates. Their decision to betray may have been made easier by a degree of alienation from ordinary British society (even, conceivably, aided by some form of blackmail in Maclean's case, although we have not found evidence of it). But essentially they were moved by a quasi-religious faith: they believed that the Soviet Union was somehow cleaner, purer and better than their own country, because it claimed to have adopted Communism. Like religious zealots in many ages before them, they would justify everything in their careers—treachery, cruelty, even murder—by pointing to the cause. Like the chorus in Brecht's classic of Communist revolution, *The Measures Taken,* they would say: "What baseness would you not commit to root out baseness?"

Men like Philby, Burgess and Maclean were deadly to British society because we had not had to deal with such people for a long time. That Englishmen of seemingly commonplace aspect might be secretly in bond to an alien and all-justifying ideology was something which had been forgotten since the religious conflicts of the sixteenth century. The Elizabethans would have perhaps been less surprised by the phenomenon.

This is not to say that the religious comparison should be pushed too far. The Jesuit "penetration agents" who came to England in the Catholic service lived austere lives in the shadow of dangers which were generally more horrible than anything our Communist agents faced. (We have given up drawing and quartering.) And it could certainly not be said that any of our three subjects lived austerely. They spent their Western years in considerable comfort, and they never chose to deny themselves the pleasures of trust and friendship, although if they were serious in their inner loyalties they must have known that these relationships would eventually be exposed as one-way bargains. Philby in particular may have exercised self-discipline, but none of them could claim to have exercised self-denial.

"A blackguard," one of his old chiefs called Kim Philby. But, no matter how many minor indulgences and petty cruelties one might list against Philby, he clearly cannot be called a blackguard validly. A blackguard would have been less dangerous: Philby was essentially an idealist. He was an energetic, reasonably intelligent young man who felt betrayed after the 1931 election in Britain, and who was shocked by the sight of street-warfare in Vienna. He had been left by his father with little but a fierce, if undirected, sense of righteousness and a desire to make an impression upon the world. He felt little attachment to Britain, but was seduced as many Englishmen of his class have been, by the delicious under-currents of intrigue. Once they contacted him, the rest was inevitable: as Mr. le Carré points out in his Intro-duction, once Philby had entered the secret world, it was too late to change. Once he adopted his "cover," his real personality ceased to develop: it would appear to be a consequence of employment as a secret agent.

The question of how much damage he did is tied up with the argument about how effective espionage and in-telligence services are, anyway. But for Philby, could the Albanian subversion have succeeded? Supposing it had succeeded, would the Western nations have tried harder, and with more success, to destroy the Russian hegemony in Eastern Europe? Clearly, this is what was in the mind of one Foreign Office man when he said that "Philby robbed European countries of their freedom." But the Albanian operation might have failed without Philby and even had it succeeded furiously, there is a question whether the West would have mounted really extensive attempts at armed subversion in Russia's major domin-ions.

The exact extent of the damage, then, may never be worked out. But there can be little doubt that in terms of international intelligence and espionage, Kim Philby's ca-reer in the West was a Soviet triumph of mighty propor-tions. It was well summed-up, in slightly curious language, by a CIA man we talked to. "What it comes to," he said, "is that when you look at that whole period from 1944 to 1951—leaving out anything he picked up other times—

the entire Western intelligence effort, which was pretty big, was what you might call a minus advantage. We'd have been better off doing nothing."

That is the debit side. On the credit side, we might follow Anthony Nutting, in his account of another great British debacle—Suez—and quote Kipling again.

> *"Let us look at this quite fairly, as a business people should.*
> *We have had no end of a lesson—it will do us no end of good."*

There can be no doubt that in immediate terms the Philby affair was one of the causes of a considerable reform and improvement of the British intelligence services. It happened that Britain began her confrontation with the Soviet Union equipped with a grotesquely unsuitable Secret Intelligence Service, and Philby destroyed that service. To that extent, he has helped us.

But there should be more in the credit balance than an organisational reform of the SIS. One of the remarkable things about the interwoven scandal of the Philby-Burgess-Maclean affair is that it illustrates, almost in parable form, so many of the curable weaknesses of our society. It is presumably only if we fail to learn from the affair that it is a real tragedy for us, because it is our claim that democracy can learn from its mistakes. The affair tells us a good deal about the role of privilege in our society, and the degree to which irrelevant insignia of social and economic status can be fatally mistaken for evidence of political acceptability. It also gives us an idea of how much our bureaucracy is prepared to hide: the White Paper on Burgess and Maclean, and the tightly circumscribed official accounts of the role Kim Philby played in British affairs, are classic warnings to those who are tempted to believe the Official Versions without powerful supporting evidence.

But the most important lesson is that democracy cannot be defended by people who are themselves politically illiterate and naive. Philby, Burgess and Maclean all survived, essentially, because they passed so much of their careers amongst people who shared, in varying degrees, the comfortable assumption that it was permissible to

ignore the ideologies which have altered the whole aspect
of the twentieth century. "All the Isms are Wasms," said
the Foreign Office spokesman with magnificent flippancy
when the Nazi-Soviet pact was announced. But he was
wrong: this remains a century in which people are moved
by Isms. Philby and his friends have done enough to
teach us the lesson. Only if we fail to understand it do
they win.

Postscript

When we were first working on the Philby investigation
back in 1967, one of our sources, John Wyndham (later
Lord Egremont)—who, as private secretary and confidant
to Prime Minister Harold Macmillan, knew a good deal
about such matters—urged us to regard Philby as "no
more than the tip of the iceberg." As our investigation
progressed, names of other likely KGB agents swam to the
surface. One such name was Sir Anthony Blunt, Keeper
of the Queen's Pictures, eminent art historian, and a
friend of Philby and Burgess since the '30s (see Chapter 4). We tried to interview Blunt. He refused to see us.
We wrote to him. He did not reply. Rightly or wrongly, we
decided that we would continue to concentrate on our
main subject rather than waste time on what might turn
out to be unproductive enquiries about Blunt.

After this book was first published, there were rumours
that Blunt had been greatly relieved that he did not figure in it more prominently. There was gossip that Blunt
had, indeed, played some role in the flight of Burgess and
Maclean. But whenever one of Fleet Street's more sensational newspapers began to look for evidence of this role,
threatening noises from Blunt's solicitors effectively halted
the investigation. Then in 1977 *The Times* published an
article which said that a Cambridge don, Donald Beves,
then dead, had been the KGB recruiter of Philby, Bur-

gess and Maclean. The outcry in Beves's defence was such that *The Times* was forced to apologise, but the result was a re-awakening of interest in the spy trio. Two authors were soon going over the ground we had ploughed in 1967—Richard Deacon, the author of several histories of espionage, and Andrew Boyle, a biographer with wartime intelligence experience.

Deacon's book had to be withdrawn for libel reasons, but Boyle's, published on November 5, 1979, sparked off an explosion. Boyle named as KGB agents only Philby, Burgess and Maclean. But by an ingenious juxtaposition of Blunt's name with that of a KGB agent code-named "Maurice," Boyle managed to hint, with minimum risk of libel, that Blunt and "Maurice" were one and the same person. Three days later, the Prime Minister, Mrs. Thatcher, told the House of Commons that Blunt had confessed to British security services in 1964 that he had worked for the KGB since 1936, that he had been active in passing information to the Russians when he was working for MI 5, that on leaving MI 5 in 1945 he was no longer in a position to obtain classified information, and that in return for telling all he knew, Blunt had been given immunity from prosecution.

Blunt elaborated on this statement at a press conference. He said, "It seemed to me and to many of my contemporaries in the mid-thirties that the Communist Party and Russia constituted the only bulwark against Fascism, since the Western democracies were taking an uncertain and compromising attitude towards Germany. I was persuaded by Guy Burgess that I could best serve the cause of anti-Fascism by joining him in his work for the Russians. This was a case of political conscience against loyalty to country; I chose conscience. When I later realised the true facts about Russia I was prevented from taking any action by personal loyalty; I could not denounce my friends. In 1964 an event took place which meant that I was no longer bound by this loyalty, and being promised immunity, I was relieved to give the authorities all the information in my possession. From 1945 I ceased to pass information to the Russians, but in 1951 I was in contact with them on behalf of Burgess. I was myself pressed to go to Russia. I refused."

After that, Blunt retreated behind the Official Secrets

Act, refusing to go into detail about what, exactly, had happened in 1964 which had released him from his loyalty; what, exactly, he had passed to the Russians, and what role he had played in the flight of Burgess and Maclean. There were also other intriguing questions. After Blunt had confessed, whose decision had it been to give him immunity from prosecution? Why had he been given such immunity? Why had a self-confessed traitor been allowed to stay on at his post in Buckingham Palace? And why was he eventually publicly exposed? We have answers to most of these questions.

At his press conference Blunt said, "They [MI 5 officers] came to me with certain information in 1964 which both showed that they knew quite a lot and also freed me from my loyalty . . ." In response to questions Blunt said that he had been freed by the "sayings" of a "colleague or friend." He added that neither Burgess nor Philby was concerned. This leaves only one logical interpretation: in 1964 MI 5 obtained a confession from a friend or colleague of Blunt's, someone about whom Blunt, until then, had felt a sense of loyalty that had prevented him, too, from confessing. This man's confession both provided MI 5 with further information about Blunt's role and, at the same time, liberated Blunt from his loyalty. Presumably this man, too, was given immunity from prosecution. Who he is remains a mystery. We asked Blunt recently. He refused to talk about the matter.

At the same time, we asked Blunt if he would tell us in general terms what sort of information he had passed to the Russians when he had been in MI 5. Blunt said that his Russian controller had been interested in only one topic: everything that MI 5 knew about German intelligence. What role had he played in the Burgess–Maclean affair? Blunt denied that he had tipped off Maclean that he was about to be interrogated. He said that, as far as he knew, the tip had come from Philby (see Chapter 16). He said that his only role had been to see his controller, on Burgess's suggestion, in case the KGB wanted him to go to Russia as well as Burgess and Maclean. The controller had ordered him to go but he had refused.

The decision to give Blunt immunity from prosecution in return for his co-operation was based on MI 5's recommendation and taken by then acting Director of Public

Prosecution, Maurice Crump. MI 5 put it to Crump that the public interest would be best served by not prosecuting Blunt, and Crump has told us that he made up his mind "with no thought as to the eminence or otherwise of the person concerned, but solely on the facts of the case and the representations made to me." It is clear what MI 5 had in mind. If Blunt was not prosecuted and allowed to continue his career in the art world, then the KGB might think that he had escaped detection. In time the Russians might try to re-activate Blunt, then MI 5 would have a KGB agent working for them. This was a risky move, because Blunt's art career involved him with the Queen, so the Queen's private secretary, Sir Michael Adeane, was told and was assured that Blunt would be closely watched. Here MI 5 was fortunate in that the assistant Keeper of the Queen's Pictures was Oliver Miller, a former SIS officer. Adeane, in the event, felt obliged to tell the Queen, and her staff say that from that moment she did her best to avoid engagements at which she would be seen publicly with Blunt—until the day in November 1979, when Blunt was exposed and she was able to strip him of his knighthood.

The KGB did not oblige MI 5 and over the years it became clear that the Russians did not intend to re-activate Blunt, that they considered him a "burnt out case." A strong resentment grew in both branches of the British services that Blunt had got away with treason and was being "loaded with honours." A move to "get Blunt" got under way, one manifestation of which was planting in *The Times* the Beves story, referred to earlier. The thinking was that it would re-awaken interest in the Philby–Burgess–Maclean affair, that someone might accept that Beves was not involved, but would then look for a man with a similar name and a similar background. And, at the very least, all the thrashing around might provoke something. It was a crude plan, but it worked. Boyle's book alone would have been unlikely to have exposed Blunt. But it drew Mrs. Thatcher's attention, and she asked for the files. When she had read them, she agreed with Blunt's enemies and saw no reason why he should be protected any longer. Her statement to the House of Commons was the outcome.

It would be wrong to elevate Blunt to the status of

Philby, Burgess or Maclean. Unless the security services are concealing further information about him, Blunt was a small-time KGB agent. The intense interest his unmasking aroused in Britain had less to do with the extent of his treachery than with the fact that it appeared to confirm Hoover's obsessive fears—that the British establishment had covered up the true depth of Soviet penetration into Britain's ruling class.

About the Authors

Bruce Page worked for *The Sunday Times* and was part of the famous Insight Team, which spent months interviewing everyone who had known Philby in a social or business way. He is now the editor of *The New Statesman*. Phillip Knightley and David Leitch are now special feature writers for *The Sunday Times* and were also part of the Insight Team.